BOETHIUS'S
De topicis differentiis

BOETHIUS'S
De topicis differentiis

TRANSLATED, WITH NOTES AND
ESSAYS ON THE TEXT,
BY ELEONORE STUMP

Cornell University Press
ITHACA AND LONDON

This book has been published with the aid of a grant from the
Hull Memorial Publication Fund of Cornell University.

First published 1978 by Cornell University Press.
Published in the United Kingdom by Cornell University Press Ltd.,
2–4 Brook Street, London W1Y 1AA.

International Standard Book Number 0-8014-1067-3
Library of Congress Catalog Card Number 77-17275
Printed in the United States of America by Vail-Ballou Press, Inc.
*Librarians: Library of Congress cataloging information
appears on the last page of the book.*

To John Crossett

והמשכלים יזהרו כזהר הרקיע
ומצדיקי הרבים ככוכבים לעולם ועד

—Daniel 12:3

Preface

This book is a philosophical study of Boethius's treatise *De to-picis differentiis*. It includes the first English translation of this historically and philosophically important text, as well as copious notes designed to make the text accessible to philosophers and scholars interested in the medieval period. Detailed philosophical analyses of the text and of important technical concepts, such as the concept of the predicables, are worked out in the chapters of Part II. Chapters on Aristotle's *Topics* and the treatise on dialectic in Peter of Spain's *Tractatus* explain the work of these philosophers on the Topics and explore the relationship of their views to those of Boethius. My principal aim is to make Boethius's treatise available and comprehensible to scholars for whom the technical Latin vocabulary and unfamiliar subject matter have made it inaccessible.

In the course of producing this book I have accumulated numerous debts of gratitude. The Danforth Foundation generously funded not only the long process of graduate education but also the preparation of my dissertation. A postdoctoral grant from the American Association of University Women, supplemented by Cornell University, freed me from teaching duties for a year and allowed me to work full time on this project. Steven Simon painstakingly and laboriously checked all the references and helped make the manuscript more precise. Carole Seamon typed a difficult manuscript accurately and efficiently and very competently turned my unlovely draft into neat copy. My notes on Book IV of *De topicis differentiis* benefited from Michael Leff's openhanded help with ancient rhetoric; and Nicholas Sturgeon corrected several infelicities and errors. John Crossett gave me detailed criticism of the chapters on Aristotle, Boethius, and Peter of Spain, and I have dedicated the book to him as an expression of the great gratitude I owe him. He awakened my mind when I was an undergraduate, and I continue to learn from him now. Regarding the intellectual virtues, too, it is true that "οὐκ ἔστιν δοῦλος μείζων τοῦ κυρίου αὐτοῦ." Norman Kretzmann, my former teacher, gave unstintingly of his time and energy; whatever its flaws, the book is immeasurably better than it would have been without him. He made numerous useful corrections and suggestions; he continually gave me encouragement and support, and his intellectual excellence and dedication set me an example that turned all the work into a labor of love. And, finally, I owe thanks to my husband, Donald Stump; his support of my academic work and his good-humored willingness to share housework and baby care while pursuing his own career have been the sine qua non of this book.

ELEONORE STUMP

Ithaca, New York

Contents

Abbreviations

(For complete bibliographical information, see the Bibliography.)

CAG	*Commentaria in Aristotelem graeca*
De inv.	Cicero, *De inventione*
De syll. cat.	Boethius, *De syllogismis categoricis*
De syll. hyp.	Boethius, *De syllogismis hypotheticis*
De top. diff.	Boethius, *De topicis differentiis*
ICT	Boethius, *In Ciceronis Topica*
In Isag.	Boethius, *In Isagogen*
In Top.	Alexander of Aphrodisias, *In Aristotelis Topicorum libros octos commentaria*
Log. Mod.	L. M. de Rijk, *Logica Modernorum*
PL	*Patrologia latina*
Rhet. ad Her.	Harry Caplan, tr., *Rhetorica ad Herennium*
Rhet. lat. min.	Charles Halm, ed., *Rhetores latini minores*

Introduction

Boethius

Anicius Manlius Severinus Boethius, "the last of the Romans" and the tutor of the Middle Ages, was born into a patrician family in Rome in 480. Orphaned at an early age, he was brought up by the illustrious and aristocratic Quintus Aurelius Memmius Symmachus, whose daughter he eventually married. He gained a reputation as a man of learning, and his brilliant public career was marked by honors. For many years, he occupied a position of trust under the Arian king Theodoric the Ostrogoth; in the year 510 he became consul, and his two sons were joint consuls in 522. Eventually, however, he fell out of favor with Theodoric and was accused of treason. The official charges against him include the implausible accusation of practicing magic and astrology, but the principal reason for his imprisonment seems to have been Theodoric's suspicion that Boethius was corresponding with the orthodox Byzantine Emperor Justin in a conspiracy to overthrow Theodoric. In 524 (or 526), after a term of imprisonment at Pavia, Boethius was put to death. Though there is still controversy, it is widely accepted now that Boethius was unjustly accused.[1]

Scholars disagree over where Boethius was educated and what his sources were. An older theory, still considered arguable, is that Boethius studied in Athens and learned his philosophy in Neo-Platonist schools there.[2] Pierre-Paul Courcelle, on the other hand, maintains that Boethius studied not at Athens but at Alex-

[1]. See C. J. De Vogel, "Boethius, der letzte der Römer," section II, forthcoming in *Aufstieg und Niedergang der römischen Welt*, vol. III, ed. Hildegard Temporini (Berlin). I am grateful to Professor De Vogel for letting me see her article in typescript.

[2]. See, for example, R. Bonnaud, "L'Education scientifique de Boèce," *Speculum*, 4 (1929), 198–206; and C. J. De Vogel, "Boethiana" I and II, *Vivarium*, 9 (1971) and 10 (1972), 49–66 and 1–40; and "Boethius, der letzte de Römer," section II.

andria in the school of the Greek commentators on Aristotle, and that the head of that school, Ammonius Hermiae, was one of the main influences on Boethius.[3] More recently a theory has been gaining currency that Boethius studied neither in Athens nor in Alexandria but got the material for his logical works from the marginalia in a copy of Aristotle's *Organon*, which he owned.[4] Whatever the final outcome of the controversy, it is clear that Boethius was heavily influenced by both Neo-Platonism and Aristotelianism.

Boethius's works include the *Consolation of Philosophy*, one of the masterpieces of Western literature; five theological treatises, important in the development of medieval theology; and three books on the quadrivium: two treatises on mathematics and a textbook on music. He intended to translate all the works of Plato and of Aristotle into Latin and to reconcile the two, but he accomplished only a small portion of that enormous task, namely, translations of and commentaries on most of Aristotle's logical works. He also translated Porphyry's *Isagoge* and wrote commentaries on it and on Cicero's *Topica*. In addition, he wrote several independent works on logic, including treatises on categorical and hypothetical syllogisms, a book on ways of analyzing things (*Liber de divisione*), and a treatise on Topics, the *De topicis differentiis* (*De top. diff.*), with which this study is concerned.[5]

Boethius's influence on medieval philosophy was considerable. The early scholastics knew as much of Aristotle as they did know largely through his translations; his commentaries and treatises were used very widely and served to establish, among other

3. See *Late Latin Writers and Their Greek Sources*, tr. H. Wedeck (Cambridge, Mass., 1969; 1st ed., Paris, 1948), pp. 275ff.; also, "Boèce et l'école d'Alexandrie," *Mélanges d'Archéologie et d'Histoire*, 52 (1935), 185–223; and *La Consolation de philosophie dans la tradition littéraire, antécédents et postérité de Boèce* (Paris, 1967). See also Philip Merlan, "Ammonius Hermiae, Zacharias Scholasticus, and Boethius," *Greek, Roman, and Byzantine Studies*, 9 (1968), 193–203.

4. James Shiel, "Boethius' Commentaries on Aristotle," *Mediaeval and Renaissance Studies*, 4 (1958), 217–244. See also Lorenzo Minio-Paluello, "Les Traductions et les commentaires aristotéliciens de Boèce," *Studia Patristica II*, 5th ser., 9 (1957), 358–365; and L. M. de Rijk, "On the Chronology of Boethius' Works on Logic" I and II, *Vivarium*, 2 (1964), 1–49, 125–162. See also my article "Boethius's Works on the Topics," *Vivarium*, 12 (1974), 77–93.

5. The name of this treatise is traditionally given as "*De differentiis topicis.*" For evidence that its proper name is "*De topicis differentiis*" see Samuel Brandt, "Entstehungszeit und zeitliche Folge der Werke von Boethius," *Philologus*, 62 (1903), 263, n. 16.

things, a basic Latin philosophical vocabulary. In some cases—for example, in certain developments in medieval logic—his work is the principal source; and his discussion of the ontological status of predicables seems to have sparked the long medieval controversy over universals. In short, he was one of the main influences on the early scholastics and was an authority for them second perhaps only to Augustine among Christian philosophers.

L. M. de Rijk has made a detailed study of the chronology of Boethius's logical works and feels that he can establish with reasonable reliability the following list:

In Porphyrii Isagogen, editio prima	ca. 504–505
De syllogismis categoricis	ca. 505–506
In Porphyrii Isagogen, editio secunda	ca. 507–509
In Aristotelis Categorias	ca. 509–511
In Aristotelis Perihermeneias, editio prima	not before 513
In Aristotelis Perihermeneias, editio secunda	ca. 515–516
De syllogismis hypotheticis	between 516 and 522
In Ciceronis Topica	before 522
De topicis differentiis	before 523

Of the Boethian works on logic not included in this list, two are pertinent to the study of Topics: *Liber de divisione* and Boethius's lost commentary on Aristotle's *Topics*. De Rijk estimates that the former was written between 505 and 509 and the latter sometime before 523, before *De top. diff.*[6]

De topicis differentiis

Boethius's *De topicis differentiis* is concerned with the discovery of arguments. As there is a method for judging or evaluating arguments (what we call 'logic'), so, Boethius thinks, there is also a method for finding arguments. The method varies somewhat, depending on whether the arguments sought will be used in rhetoric for legal or political speeches or in dialectic for philosophical inquiry. Most of Boethius's attention is given to the method as used in dialectic, but the fourth and last Book of the treatise examines the method as used in rhetoric and compares it with that used in dialectic.

Whether the method for finding arguments is rhetorical or dia-

6. "On the Chronology" II, pp. 159–161.

lectical, its main instrument is something called a Topic (in Latin, *'locus'*). 'Topic' is the standard English translation for the Greek *'τόπος'* (the Aristotelian counterpart of *'locus'*), which means, literally, a place or area. A certain sort of Topic that plays a role in the ancient methods for memorization antedates and is probably the source for the kind of Topic used in discovering arguments. In the art of memorizing, a Topic is a place, in the literal sense, which the memorizer pictures in his mind and from which he recalls what he wants to remember. He familiarizes himself with some large edifice in which a number of places are picked out as the τόποι to aid memory, and these places are fixed in the memory in their actual order of occurrence in the edifice. Then the speech, or whatever is being memorized, is divided into parts, and a vivid image is associated with each of the parts. The memorizer pictures these images put into the places of the edifice in their appropriate order. When he is delivering his speech, he imagines himself walking through the edifice, going from place to place, and finding in each place the image he put there. Each image reminds him of a certain part of his speech; and in this way he uses the τόποι to recall the entire speech, part by part, in order.[7]

These Topics are, of course, very different from those used to find arguments, but the two sorts of Topics were seen as analogous. Aristotle himself elucidates dialectical Topics by comparing them with mnemonic Topics (*Top.* 163b28ff.), and Alexander of Aphrodisias elaborates Aristotle's comparison.[8]

A mnemonic Topic is literally a place that can be used over and over again to "store" and "retrieve" what one wants to remember; it is a place from which things to be remembered are recalled. A dialectical or rhetorical Topic is figuratively a place that can be used again and again to produce a variety of arguments. For Aristotle, a dialectical Topic seems to be originally or primarily a strategy of argumentation with which one can construct a number of particular arguments; secondarily, it is a basic principle that can serve to support a variety of arguments.[9] In *De top. diff.* and the

7. Cf. Frances Yates, *The Art of Memory* (London, 1966); Frances Yates, "The Ciceronian Art of Memory," *Medioevo e rinascimento* (Florence, 1955), II, 871–903; Harry Caplan, tr., *Rhetorica ad Herennium* (Cambridge, Mass., 1954); and Richard Sorabji, *Aristotle on Memory* (London, 1972).

8. *In Aristotelis Topicorum,* in *Commentaria in Aristotelem Graeca* (*CAG*), ed. Maximilian Wallies (Berlin, 1891), II, pt. ii, 586–587.

9. See the chapter, "Dialectic and Aristotle's Topics," below.

commentary on Cicero's *Topica* (*In Ciceronis Topica*), Boethius is working with a complicated and ingenious variation on such Topics for finding arguments.

De top. diff. is Boethius's definitive work on the Topics. In it he considers two different sets of dialectical Topics, one of which he finds in Cicero's *Topica* and the other of which stems from the Greek commentator Themistius (ca. 320–390); and he attempts to reconcile the two sets of dialectical Topics. He also discusses rhetorical Topics, and he concludes the treatise by comparing rhetorical and dialectical Topics to make their similarities and differences clear. Because it is an advanced work with a broad scope of material, *De top. diff.* does not devote much attention to the way in which a Topic functions to find an argument. One is likelier to find such discussion in the more elementary *In Ciceronis Topica*. Instead, in *De top. diff.* Boethius contents himself with describing the various Topics and giving examples using each, with a minimum of explanation about the basic method. In the chapter on Boethius, I have explained what I think his technique for finding arguments is and how it works.

In Boethius's work, as well as in Aristotle's, the technique for finding arguments depends on the notion of the predicables: genus, species, definition, differentia, property, and accident. These are technical concepts in ancient and medieval philosophy, and I have provided some account of them in the chapters "Differentia and the Porphyrian Tree" and "Differentia."

De top. diff. has never been critically edited, and the only modern printing of it is available in the *Patrologia Latina* series edited by J.-P. Migne; the *Patrologia* text for *De top. diff.* is apparently copied from the edition of Glareanus, Basel, 1546 and 1570. According to De Rijk, there are about 170 extant manuscripts of *De top. diff.* dating from the tenth to the fifteenth centuries, a fact that attests to the work's popularity and influence.[10] The translation I provide here is the first complete translation of the treatise into any other language, as far as I know. It is not part of my purpose to do editorial work on the text, and, consequently, I have based my translation on the *Patrologia* edition. But I have checked the Glareanus edition of 1570, and I have commented in the notes on some discrepancies that make an important difference to the sense

10. "On the Chronology" II, p. 153 n. 1.

of the text. I have also checked difficult passages in the Paris 1537 edition and in one manuscript, Orleans 267; when my checking has turned up important textual differences, they are mentioned in the notes.[11]

Dialectic

For the most part, *De topicis differentiis* falls into the division of logic that the ancients and medievals called dialectic. It builds on a long tradition of dialectic stemming from Aristotle, and it is itself an important source for much of the later medieval discussion of dialectic. To facilitate understanding Boethius's treatise and evaluating its contribution to the subject, I want to sketch briefly what dialectic was conceived to be and how Boethius fits into the tradition of its study.

Aristotle's *Topics* amounts to a systematizing of the sort of philosophizing carried on in Platonic dialogues.[12] Aristotle thinks of dialectic as involving give and take between a questioner and an answerer;[13] he classifies dialectical argument as the kind of argument used in dialogues (*Soph. El.* 165a38–39), and almost the whole last book of the *Topics* is devoted to techniques for succeeding in Socratic disputation. Seeing the connection between dialectic and disputation helps to clarify the characteristic most generally associated with dialectic and used to distinguish dialectic from demonstration, namely, that dialectic takes its premises from what is "probable" (ἔνδοξα).[14] A dialectical argument differs from a demonstrative one because a demonstrative argument depends on true and indemonstrable premises,[15] but a dialectical argument depends only on premises that are readily believable, that is, believed by everyone or the many or the wise.[16]

11. I am indebted to Pierre Hadot for generously making available to me a photocopy of the Paris 1537 edition.
12. Cf., for example, Gilbert Ryle, "Dialectic in the Academy," in *Aristotle on Dialectic, Proceedings of the Third Symposium Aristotelicum,* ed. G. E. L. Owen (Oxford, 1968), pp. 69–79. Also, Friedrich Solmsen, "Dialectic without the Forms," in *Aristotle on Dialectic,* pp. 49–68.
13. Cf., for example, *Top.* 155b9–10 and *An. Pr.* 24a24–26.
14. See, for example, *An. Pr.* 24b10–12. 'Probable' is the common but misleading translation of 'ἔνδοξα.' In my translation of *De top. diff.,* on the basis of what Boethius says about the Latin equivalent of Aristotle's Greek term, I have abandoned 'probable' and substituted 'readily believable.'
15. See *An. Pos.* 71b26–30.   16. *Top.* 100a26–b17, 100b21–23.

A dialectical argument is not so much a second-class argument, one whose premises are not completely sure, as an argument made for a particular purpose, that is, for disputation. In a disputation, one wants to compel an opponent to agree, and so the premises of the argument must be plausible, above all, but they need not fall short of the complete truth.[17] The premises of a demonstrative argument are truths known per se or what is derived from such truths, and everyone who understands a truth known per se agrees without further evidence that it is true. But among the types of dialectical premises are those held to be true by everyone, and included in the class of propositions held to be true by everyone will be truths known per se, that is, demonstrative premises. So some premises and hence some arguments can be both dialectical and demonstrative. Dialectical and demonstrative arguments, then, constitute overlapping, rather than mutually exclusive, groups of arguments.

Dialectic's readily believable premises have another important function. In the *Posterior Analytics*, Aristotle distinguishes dialectic from the (demonstrative) sciences. Dialectic is not defined as the sciences are (presumably by a particular set of first principles), and it does not concern itself with any one genus of things (*An. Pos.* 77a26–35). The status of dialectic and its place in Aristotle's divisions of philosophy become clearer in a passage in the *Topics*. The first principles or axioms of any science cannot be discussed demonstratively by that science because they are what is best known in the science and all the other truths of the science are derived from them. Discussion of the axioms of any science, Aristotle says, takes place only or most appropriately within dialectic (*Top.* 101a37–63). Dialectic can discuss the axioms of a science because its purpose is to produce agreement between a questioner and an answerer in a disputation. To achieve that aim, a questioner does not necessarily require premises that are more basic and better known than his thesis, as he would if he were trying to establish his thesis by demonstrative argument; he needs only premises that the answerer will grant him and from which his conclusion will follow. For example, in *Met.* 1006a10ff., Aristotle says that it is not possible to *demonstrate* the law of noncontradic-

17. Cf. *Soph. El.* 165b3–4 and *Top.* 160b17ff., 161b34–38, and 104a3–12.

tion, since there is nothing more basic or better known, but that it can be established by dialectic.[18] So to examine the axioms of a demonstrative science, one needs to rely on plausible ("probable") or readily believable truths, and these are the peculiar province of dialectic (*Top.* 101b1–4). Hence dialectic is not only distinguished from demonstration and the sciences, but it is also established as basic to all of them.

art

The purpose of Aristotle's systematizing of dialectic is to provide a τέχνη, an art for finding in an orderly way dialectical arguments to support one side or another of a question. Aristotle says as much at the beginning of the *Topics* (100a18–21), and at the end of the *De sophisticis elenchis* he claims to be the originator of the art presented in that work and the *Topics*. He does not maintain that the subject of finding arguments has never been studied or taught before, but that it has never before been dealt with systematically as an art or discipline (*Soph. El.* 183b17–184b8). He draws a useful contrast between what he wants to accomplish and what the Sophists do: they enable their students to argue well by having them memorize prepared arguments on major issues; Aristotle does so by teaching them a method for discovering arguments.

So for Aristotle dialectic is the art of finding arguments that are used in disputation and take generally accepted truths as their premises. It falls under no particular science, nor is it a science in its own right, but it provides a method for investigating the first principles of any science.

Cicero begins his *Topica* by apparently promising to explain Aristotle's *Topics* to his friend Trebatius, but he goes on to write a treatise that bears little resemblance to Aristotle's work. Consequently, there has been a search for the treatise that Cicero was in fact explaining when he thought he was explaining Aristotle's. Different scholars have suggested different treatises as candidates, with little consensus.[19] But I think that the entire search may be misguided.

18. I was made aware of the passage and its relevance in this context by Russell Dancy; see his book *Sense and Contradiction: A Study in Aristotle* (Boston, 1975), in which this passage is discussed at length.

19. Cf. H. M. Hubbell's introduction to his translation of Cicero's *Topica*, Loeb Classical Library (London, 1960), pp. 377–378; for a short list of books and articles on the controversy, see his bibliography, p. 380. In addition, cf. Benedetto Riposati, "Quid Cicero de thesi et hypothesi in ⟨⟨Topicis⟩⟩ senserit," *Aevum*, 18 (1944), 61–71; P. Thielscher, "Ciceros Topik und Aristoteles," *Philologus*, 67 (1908), 52–67;

As far as I know, Cicero mentions what he means to give Trebatius in his *Topica* only in the opening of that work itself and in a letter to Trebatius.[20] In the letter Cicero says *"ut primum Velia navigare coepi, institui Topica Aristotelea conscribere."* The Loeb translation reads: "as soon as I began my voyage from Velia I set about writing a summary of the *Topics* of Aristotle." But taking *"conscribere"* as "writing a summary" is not warranted either by the ordinary meaning of the Latin word or by anything in the context in which it occurs; and to take the word as the Loeb translator does is to prejudge the issue. In fact, *"conscribere"* can range from "composing" to "writing down"; and in this letter to Trebatius, it need mean no more than "writing about."

Nor is it clear to me that *"Topica Aristotelea"* should be translated as "Aristotle's *Topics.*" Might the phrase not mean simply 'Aristotelian Topics,' the Greek-based 'Topica' being used as a technical term to avoid the ambiguity of the Latin-based equivalent, 'loci'? After all, Cicero introduces 'locus' in its technical sense slowly and carefully and explains it by reference to Greek terms (Cicero, *Topica*, II 6–7). In addition, there is a similar phrase at the beginning of Cicero's *Topica*, and there *"Topica"* seems to mean just "Topics" and not to be the title of Aristotle's book. The passage reads *"incidisti in Aristotelis Topica quaedam, quae sunt ab illo pluribus libris explicata"*; and the clause "which are expounded by him in several books" strongly suggests that *"Topica"* here has to do with the subject that is expounded in the eight books of Aristotle's *Topics* rather than with the title of that work. So the passage in the letter to Trebatius could, I think, be translated as "I began to write about Aristotelian Topics"; at the least the passage does not constitute conclusive evidence that Cicero meant his *Topica* to be a summary of or even a close commentary on Aristotle's *Topics.*

Though some scholars think that in the beginning of the *Topica*, Cicero is promising to explain Aristotle to his friend—H. M. Hubbell even thinks that the promise is to translate Aristotle[21]—nothing in the text explicitly makes any such promise. In fact,

---

and Werner Eisenhut, *Einführung in die antike Rhetorik und ihre Geschichte* (Darmstadt, 1974), esp. pp. 65–66. The last-mentioned work also contains a useful bibliography.

20. Cicero, *The Letters to His Friends*, tr. W. G. Williams, Loeb Classical Library (London, 1928), vol. II, VII.xix.

21. Hubbell, tr., Cicero, *Topica*, p. 422, note a.

Trebatius does not show much interest in either Aristotle or philosophy. He has tried reading Aristotle's *Topics,* but has found the work too obscure (I.3); and Cicero repeatedly apologizes when he digresses into subjects of strictly philosophical interest. Trebatius is a lawyer. What excites him is the promise of the Topics. He becomes "enflamed" when Cicero tells him that Aristotle has a method for finding arguments in a rational and orderly way (I.2); it is the method that he is interested in learning. And, I think, it is the method, not any scholarly exegesis of Aristotle's treatise, that Cicero is undertaking to give to Trebatius. In fact, Hubbell's translation of the Latin of the relevant passage makes my point explicit: "And when I had made clear to you that these books contained a system developed by Aristotle for inventing arguments so that we might come upon them by a rational system without wandering about, you begged me to teach you *the subject*" (my emphasis).[22] And Cicero does try to teach his friend the method, especially as it applies to jurisprudence. When Cicero expands a bit into other areas, even oratory, he spends time justifying his doing so (cf. X.41, XII.51, XVII.65, XIX.72). So I think it is a mistake to suppose that Cicero meant to write a commentary on Aristotle but was confused about the authorship of the treatise he was commenting on.[23]

It is hard to find much philosophical discussion on the nature of dialectic in Cicero's *Topica.*[24] In general, Cicero thinks of the Topics solely as means for finding arguments. The context of dialectical disputation is almost completely lost; he considers dialectical Topics useful for making speeches, especially for arguing a case at law. In addition, dialectic has lost the special status it has

22. "*Cum tibi exposuissem, disciplinam inveniendorum argumentorum, ut sine ullo errore ad ea ratione et via perveniremus, ab Aristotele inventam illis libris contineri, verecunde tu quidem ut omnia, sed tamen facile ut cernerem te ardere studio, mecum ut tibi illa traderem egisti*" (I.2).

23. B. Riposati argues for the same conclusion on other grounds; see his *Studi sui 'Topica, de Cicerone,* (Milan, 1947), esp. pp. 294–295.

24. For two learned and thorough expositions of Cicero's *Topica,* see Riposati, *Studi,* and Alain Michel, *Les Rapports de la rhétorique et de la philosophie dans l'oeuvre de Cicéron* (Paris, 1960). Michel's book should be used with some caution in the section on Topics because it occasionally confuses and conflates important philosophical categories. To give just one example, Michel assimilates one of Cicero's main groups of Topics (those taken from "things which are in some way related to the things asked about") to the predicable *accident* (p. 189); but such Topics include genus, species, and differentia, which have to do with substance and cannot be classed as accidents.

in Aristotle. Cicero makes it a twin to logic, both of them branches of the art of discourse (*ars disserendi*); and he makes no use of Aristotle's suggestion that dialectic is useful in examining the first principles of sciences. Most important, Cicero's concept of a Topic is very different from Aristotle's and similar to Boethius's, though he gives almost no indication of the way in which he thinks such a Topic functions.

Cicero's treatise, then, differs a great deal from Aristotle's, and I think something useful can be drawn from that fact. If Cicero himself had discovered any of the adaptations of or changes in the Aristotelian method which he makes use of in his *Topica*, it seems hard to believe that he would not have mentioned his discoveries and announced them as the product of his own effort and learning. But he does nothing of the sort; instead he takes them for granted. So it is more than likely, I think, that the art of Topics underwent changes that had become standard by Cicero's time. I have tried to suggest how and when such changes might have occurred in the chapter "Between Aristotle and Boethius."

For Boethius, as for Cicero, dialectic is primarily a discipline for finding arguments. Men naturally hit on arguments without the help of any art. But dialectic enables them to find arguments "without travail and without confusion";[25] it provides a way "without wandering" and a "straight path" (*ICT* 271.41–43; *PL* 1043A13–15) for the discovery of arguments. Like Aristotle, Boethius thinks that dialectic is used primarily in dialogue or disputation (*De top. diff.* 1206C3–D4), but he does not tie the discipline of dialectic as closely to the context of disputation as does Aristotle. Aristotle in the *Topics* is interested in enabling a man to function well in a dialectical dispute, and he spends a good deal of time discussing disputation. He examines the sorts of problems that give rise to arguments (101b11ff.); he discusses the sort of proposition one ought to defend in an argument (104a3ff.) and general preparation for arguing (105a20ff.); and he devotes most of the eighth Book to ways of getting the better of one's opponent in

---

25. *In Ciceronis Topica* (*ICT*), in *Ciceronis Opera*, ed. J. C. Orelli (Zurich, 1833), V, pt. 1, 272.3; for the same text in the *Patrologia Latina* (*PL*) edition, see *PL*, LXIV, 1043B5–6. For corrections of the text, see Thomas Stangl, *Boethiana vel Boethii commentariorum in Ciceronis Topica emendationes* (Gotha, 1882); and A. Perdamo, ed., "A Critical Edition of Boethius' Commentary on Cicero's *Topica*. Bk.I" (Ph.D. diss., St. Louis University, 1963). I am currently working on a translation of and commentary on Boethius's *In Ciceronis Topica*.

an argument. There are no similar discussions in *De top. diff.* Nor does Boethius seem to have in mind a certain structure for the dispute as Aristotle does; for example, he spends no time distinguishing the functions of the questioner from those of the answerer, and he says nothing about criteria for evaluating a dialectical disputation. In short, Boethius (at least in his extant works on the Topics) is not much interested in the disputation itself; his main concern is simply with the process of constructing arguments. Consequently, *De top. diff.* is devoted almost completely to the Topics, to explaining what they are and how they can be used to produce arguments. Its aim is to make the discipline of dialectic more systematic and more concise so that it might be an easily usable tool for finding arguments.

Later medieval philosophers were also interested in dialectic, and the literature on the subject is immense. For example, Charles Lohr catalogues medieval commentaries on Aristotle alphabetically by author; his list is hundreds of pages long, and many of the entries are commentaries on Aristotle's *Topics*. [26] Furthermore, the subject came to be considered a regular part of logic and was treated in a section of its own in logic texts. Boethius was for a long time the direct, perhaps the sole, source for the study of dialectic, and his work remained an important indirect source even when it was superseded by later treatments of the subject, such as that in Peter of Spain's *Tractatus*, a standard logic textbook from the late thirteenth to the end of the fifteenth centuries. [27] The chapter on topics in the *Tractatus* is organized in the same way as *De top. diff.*; first there is a series of definitions and then a listing of the Topics with a description and example for each. The whole chapter is heavily dependent on Boethius's treatise; and in some places, what Peter says is simply a quotation from Boethius. Some of his definitions, for example, are identical to those of Boethius. [28]

26. "Medieval Latin Aristotle Commentaries. Authors A–F," *Traditio*, 23 (1967), 313–413; "Authors G–I," *Traditio*, 24 (1968), 149–245; "Authors: Jacobus–Johannes Juff," *Traditio*, 26 (1970), 135–216; "Authors: Johannes de Knathi–Myngodus," *Traditio*, 27 (1971), 251–351; "Authors: Narcissus–Richardus," *Traditio*, 28 (1972), 281–396; "Authors: Robertus–Wilgelmus," *Traditio*, 29 (1973), 93–197; "Supplementary Authors," *Traditio*, 30 (1974), 119–144.

27. Peter of Spain, *Tractatus*, ed. L. M. de Rijk (Assen, 1972), pp. 55–78.

28. Cf., for example, Peter, p. 55.17, and Boethius, *De top. diff.*, 1180C4–5; Peter, p. 55.23, and Boethius, *De top. diff.*, 1183A9–10; and Peter, p. 56.16–18, and Boethius, *De top. diff.*, 1184B13–C1. References to *De top. diff.* here and throughout are to the *PL* edition.

Commenting even sketchily on important or especially pertinent medieval discussions of the Topics is a very large job and outside the scope of this study. One would need to take account, for example, of Abelard, Averroes, Albert the Great, Peter of Spain, William of Sherwood, Lambert of Auxerre, John Buridan, Walter Burley, Albert of Saxony, William Ockham, and the Pseudo-Scot, among others.[29] Because Peter of Spain's *Tractatus* was widely used and because Peter's treatment of Topics seems fairly typical for its time, I have examined his discussion of Topics in detail in the chapter on Peter of Spain to show how the art of Topics changed from Boethius's time to Peter's. Here I want to make only a few observations about the nature of that change.

Cicero and Boethius think of the art of discourse (*ars disserendi*) as divided into the art of finding arguments (dialectic) and the art of judging them (what we call 'logic'). In the discussion of the Topics after Boethius, there is a growing tendency to absorb the techniques of the art of finding into the art of judging, to make the Topics part of the method for judging the validity of arguments. Otto Bird speaks of it more specifically as an absorption of the study of the Topics into the study of conditionals,[30] and he considers Abelard a transitional figure between Boethius and Ockham.[31] For Abelard, a Topic is an inference rule that helps one find what is missing in enthymemes.[32] Enthymemes, or "imper-

29. Cf. especially Jan Pinborg, "Topik und Syllogistik im Mittelalter," *Sapienter Ordinare: Festgabe für Erich Kleineidam*, ed. F. Hoffmann, L. Scheffczyk, and K. Feiereis (Leipzig, 1969), and *Logik und Semantik im Mittelalter* (Stuttgart-Bad Cannstatt, 1972); and the following articles by Otto Bird: "The Tradition of the Logical Topics: Aristotle to Ockham," *Journal of the History of Ideas*, 23 (1962), 307–323; "The Formalizing of the Topics in Mediaeval Logic," *Notre Dame Journal of Formal Logic*, 1 (1960), 138–149; "The Logical Interest of the Topics as Seen in Abelard," *Modern Schoolman*, 37 (1959), 53–57; "Topic and Consequence in Ockham's Logic," *Notre Dame Journal of Formal Logic*, 2 (1961), 65–78.

30. Bird, "Formalizing," pp. 145–146 and 148.

31. I am indebted to Bird's article "The Logical Interest" for my understanding of Abelard in what follows.

32. Abelard, *Dialectica*, ed. L. M. de Rijk (2d ed., Assen, 1970), pp. 253–255 and 262. "Hence, a Topic is properly said to be the force only of those inferences which are imperfect, so that the assignment of the Topic supplies what is lacking with regard to the perfection of the inference. For example, when we say, 'If it is a man, it is an animal,' and by means of 'man' we assert 'animal,' the consequence is not ratified by means of the connection of the terms asserted in the construction [that is, the enthymeme], but the necessity of the consequence is manifested when the former [viz., man] is shown to be a species of the latter [viz., animal], and the method of proof—from the species to the genus—is expressed by the maximal proposition [that is, the Topic]" (262.29–35).

fect syllogisms," are valid not formally but because of a certain relationship between the terms.[33] The Topic makes such inferences formally valid because it provides a rule or law founded on a certain relationship between the things signified by the terms,[34] for example: Whatever the species is predicated of, the genus [of that species] is also predicated of.[35] With Ockham, the whole study of the Topics has become subsumed under the study of conditionals. Ockham distinguishes formal consequences, those that are valid in virtue of their structure, from material consequences, those that are valid because of a certain relationship among the terms. A Topic for Ockham is what validates the passage from the antecedent to the consequent in a material consequence.[36]

This later stage in the development of the study of Topics resembles certain subjects of interest among contemporary philsophers. Bird argues that attempts such as Stephen Toulmin's to analyze inferences that seem outside the pale of formal logic amount to a rediscovery of the Topics.[37] The sort of argument Toulmin analyzes and finds warrants for is the sort of argument the medievals discussed as material consequences, according to Bird. In addition, Bird claims, the medievals found a way to formalize the study of material consequences, and the study of the Topics became for them something like a logic of classes.

With these later changes in the discipline of the Topics, however, the ancient idea of a discipline of discovery and Boethius's cogent technique for discovering arguments have been lost.[38]

33. Cf. Abelard, *Dialectica*, pp. 256–257.
34. Cf. Pinborg, "Topik und Syllogistik," pp. 160–164.
35. *"de quocumque predicatur species, et genus,"* Abelard, *Dialectica*, p. 347.2.
36. See Bird, "Tradition of the Logical Topics," pp. 317–322, and "Topic and Consequence in Ockham's Logic."
37. "Tradition of the Logical Topics," pp. 322–323; "The Re-discovery of the 'Topics': Prof. Toulmin's Inference-Warrants," *Proceedings of the American Catholic Philosophical Association*, 34 (1960), 200–205.
38. I regret that I was unable to consult Luca Obertello's *Severino Boezio* while I was writing this book.

PART ONE

De topicis differentiis

BOOK I

1173C   The whole science of discourse (*ratio disserendi*), which the
ancient Peripatetics called 'λογική,' is divided into two parts:
one of discovering, the other of judging. The part which
purges and instructs judgment, called 'ἀναλυτική' by them, we
5   can name 'analytical.' The part which aids competence (*facultatem*) in discovering, called 'τοπική' by the Greeks, is called
'Topical' (*localis*) by us. The part which is mistress of judging
will be discussed elsewhere.

My present plan is to show what the Topics are, what their
10   differentiae are, and which are suited for which syllogisms. It
seems that we ought not to do this simply and uniformly, but
rather that we ought to convey two divisions [of Topics], one
dug out from Greek books, the other taken from Cicero's *Topica*. To complete the investigation, we must explain in which
15   ways each division differs from the other, /1173D/ in which
ways each matches the other, and in what way each can in
turn contain the other.

We will not dwell on details now, but we will discuss the
whole division in general, collecting definitions, examples,
20   and differentiae only of those Topics from which arguments
arise. The details, as befits the character of the work, are more
thoroughly set forth in the eight books of Aristotle's *Topics*,
which we translated into Latin, or in the seven books of Cicero's *Topica*, for which we with a great deal of effort produced
25   a clear and complete commentary. There all these things are
set forth in clear and appropriate parts, but here the things
that have been made clear piece by (*per membra*) elsewhere
are treated in a general examination.

We must take care to pursue not only the dialectical Topics
30   but also the rhetorical Topics and the way in which the rhetor-

1173D ical Topics differ among themselves and from the dialectical Topics, so that when all the Topics have been completely and fully considered and their differences /1174C/ and similarities have been thoroughly examined, an abundance of arguments
5 will be provided and there can be a clear distinguishing among the Topics.

In order to establish all these things with very clear reasons, we must prolong our introduction a little more. A proposition (*propositio*) is an expression (*oratio*) signifying what is true or
10 false; for example, when someone says that the heaven is re-volvable, this is called a statement (*enuntiatio*) and an assertion (*proloquium*). A question is a proposition brought into doubt and uncertainty, as when someone asks whether the heaven is revolvable. A conclusion is a proposition confirmed by argu-
15 ments, as when someone shows by means of other facts (*rebus*) that the heaven is revolvable. A statement, whether it is said only for its own sake or brought forward to confirm something else, is a proposition; if one asks regarding it, it is a question; if it is confirmed [by other facts], it is a conclusion. So a prop-
20 osition, question, and conclusion are one and the same, though /1174D/ they differ in the way mentioned above.

An argument is a reason (*ratio*) producing belief regarding a matter [that is] in doubt. Argument and argumentation are not the same, however; for the sense (*vis sententiae*) and the reason
25 enclosed in discourse (*oratio*) when something [that was] un-certain is demonstrated is called the argument; but the expres-sion (*elocutio*) of the argument is called the argumentation. So the argument is the strength (*virtus*), mental content (*mens*), and sense of argumentation; argumentation, on the other
30 hand, is the unfolding of the argument by means of discourse (*oratio*).

A Topic is the seat of an argument, or that from which one draws an argument appropriate to the question under consid-eration.
35 Now we must treat the details more thoroughly and make a division of them by species, parts, and schemes (*figuras*), as we said.

First we should discuss the proposition. This, we said, is an expression containing truth or falsehood. There are two spe-
40 cies of proposition: the one, affirmation; the other, negation. If

1174D someone proclaims /1175A/ 'The heaven is revolvable,' that is
an affirmation. If someone declares 'The heaven is not revolvable,' that is a negation.

5   Of these [affirmations and negations], some are universal,
some particular, some indefinite, and some singular. If someone declares 'Every man is just,' 'No man is just,' these are
universal [affirmations and negations]. If someone says, 'Some
man is just,' 'Some man is not just,' these are particular [affir-
mations and negations]. If someone says, 'A man is just,' 'A
10   man is not just,' these are indefinite [affirmations and nega-
tions]. Singular [affirmations and negations] are those that
present an individual or something singular, as, for example,
'Cato is just,' 'Cato is not just'; for Cato is individual and singular.

15   Of these, we call some predicative and some conditional.
Predicatives are those which are presented simply, that is,
those to which no conditional force (vis conditionis) attaches;
as, for example, when someone /1175B/ says simply that the
heaven is revolvable. But if a condition is joined to this, one
20   conditional is made out of two propositions, in this way: 'If
the heaven is spherical, it is revolvable.' Here as a result of the
condition, one understands that the heaven is revolvable just
for this reason, namely, if it is spherical.

Thus, some propositions are predicative and others condi-
25   tional; and so we call the parts of predicative propositions
terms: these are the predicate and the subject. Terms are what
I call the verbs and names out of which the proposition is knit
together. For example, in the proposition 'Man is just,' these
two names 'just' and 'man' we call the parts of the proposition.
30   We also call them the terms; and of the terms, one is the subject, the other is the predicate. The subject is the lesser (minor)
term, the predicate is the greater (major). Thus, for example, in
the proposition 'Man is just,' /1175C/ 'man' is less than 'just,'
for justice can be not only in man but also in corporeal and
35   divine substances. Therefore, the term 'just' is the greater but
'man' is the lesser; and so 'man' is the subject term and 'just'
the predicate.

Though these simple propositions have one term as predicate and one as subject, the proposition is called predicative
40   because of the special status of the greater [term]. It often hap-

1175C pens, however, that the terms are found to be equal to each
       other, in this way: 'Man is a risible thing.' 'Man' and 'a risible
       thing' are each equally the subject term, for risible thing does
       not extend beyond man nor does man extend beyond risible
5   thing. It is necessary, however, that if the terms are unequal,
       the greater is always predicated of /1175D/ [the term that is
       then] the subject. If they are equal, each by reversing the pred-
       ication (*conversa praedicatione*) is said of the other. But in no
       proposition does it happen that the lesser is predicated of the
10   greater.
          It can happen that the parts of propositions, which we call
       terms, occur not only as names but also as phrases (*orationes*).
       Often a phrase is predicated of a phrase in this way: 'Socrates
       with Plato and the [other] students investigates the essence
15   (*ratio*) of philosophy.' The phrase 'Socrates with Plato and the
       [other] students' is, of course, the subject, and 'investigates
       the essence of philosophy' is predicated. Sometimes a name is
       the subject and a phrase the predicate, in this way: 'Socrates
       investigates the essence of philosophy.' Here 'Socrates' alone
20   is the subject; the predicate is the phrase /1176A/ 'investigates
       the essence of philosophy.' It also happens that a phrase is the
       subject (*supponatur*) and a simple word is predicated, in this
       way: 'Socrates's similarity to the celestial divine substances is
       justice.' Here the phrase 'Socrates's similarity to the celestial
25   divine substances' is the subject, and 'justice' is predicated.
       But we have discussed such propositions more thoroughly in
       the commentaries which we composed on Aristotle's book *De
       interpretatione*.
          The parts of conditional propositions, which the Greeks call
30   hypothetical, are simple propositions. The part of a condi-
       tional proposition that is said first is called the antecedent and
       the part that is said second is called the consequent. So, for ex-
       ample, in this proposition 'If it is spherical, it is revolvable,'
       that it is spherical is the antecedent; that it is revolvable, the
35   consequent. /1176B/
          Of these, some are simple conditionals, some conjoined con-
       ditionals.
          Simple conditionals are those that have predicative proposi-
       tions for their parts, as in the example mentioned above: 'If it

1176B is spherical, it is revolvable'; for, separated and taken singly, 'It is spherical' and 'It is revolvable' are both predicatives.

There are many kinds (*multiplex differentia*) of conjoined conditionals, which we delved into most thoroughly in the books we composed on hypothetical syllogisms.

There are, on the other hand, four kinds of simple hypothetical propositions. There are those made up of two affirmative categoricals, as 'If it is spherical, it is revolvable,' for each of these is affirmative. Or, of two negatives, as 'If the heaven is not spherical, it is not revolvable, for that it is not spherical and that it is not revolvable are /1176C/ both negations. Or, of an affirmative and a negative, as 'If it is square, it is not revolvable,' for that it is square is an affirmation and that it is not revolvable is a negation. Or, of a negative and an affirmative, as 'If it is not spherical, it is stationary,' for that it is not spherical is a negation but that it is stationary is an affirmation.

Also, some propositions are known per se, and no proof can be found for these. Others, although the mind of the hearer approves them and assents to them, can nevertheless be proved by other, more fundamental propositions. Those for which there is no proof are called maximal and principal, because it is necessary that these prove those which do not deny that they can be demonstrated. This is a maximal proposition: 'If you take equals from equals, the remainders are equal.' /1176D/ This is known per se, in such a way that there cannot be anything more known by which it could be proved. Since these propositions produce appropriate belief in themselves by nature, they not only need no argument from without for belief but also are generally the starting point for the proof of other things. Therefore, propositions known per se, than which nothing is more known, are called indemonstrable, maximal, and principal. There are others which, although the judgment of the hearer may assent to them, nevertheless have something naturally more known which provides belief for them from without if some question arises about them. These others are called demonstrable, lesser, and secondary.

And now enough has been said about propositions.

A question is a proposition in doubt, and virtually the same

1176D things have to be taken into consideration here which were just now said about the proposition. /1177A/

For some questions are simple; some are composite. The simple ones are those which are derived from a simple proposition in this way, as, for example, when someone asks whether the heaven is revolvable, for this question comes from the proposition which says that the heaven is revolvable. If the question has its origin from a conditional composite proposition, it will be conditional and composite; for example, 'If the heaven is spherical, is it revolvable?', for this question takes its starting point from the conditional proposition 'If the heaven is spherical, it is revolvable.' So a question is sometimes predicative and sometimes conditional.

And so a question has the same parts which were just now mentioned for propositions. Predicative questions, then, have a predicate and a subject; for example, that in which one asks whether the heaven is revolvable, for 'revolvable' is the predicate and /1177B/ 'heaven' is the subject. 'Revolvable' is a greater (*major*) term than 'heaven,' for it is not the heaven alone which can be said to be revolvable. A conjoined question, on the other hand, will have these parts: a predicate and a subject, an antecedent and a consequent. For example, in that which asks (*dicit*) whether the heaven is revolvable if it is spherical, that it is spherical is the antecedent and that it is revolvable is the consequent. So in a predicative question, what is in doubt is whether the predicate inheres in the subject term. But in hypothetical questions, what is questioned is only whether what is proposed as the consequent accompanies the thing that precedes.

All the things that were said about predicative propositions—that some are universal, some particular, some indefinite, and some singular—virtually the same things can also be said about predicative questions. /1177C/ For this is the only difference between a question and a proposition: a proposition is an expression signifying what is true or false, either simply stated or for the sake of proving something else; a question, on the other hand, though it is an expression, is a proposition in doubt. So with the addition of doubt, the things considered in connection with the proposition are also appropriate to be discussed in connection with the question.

1177C   There are two kinds of question. One is that called 'thesis' by the [Greek] dialecticians. This is the kind of question which asks about and discusses things stripped of relation to other circumstances; it is the sort of question dialecticians

5   most frequently dispute about—for example, 'Is pleasure the greatest good?' [or] 'Should one marry?' By us, this sort of question is called 'proposal' (*propositum*). The other kind of question the Greeks call 'hypothesis,' and we call 'case' (*causa*). This sort /1177D/ is a question involving persons,

10   times, deeds, and other circumstances; for example, 'Was Cicero rightfully thrust into exile at a time of uncertainty for the republic because he had put to death Roman citizens without the command of the people?'

    This twofold division of questions must have further sub-

15   divisions. The thesis belongs to philosophers, the hypothesis to orators. I will give the divisions of the sort of question which is the hypothesis later. Now I will examine the division of the thesis, which is divided into four kinds. In every predicative dialectical question, one asks whether what is predica-

20   tive inheres in what is the subject. When something is put forth as inhering in something else, it will be greater (*majus*) than that of which it is predicated and will be asserted to inhere in [the subject's] substance, or it will be greater than that of which it is predicated /1178A/ but it will not be predi-

25   cated of its substance, or it will be equal to it and predicated of its substance, or it will be equal to it but will not include its substance. For it happens in no proposition that we predicate what is lesser of what is greater.

    If what is put forth in the question is such that it is greater

30   than the subject and predicated of the substance of the subject, it will be a genus, for every genus is greater than what it is predicated of and is said of its [subject's] substance as, for example, animal of man. If it is greater but not predicated of the subject's substance, it will be an accident, as, for example,

35   white in relation to man. If it is equal but substantial, it will be the definition of the subject, as, for example, rational mortal animal in relation to man, for this is reversible (*convertitur*) and shows the formula (*ratio*) of the subject, that is, the substance of man. If it is /1178B/ equal but separated from the

40   formula of the substance, it will be a property, as, for example,

1178B risible in relation to man. So simple dialectical questions are
       about genus, accident, definition, or property.

       There can also be questions about differentia—when one
       questions whether the celestial bodies are rational or not, or
5   when what is in doubt is whether the differentia between a
       tyrant and a ruler (*princeps*) is that a ruler takes his power
       from the laws, but a tyrant oppresses the people with domina-
       tion by force. But raising a question about a differentia is the
       same as asking about the genus, for the differentia will be ei-
10   ther constitutive or divisive. If it is constitutive, it stands as it
       were in place of the genus, as rationality (*rationabilitas*) for
       man (or if the celestial bodies partake of reason, then also for
       the celestial bodies). But if it is divisive, it is considered as a
       species, /1178C/ for every species occurs with a dividing dif-
15   ferentia. But if we use differentia now in place of the genus,
       now in place of the species, we cannot doubt that to raise a
       question about differentia is to ask about genus.

       It can happen that something is brought into contention by
       comparison, as when there is doubt whether courage is better
20   than justice. But this question must be put among questions
       involving accidents, because nothing but accident comes into
       play in comparisons, for only accident admits of more and less.

       Again, there can be contention about what is the same; for
       example, whether what is advantageous (*utile*) is the same as
25   what is virtuous (*honestum*). But this question should be as-
       sociated with [those involving] definition, for things whose
       definition is the same are themselves also the same, but things
       whose formula (*ratio*) of substance is different are themselves
       also different.

30   So /1178D/ there are rightly said to be four kinds of simple
       dialectical question, and enough has been said about them.

       Now we must discuss conditional questions. Of these, some
       are made up of two affirmatives, some of two negatives, some
       of an affirmation and a negation, and some of a negation and
35   an affirmation. If the conditional proposition is made up of
       two affirmations, then what is in question is whether an affir-
       mation follows from an affirmation. If the proposition is com-
       pounded of two negations, what is in contest is whether a
       negation follows from a negation. If it is composed of an affir-
40   mation and a negation or a negation and an affirmation, what

1178D is in doubt is whether a negation follows from an affirmation, or an affirmation from a negation.

And first we must make a division of the question in which it is decided whether an affirmation follows from an affirmation, which does not fall outside the division or predicative questions; for it generally happens in just those things which I mentioned shortly before that something precedes and something else follows from it. (1) Genus, differentia, definition, property, or inseparable accident follow from the species. Similarly, (2) species follows from property and definition; (3) differentia and definition follow from property; and (4) property or differentia follow from definition. For example: (1') if it is a man, it is an animal; if it is a man, it is rational; if it is a man, it is a mortal rational animal; if it is a man, it is risible; if it is an Ethiopian, it is black. (2') If it is risible, it is a man; if it is a mortal rational animal, it is a man. (3') If it is risible, it is rational; if it is risible, /1179B/ it is a mortal rational animal. (4') If it is a mortal rational animal, it is risible, or two-footed.

Besides these, an effect sometimes follows from a cause, and a cause sometimes follows from an effect. An effect follows from a cause in this way: if the sun is present, it is day (*lucet*); a cause from an effect in this way: if something is burned up (*exustum*), there has been a fire, or in this way: if the sun appears, it is day.

Similarly, the parts follow from the whole, as, 'If the house is complete, a roof, walls, and a foundation exist (*consistunt*).'

So also an oblique form (*modus*) follows from the principal name, as, 'If justice is good, what is [done] justly is also good.' The principal name also follows from the oblique form, as, 'If what is [done] justly is good, justice is also good.'

Also, the subject follows from [its] accidents, as, 'If something is white, it is a body.'

Therefore, /1179C/ we have to make just this division of the question—a simple conditional composed of two affirmations—namely, that in it one asks about genus, differentia, species, property, definition, accident, cause and effect, whole and parts, or oblique form and principal name. And these are the things we ought to understand about the question which is a simple hypothetical and composed of two affirmatives.

The same differentiae must make up those questions deriv-

1179C ing from propositions which are both negations. For if the genus is not, the species is not. Similarly, if the differentia, definition, or property is not, the species will not be. And all the other things mentioned above should be understood in the
5 same way because whatever precedes in such a way that something else follows, if that which /1179D/ follows is not, that which precedes is not either.

There is this division of questions made up of an affirmation and a negation: they consist in different genera, different
10 species, contraries, or privation and possession. For in order for a negation to follow from an affirmation, a different genus is posited, so that what is different from it is rejected in this way: 'If it is a man, it is not whiteness,' or 'If it is a substance, it is not a quality.' Or else, different species under the same
15 genus are posited in this way: 'If it is a man, it is not a horse.' Or else, contraries are posited, as, 'If it is white, it is not black.' Or, privations are posited, as, 'If it is blind, it does not see.' Finally, in all things which are not the same, it is the case that if something is one of them, it /1180A/ is not another.
20 Therefore, in order for a negation to follow from an affirmation which has been put forth, there will be different genera, different species, contraries, privations, or any other things that are mutually exclusive (sibi invicem inconvenientia).

But it cannot happen that an affirmation follows from a
25 negation—the fourth differentia of the conditional proposition—except in the case of contraries which lack an intermediate and one or the other of which must always occur (inesse). For example, 'If it is not day, it is night'; 'If it is not dark, it is light.'
30 Now that the division of predicative and conditional questions has been made, we ought yet to add this, it seems: every question is drawn from the science of discourse (ratio disserendi) or from natural or moral theory. For example, from the science of discourse: whether affirmation and negation are
35 species of statement. From natural theory: whether /1180B/ the heaven is spherical. From moral theory: whether virtue alone suffices for happiness.

Furthermore, every question is either simple or complex. The simple question is often divided into affirmation and

1180B negation in such a way that one must affirm the whole of one
and negate the whole of the other—for example, 'Is the heaven
spherical or not?'—because one part of the question contains
an affirmation, the other a negation; for one person produces
5 an affirmation when he maintains that it is, and another produces a negation when he contends that it is not. A complex
question is one which is divided into more than one affirmation. For example, 'Is the heaven spherical or square or rectan-
gular or of some other shape?' Here it is necessary to test sev-
10 eral affirmations which maintain different things.

Insofar as it pertains to the present business, enough has
been said about the question.

/1180C/ A conclusion is a proposition confirmed by arguments, and virtually the same things can be said about it as
15 were said about the proposition. Since these things were
thoroughly explained above, we ought next, it seems, to examine the argument.

An argument is a reason producing belief regarding something which is in doubt. It must always be more known than
20 the question; for if things which are not known are proved by
things which are known and an argument proves something
which is in doubt, then what is adduced to provide belief for
the question must be more known than the question.

Of all arguments, some are readily believable (*probabilia*)   *probable*
25 and necessary, some readily believable and not necessary,
some necessary but not readily believable, and some neither
readily believable nor necessary.

Something is readily believable if it seems true to everyone
or to most people or to the wise—and of the wise, either to all
30 of them or most of them or to those most famous and distinguished—or to /1180D/ an expert in his own field, for example,
to a doctor in the field of medicine or to a pilot in the naviga-
tion of ships, or, finally, if it seems true to the person with
whom one is having the conversation or who is judging it. In
35 this, the truth or falsity of the argument makes no difference,
if only it has the appearance of truth.

Something is necessary if it is as it is said to be and cannot
be otherwise.

This is an example of something readily believable and nec-

1180D essary: if something is added to a certain thing, the whole is made greater. No one disagrees with this proposition, and it is necessary that it be so.

5   Those things are readily believable and not necessary to which the mind of the hearer readily agrees but which do not contain firm truth. For example, 'If she is a mother, she loves [her] child.'

Those things are necessary and not /1181A/ readily believable which must be as they are said to be but to which the
10   hearer does not readily agree. For example, 'An eclipse of the sun occurs because of the interposition of the body of the moon.'

Those things are neither necessary nor readily believable which are established neither in human opinion nor in truth.
15   For example, 'Diogenes has horns, for everyone has what he never lost.' These cannot be called arguments, for arguments produce belief regarding something which is in doubt. But there is no belief from these, which are established neither in human opinion nor in truth.
20   It can be said that those [arguments] which are necessary but not confirmed by the people hearing them are not arguments either. For if there is to be belief regarding something which is in doubt, the mind of the hearer must be compelled by the things to which he agrees so that he can accede also to
25   the conclusion, which he had not previously /1181B/ assented to. But because the one judging does not assent to what is only necessary and not also readily believable, it must be that he will not agree either to what is produced from such a reason (*ratio*). So it follows from such a reason that things which are
30   necessary only and not also readily believable are not arguments.

But this is not the case, and this exposition is not based on a correct understanding of 'readily believable.' Those things are readily believable to which agreement is spontaneously and
35   willingly given, so that they are agreed to as soon as they are heard. But those things that are necessary and not readily believable are demonstrated before by other things that are necessary and readily believable; and, known and believed, they produce belief regarding something else which is in doubt.
40   The theories (theorems) which are considered in geometry are

1181B of this sort. For the things presented there /1181C/ are not such that the mind of the student agrees to them spontaneously; but since they are demonstrated by other arguments and so are known and understood, they produce belief regarding
5   other theories. So those things that are not readily believable per se but are necessary cannot be arguments to confirm something else for hearers to whom they have not yet been demonstrated. But to those hearers who by prior reasons have come to believe those things which they [once] did not agree to,
10   they can be invoked as arguments if [the hearers] are in doubt about something.

Since the whole art (artificium) of discourse consists in four disciplines, we ought to say which one admits of the use of which arguments, so that the abundance may appear clearly to
15   him who understands well the study of Topics. The whole science of discourse is placed under four disciplines and under the artisans, as it were, of these disciplines, /1181D/ namely, the dialectician, the orator, the philosopher, and the sophist.

The dialectician and the orator occupy themselves with a
20   kind of argument common to them both, for each of them aims at arguments that are readily believable whether they are necessary or not. They employ these two kinds of argument: those that are readily believable and necessary and /1182A/ those that are readily believable and not necessary.

25   The philosopher and demonstrator investigates only truth alone; and it makes no difference whether the arguments are readily believable or not, provided they are necessary. He also uses two kinds of argument: those that are readily believable and necessary, and those that are necessary and not readily
30   believable. So it is clear in what respect the philosopher differs from the orator and the dialectician in their areas of inquiry, namely, for them it consists in ready believability and for him in truth.

But the fourth kind of argument, which we showed above is
35   not even rightly called an argument, is generally reckoned among those that are sophistical.

The purpose of the Topics is to reveal (demonstrare) a bountiful supply of arguments which have the appearance of truth. /1182B/ Abundant and bountiful matter for discourse must
40   arise when the Topics from which readily believable argu-

1182B ments are drawn have been designated. But since, as was said above, some readily believable arguments are necessary and others not, when Topics of readily believable arguments are brought forth, Topics of necessary arguments are also pro-
5 duced. So this discipline [of Topics] is mainly serviceable to orators and dialecticians, and secondarily to philosophers. Insofar as all readily believable arguments are searched out, the dialecticians and the orators are served; insofar as readily believable and necessary arguments are produced, an abun-
10 dance is provided for philosophical demonstration. So not only the dialectician and the orator but also the demonstrator and producer of true argumentation have something they can take from the Topics since among the Topics of readily believable arguments this teaching (*traditio*) contains also the start-
15 ing points of necessary arguments. /1182C/ The arguments that are necessary but not readily believable and the last kind of argument, that which is neither readily believable nor necessary, are not part of what this work proposes to consider, except that occasionally certain sophistical Topics are brought up
20 for the sake of exercising the reader.

So the usefulness and purpose of the Topics have both been made clear, for they aid both competence in speech and the investigation of truth. Insofar as knowledge of the Topics serves dialecticians and orators, it provides an abundance [of ma-
25 terials] for speech (*oratio*) by means of the discovery [of arguments]; on the other hand, insofar as it teaches philosophers about the topics of necessary [arguments], it points out in a certain way the path of truth. Therefore, this study should be the more thoroughly investigated and examined; and when it
30 is known and understood, it ought to be strengthened by use and /1182D/ exercise. For study of the Topics promises something great, namely, the paths of discovery, which those who are ignorant of this account (*ratio*) impute altogether to natural talent alone; they do not understand how much by means of
35 this study one acquires that which brings force to art and power to nature. But enough about that. Now let us explain the rest.

BOOK II

1181D   All the things set forth in succession in the book above will
seem somewhat superfluous and rather secondary to less educated people perhaps, for when they read the title of [these]
Books—*De differentiis topicis*—/1182D/they omit the stages of
5   the study and immediately direct their attention to the end of
the work. But to me it seems inevitable that the mind of the
student will be unable to achieve the higher stages [of the
study] unless [the prior stages of the study] have been previously learned. And if those who /1183A/ now think the
10   whole discussion of the first Book superfluous read everything
thoroughly and survey with mind and reason (*ratio*) the composition of the work, they will surely cease to judge superfluous what they cannot help but see in position as part of the
[whole] work. And that is enough about that. Since enough
15   has been said about what we presented before, that is, about
the proposition, question, conclusion, [and] argument, let us
now discuss argumentation. Argumentation is the unfolding
of an argument by means of discourse (*oratio*).
        There are two kinds of argumentation; one is called syl-
20   logism, the other induction.
        Syllogism is discourse in which, when certain things have
been laid down and agreed to, something other than the
things agreed to must result by means of the things agreed to.
The second /1183B/ Book of the work in which I wrote a text-
25   book (*institutionem*) on categorical syllogisms contains the explanation (*ratio*) of this definition in full. But to facilitate understanding, we will briefly clarify the same matter here with
an example. This is a syllogism: every man is an animal; every
animal is a substance; therefore, every man is a substance.
30   This whole thing is the discourse in which, when certain

1183B things have been laid down and agreed to—namely, the two
propositions 'Every man is an animal' and 'Every animal is a
substance'—by means of the things agreed to something else
is produced—namely, the conclusion 'Therefore, every man is

5   a substance.' For by means of the propositions agreed to, the
deriving of the conclusion is necessarily produced. These are
the propositions: 'Every man is an animal' and 'Every animal
is a substance'; and from these something other /1183C/ than
the things agreed to is produced. For one concludes 'There-

10 fore, every man is a substance';' and this is far different both
from the proposition 'Every man is an animal' and from the
proposition 'Every animal is a substance.'

    Of syllogisms, some are predicative—these are called cate-
gorical—and some are conditional—these we call hypothetical.

15 Those made up of only predicative propositions are predicative, as the one I mentioned in the example above, for it is
made up of only predicative propositions. On the other hand,
those whose propositions are connected by a condition are hypotheticals. For example: if it is day, there is light; it is day;

20 therefore, there is light. The first proposition contains the condition that it is light just for this reason [namely], if it is day.
So this syllogism is called hypothetical, /1183D/ that is, conditional.

    Induction, on the other hand, is discourse by means of

25 which there is a progression from particulars to universals. For
example, if a pilot to govern ships is chosen not by lot but according to [his possession of] the art, and a charioteer to rule
horses is gotten not by the outcome of lots but by the recom-
mendation of [his possessing] the art, and not lot but skill

30 at governing produces a ruler to guide a state, and similar
[conclusions] are gathered in many [cases], then it results from
these that for anything which one wants responsibly ruled or
governed one finds a suitable ruler not by lot but by art. So
you see how the discourse runs through singulars to arrive at a

35 universal. When one has brought together the cases of ships,
chariots, and states, which are all ruled by art rather than lot,
as though the matter were so in all other cases too, one concludes what /1184A/ was the universal in this way: in all cases
one ought to appoint a ruler not by lot but by art.

40   Often the many particulars brought together prove some

1184A other particular; for example, if someone says: 'If neither ships nor chariots nor fields have their governors appointed by lot, neither should states have their governors taken by lot.'

This kind of argumentation is generally the most readily be-
5   lievable, although it is not as certain as the syllogism. For a syllogism moves from universals to particulars; and if it is made up of true propositions, there is in it certain and unchangeable truth. Induction, on the other hand, is the most readily believable, but it sometimes lacks truth. For example:
10   whoever knows singing is a singer, whoever knows wrestling is a wrestler, and whoever knows building /1184B/ is a builder; and from many cases brought together by a similar principle (ratio), this can result: whoever knows evil is an evildoer, and this does not follow. A good man cannot lack knowledge of
15   evil; for virtue loves itself and despises its contrary, but it can- not shun vice unless it knows what vice is.

[In addition] to these two sources and genera of arguing, we discern two other modes of argumentation, one a substitute for the syllogism, the other a substitute for induction. It is evi-
20   dent that one has its origin in the syllogism, though it is not a complete syllogism, and the other has its origin in induction, though it is not a complete induction. These are the enthy- meme and the example.

An enthymeme is an imperfect syllogism, that is, discourse
25   in which the /1184C/ precipitous conclusion is derived without all the propositions having been laid down beforehand, as when someone says 'man is an animal; therefore he is a sub- stance,' he omits the other proposition, 'Every animal is a sub- stance.' So since an enthymeme argues from universals to par-
30   ticulars which are to be proved, it is, as it were, similar to a syllogism; but because it does not use all the propositions ap- propriate to a syllogism, it deviates from the definition (ratio) of a syllogism and so is called an imperfect syllogism.

Example is joined to induction and differs from it according
35   to a similar principle (ratio). An example argues to show some particular by means of a particular presented; for example, 'It is right for Tully the consul to kill Catiline since Scipio slew Gracchus.' For it is confirmed that Catiline ought to be de- stroyed by Cicero because /1184D/ Gracchus was killed by
40   Scipio. That both of these are particulars and not universals is

1184D shown by the inclusion of individual persons. So since a part
is proved by a part, what we call an example has a kind of
similarity to an induction. But because the parts it collects
from which it produces [the conclusion] are not more than one
5 (*plures*), it differs from induction.

And so there are two main species of arguing, one called
syllogism, the other induction. Under these and, as it were,
flowing from them are the enthymeme and the example. All
these are drawn from the syllogism and obtain their force from
10 the syllogism. For whether it is an enthymeme, induction, or
example, it takes its force as well as the belief [it produces]
most of all from the syllogism; and this is shown in Aristotle's
Prior Analytics, which we /1185A/ translated. So it suffices to
discuss the syllogism which is, as it were, principal and inclu-
15 sive of the other species of argumentation.

It remains now to disclose what a Topic (*locus*) is. A Topic,
as Cicero would have it, is the foundation (*sedes*) of an argument. I will make clear in a few words what the force of this
definition is. The foundation of an argument can be under-
20 stood partly as a maximal proposition, partly as the Differentia
of a maximal proposition. There are some propositions which
not only are known per se but also have nothing more fundamental by which they are demonstrated, and these are
called maximal and principal [propositions]. And there are
25 others for which the first and maximal propositions provide
belief. So of all things which are brought into question, the
very first to be agreed to must be those which can provide
belief for other things in such a way that nothing more known
than they can be found. /1185B/ For an argument is what pro-
30 duces belief regarding something which is in doubt, and it
ought to be more known and more readily believable than
what is proved. Hence, those maximal [propositions] known
per se so that they need no proof from without must impart
belief to all arguments.

35 Such a proposition is sometimes contained within the
boundaries of an argument, and sometimes it supplies force to
the argument and makes [it] complete from without.

Here is an example of an argument which contains such a
maximal proposition. Suppose there is a question whether
40 rule by a king is better than rule by a consul. We will say this:

1185B rule by a king lasts longer than rule by a consul, when both are good; but a good that lasts longer is better than one which lasts a short time; therefore, rule by a king is better than rule by a consul. This /1185C/ argumentation contains its maximal

5 proposition, that is, [its] Topic, which is 'Goods that last a longer time are of more worth than those which last a short time.' This is so known that it needs no proof from without and can itself be a proof for other things. And so this proposition contains the whole proof; and since the argument arises

10 from it, it is rightly called a Topic, that is, the foundation of an argument.

Let this be the example that a maximal proposition posited outside [the argument] brings force to the argument. Suppose the task is to demonstrate that an envious man is not wise. An

15 envious man is one who disparages the good of others. But a wise man does not disparage the good of others. Therefore, an envious man is not wise. The maximal proposition does not appear included within this argumentation, but it gives force to the argumentation, /1185D/ for belief for this syllogism is

20 provided by that proposition by which we know that things whose definitions are different are themselves also different. But in the definition of the envious man there is that—to pine at others' good—which is not found in the wise man; and therefore the wise man is separated from the envious man.

25 So in one way a Topic, as was said, is a maximal, universal, principal, indemonstrable, and known per se proposition, which in argumentations gives force to arguments and to propositions, [being itself] either among the propositions themselves or posited outside them. So propositions that are

30 both universal and maximal are called Topics since they are those which contain other propositions and by means of them the consequent arises and /1186A/ the conclusion becomes ratified. And as a place (locus) contains within itself the quantity of a body, so these propositions which are maximal contain

35 within themselves the whole force of secondary propositions and the deriving of the conclusion itself.

In one way a Topic, that is, the foundation of an argument, is said to be a maximal and principal proposition furnishing belief for other [propositions]. But in another way the Dif-

40 ferentiae of maximal propositions are called Topics, and they

1186A are drawn from the terms that make up the question. These must be discussed next. There are many propositions which are called maximal, and these differ among themselves; and all the Differentiae by which they differ among themselves we
5   call Topics. For if the maximal propositions themselves are Topics of arguments, their Differentiae must also be Topics of arguments. /1186B/ For the substance of anything consists of its characteristic differentiae, as the substance of man consists of rationality, which is its differentia. The Topics which are the
10   Differentiae of [maximal] propositions are more universal than those propositions, just as rationality is more universal than man. And therefore the Topics which are Differentiae are found to be fewer than the propositions of which they are the Differentiae, for it happens that all things which are more uni-
15   versal are always fewer, and those things whose number is not so great that they rapidly escape the memory of the student can easily come within the scope of a science.

What these Differentiae are is brought out better by division.

20   In predicative questions, one term is called the subject, the other the predicate. /1186C/ There is nothing in doubt in predicative questions other than whether the predicate inheres in the subject. If it does inhere, there is doubt about whether it inheres as genus, accident, property, or definition. If it is
25   shown not to inhere, nothing is left of the question; for what does not inhere at all cannot inhere as accident, definition, genus, or property. But if it does inhere, there remains a question as to which of the four ways it inheres.

Solely to inhere belongs most of all to accident; for when
30   [something] inheres not as genus, definition, or property, but nonetheless inheres, it must inhere as accident.

So we must make a division of the Topics which we established as the Differentiae of maximal propositions (*in maximarum propositionum differentia constituimus*). /1186D/ That
35   maximal propositions differ from their Differentiae will appear more clearly by means of example to those going through these things in detail (*per singula . . . quaeque currentibus*), for we will present questions, arguments, maximal and principal propositions, Topics and their Differentiae individually by an
40   example.

1186D   All Topics, that is, Differentiae of maximal propositions, must be drawn from the terms in the question, namely, the subject and the predicate, or be taken from without, or be situated as intermediates between the [previous] two.

5   Of Topics drawn from the terms about which there is doubt in the question, there are two kinds (*duplex . . . modus*). One is drawn from their substance; the other is drawn from things which follow from their substance.

/1187A/ Those which are [drawn] from substance consist in
10   the definition alone; for the definition shows the substance, and the whole demonstration of the substance is the definition. Let us make clear what we say by means of examples so that the whole system (*ratio*) of questions, argumentations, or Topics may become clear (*colliquescat*). Suppose there is a
15   question whether trees are animals and suppose there is a syllogism of this sort: an animal is an animate substance capable of perceiving; a tree is not an animate substance capable of perceiving; therefore, a tree is not an animal. The question has to do with genus, for the question is whether trees should be
20   put under the genus of animals. The Topic which consists in a universal proposition is this: that to which the definition of the genus does not belong is not a species of the genus defined. The higher Differentia of the Topic, which is nevertheless called a Topic: /1187B/ *from definition*. So you see that the
25   whole irresolution (*dubitatio*) in the question is handled in the argumentation of the syllogism by means of propositions that go together and suit one another, which maintain their force from a first and maximal proposition, namely, from that which says that that to which the definition of the genus does not
30   belong is not a species [of the genus defined]. The universal proposition itself is drawn from the substance of one of the terms in the question, namely, from animal, that is, from its definition which is *animate substance capable of perceiving*.

And in the same way in other questions, when the Differen-
35   tiae of Topics have been briefly and shortly recounted, a watchful mind should promptly understand the nature of each of them.

There are two kinds of the Topic drawn from substance; for the arguments are drawn partly from definition and partly
40   from description. Definition differs /1187C/ from description

1187C because a definition contains genus and differentiae; a description comprises understanding of the subject, either by
means of certain accidents producing one property or by
means of differentiae of the substance (*substantialibus differen-*
5   *tiis*) brought together apart from the appropriate genus. Although these definitions which arise from accidents seem in
no way to show the substance, nevertheless proofs taken from
description also seem to be taken from the Topic of *substance*
since descriptions are often put in place of a true definition
10   which shows the substance. Here is an example. Suppose
there is a question whether whiteness is a substance. Here the
question is whether whiteness is put under substance as a
genus. So we say: substance is that which can be the subject
for any accident; whiteness /1187D/ is the subject for no ac-
15   cident; therefore, whiteness is not a substance. The Topic, that
is, the maximal proposition, is the same as above: that whose
definition or description does not belong to what is called [its]
species is not the genus of that which is asserted to be [its]
species. But the description of substance does not belong to
20   whiteness. Therefore, whiteness is not substance. The higher
defferentia of the Topic: *from description;* and this we just now
put in the formula (*ratio*) of substance.
       Those are also definitions which are drawn not from the
substance of the thing but from the signification of its name;
25   and in this way they apply to what the question is about. For
example, if there is a question whether philosophy should be
pursued, there will be an argumentation of this sort. Philosophy is the love of wisdom; no one doubts that this should be
pursued; therefore, philosophy should be pursued. Here
30   /1188A/ not the definition of the thing but the explanation of
the name has provided the argument. Cicero too uses explanation of the name to defend philosophy in the *Hortensius.* In
Greek it is called '$\overset{\text{'}}{o}\nu o\mu\alpha\tau\iota\kappa\overset{\text{`}}{o}\varsigma$ $\overset{\text{'}}{o}\rho o\varsigma$' and in Latin '*nominis in-*
terpretatio' [explanation of the name]. By means of clear ex-
35   amples, I think, we have plainly expounded the arguments
taken from the substance of the terms in the question.
       Now we must discuss those which follow from the sub-
stance of the terms. There is a great variety of these, for there
are many things which adhere to individual substances. Argu-
40   ments are generally drawn from these things which are the

1188A concomitants of the substance of anything: from the whole, from parts, or from causes—efficient causes, matter, natural form, or end.

An efficient cause is one which sets [something] in motion and does something, as is discussed elsewhere. Matter is /1188B/ that from which something comes to be or in which it comes to be. The end is that for which something comes to be.

Among the Topics taken from things which follow from the substance are also these: from effects, from destructions, from uses, or, in addition to all these, from associated accidents (communiter accidentibus).

Let us examine first the Topic which arises from the whole. 'Whole' generally has two meanings, either genus or complete thing made up of more than one part. What is a whole as a genus often supplies arguments to questions in this way. For example, if there is a question whether justice is advantageous, one produces the syllogism: every virtue is advantageous; justice is a virtue; therefore, justice is advantageous. The question here is about accident, that is, whether advantage is an accident of justice. The Topic which is a maximal proposition is this: whatever is present to the genus /1188C/ is present to the species. The higher Topic of this is *from the whole*, that is, from genus, namely, virtue, which is the genus of justice.

Again, suppose there is a question whether human affairs are ruled by providence. We will say: if the world is ruled by providence, but men are part of the world, then (*igitur*) human affairs are ruled by providence. The question has to do with accident. The Topic: what suits the whole fits the part also. The highest Topic: *from the whole*, that is, from the complete thing which is made up of parts, and that is the world, which is the whole relative to men.

Arguments arise from parts also in two ways: either from the parts of a genus, and these are species; or from the parts of a complete thing, that is, of a whole whose parts are the only ones properly called 'parts.'

From the parts that are species in this way. Suppose there is a question whether virtue is the habit of a well-ordered mind. The question has to do with /1188D/ definition, that is, whether *habit of a well-ordered mind* is the definition of virtue.

1188D We will make an argumentation from species in this way: if justice, courage, temperance, and wisdom are habits of a well-ordered mind, but these four are put under virtue as [their] genus, then (*ergo*) virtue is the habit of a well-ordered mind.

5   The maximal proposition: what inheres in the individual parts must inhere in the whole. It is an argument from parts, that is, from the parts of a genus, which are called species; for justice, courage, moderation, and wisdom are species of virtue.

       Similarly from those parts which are called parts of a complete thing. Suppose there is a question whether the art of

10   medicine is advantageous. This consists in a doubt about an accident. We will say: if it is advantageous to drive out disease /1189A/ and minister to health and heal wounds, then the art of medicine is advantageous; but to drive out disease, minister

15   to health, and heal wounds is advantageous; therefore, the art of medicine is advantageous.

       Often even any one part is enough to establish the strength (*firmitas*) of the argumentation. For example, if there is doubt about whether someone has been set free, then if we show

20   him to have been emancipated by [enrollment in] the census, by a will, or by the manumission staff, we have shown that he was set free—and these are the parts of granting liberty. Again, if there is doubt about whether what is seen from afar is a house, we will say that it is not, for it lacks a roof or walls

25   or a foundation. Again, the argument is produced from one part.

       One can take parts and whole into account not only in substances but also in mode, times, quantities, and place. /1189B/ What we call *always* is a temporal whole; what we call *some-*

30   *times* is a temporal part. Again, if something is put forth without qualification, it is a whole with regard to mode; if something is put forth with a qualification, it is a part with regard to mode. Similarly, if we talk about *everything*, we talk about a whole with regard to quantity; if we pick out *something* from

35   quantity, we present a part of quantity. In the same way also with regard to place: that which is *everywhere* is a whole; what is *somewhere*, a part.

       The examples for all these should be given together. From whole to part with reference to time: if God is always, he is

40   also now. From part to whole with reference to mode: if the

1189B soul is in any way moved, it is without qualification moved; but it is moved when it is angered; therefore, it is in general and without qualification moved. Again, from the whole to the parts with regard to quantity: if Apollo is a true prophet in

5   everything, /1189C/ then it will be true that Pyrrhus conquers the Romans. Again, with regard to place: if God is everywhere, he is also here.

Next is the Topic which is called *from causes*. There are many causes: they provide and produce the source of motion,

10   or they receive the forms of species as subjects [for the forms], or for their sakes something comes to be, or it is the form of something.

Here is an argument from efficient cause. For example, if someone wants to show that justice is natural, he might say:

15   the society of men is natural; the society of men produced justice; therefore, justice is natural. The question has to do with accident. The maximal proposition: those things whose efficient causes are natural are themselves also natural. The Topic: *from efficient causes;* for the cause of anything effects the

20   thing it causes.

Again, if someone argues that the Moors do not have weapons, /1189D/ he will say they do not use weapons because they lack iron. The maximal proposition: where the matter is lacking, what is made (*efficitur*) from the matter is also lacking.

25   The Topic: *from matter.* Both of these, *from efficient causes* and *from matter*, are called by one name, 'from cause'; for that which effects something and that which receives the action of the agent are equally causes of what is effected.

Again, from the end. Suppose this is put forth: is justice

30   good? There might be an argumentation of this sort. If it is good to be happy, then justice is also good; for it is the end of justice that he who lives according to justice be brought to happiness. The maximal proposition: that whose end is good is itself also good. The Topic: *from the end.*

35   Also from the form of anything in this way: Daedalus could not fly because /1190A/ he had no wings in his natural form. The maximal proposition: a thing was capable only of what its natural form allowed. The Topic: *from the form.*

From effects, destructions, and uses, in this way. If a house

40   is good, building a house is also good; and vice versa, if

1190A building a house is good, a house is good. Again, if demolition of a house is bad, a house is good; and if a house is good,
demolition of a house is bad. If riding is good, a horse is
good; and if a horse is good, riding is good. The first example
5   is from generations, which can also be called from effects; the
second example is from destructions; the third, from uses. The
maximal proposition for all of these: that whose production
(*effectio*) is good is itself also good, and vice versa; that whose
destruction /1190B/ is bad is itself also good, and vice versa;
10   and that whose use is good is itself also good, and vice versa.

Arguments arise from associated accidents when we consider accidents which cannot or generally do not leave their
subject. For example, if someone speaks in this way: a wise
man will not repent, for repentance follows on a bad deed; but
15   since [doing] a bad deed does not belong to a wise man, neither does repentance. The question has to do with accident.
The maximal proposition: what follows from (*consequens*)
something which does not inhere in a thing cannot inhere in
that thing either. The Topic: *from associated accidents.*
20   Since we have discussed the Topics taken from the terms in
the question, we must now talk about those which, though
they are posited extrinsically, nevertheless supply arguments
for questions. These are *from judgment* (*rei judicium*), /1190C/
from similars, from the greater, from the lesser, from proportion,
25   *from opposites,* or *from transumption.*

The Topic comprised of judgment is of this sort. For example, if we say that things are as they are judged to be either
by all people or most people, and also either by the wise or
those deeply learned in any one of the arts. For example, the
30   heaven is revolvable, since those who are wise and very
learned astronomers have judged it to be so. The question has
to do with accident. The maximal proposition: what seems
true to everyone or the many or the wise should not be gainsaid. The Topic: *from judgment.*
35   From similars in this way. If one is in doubt whether being
two-legged is a property of man, we will say: the way four-
leggedness inheres in a horse is similar to the way two-
leggedness inheres in a man; but four-leggedness is not a
property of the horse; therefore, two-leggedness is not /1190D/
40   a property of man. The question has to do with property. The

1190D maximal proposition: if something inheres in a way similar [to the thing asked about] and is not a property, neither can the thing asked about be a property. The Topic: *from similars*. This Topic is divided in two, for similarity consists either in quality or in quantity. In quantity, it is called parity, that is, equality; in quality, it is called similarity.

Again, from what is greater. Suppose there is a question whether the definition of animal is *that which can move itself.* We will speak in this way: *What lives naturally* is more appropriate as the definition of animal than *that which can move itself.* But *what lives naturally* is not the definition of animal. Therefore, what seems to be even less the definition—*that which can move itself*—ought not to be thought the definition of animal either. /1191A/ The question has to do with definition. The maximal proposition: if what seems the more to inhere does not inhere, neither will that inhere which seems (*videbitur*) the less to inhere. The Topic: *from what is greater.*

And in the opposite way from things that are less. If *two-legged animal capable of walking* is the definition of man, although it seems to be less the definition of man than *mortal rational animal* (and suppose the definition of man is what he says elsewhere: *two-legged* [thing] *capable of walking*), then the definition of man will be [also] *mortal rational animal.* The question has to do with definition. The maximal proposition: if what seems the less to inhere inheres, then what seems (*videbitur*) the more to inhere will inhere.

There is a great variety of Topics which supply arguments from what is greater and what is less; and we treated these more fully in a commentary on Aristotle's *Topics.*

Similarly, from proportion. Suppose there is a question whether /1191B/ the rulers of cities should be chosen by lot. We might say: not at all, because not even a pilot of ships is appointed by lot, for there is a proportion [here]. A pilot is related to a ship as a ruler to a city. But this Topic differs from the Topic drawn from similars, for in the latter case, one thing is compared with another thing. In a proportion, however, there is not a similarity of things but a certain likeness of relationship. The question has to do with accident. The maximal proposition: what occurs in one thing must occur in what is proportional to that thing. The Topic: *from proportion.*

1191B   The Topic from opposites is manifold, for things are opposed to each other in four ways: they reflect each other as
contraries fronting one another (*adverso . . . loco*), as privation
and possession, as relation, or as affirmation and negation.
5   The differences among these things /1191C/ are recounted in
the book on the ten categories. Arguments arise from these in
this way.

From contraries. Suppose there is a question whether *being
praised* is a property of virtue. I might say: not at all, for nei-
10   ther is *being reviled* a property of vice. The question has to do
with property. The maximal proposition: contraries are suited
to contraries. The Topic: *from opposites, that is, from a contrary*.
Again, there might be a question whether *seeing* is a property
of those having eyes. I might say: no, for it happens that there
15   are those who see and others who are blind, for the privation
can be in the same things that the possession is in, and whatever is a property cannot be separated from its subject. And
since vision departs when blindness comes, we have shown
clearly that *seeing* is not a property of those having eyes. The
20   question has to do with property. The maximal proposition:
where the privation can be present, /1191D/ the possession is
not a property. The Topic: *from opposites with reference to possession and privation*.

Again, there might be a question whether *being a procreator*
25   is a property of a father. I might say: it rightly seems to be so,
because *being procreated* is a property of a child, for a father is
related to [his] child as procreator to what is procreated. The
question has to do with property. The maximal proposition:
properties of opposites which are related to each other are
30   themselves also related to each other. The Topic: *from relative
opposites*.

Similarly, there might be a question whether *being moved* is
a property of animal. It might be denied [that it is], because
neither is *not being moved* a property of what is inanimate. The
35   question has to do with property. The maximal proposition:
the properties of opposites must be opposites. The Topic: *from
opposites with reference to affirmation and negation*. For being
moved /1192A/ and not being moved are opposed to each other
with reference to affirmation and negation.
40   [An argument] arises from transumption when doubt is

1192A transferred from the terms in the question to something more known; and from the proof of it, the things in the question are established. For example, when Socrates was asking what justice in one thing might be (*posset*), he transferred the whole
5   discussion to the large scale of a republic; and from his results there, he established that [it] held good for individuals, too. This will perhaps appear to be the Topic *from the whole.* But since it does not inhere in the terms at issue and instead is taken from without only because it seems more known, for
10   that reason the Topic is called by the suitable designation *'from transumption.'*

    Transumption arises also with regard to a name whenever the argumentation /1192B/ is transferred from an obscure word to one more known. For example, suppose there is a question
15   whether a philosopher is envious and what the name 'philosopher' signifies is not known. Transferring to a word more known, we will say that he is not envious because he is wise, for 'wise' is more known than 'philosopher.'

    The Topics taken from without have been clearly discussed;
20   now intermediate Topics will be considered. Intermediate Topics are taken and arise either from case or conjugates or division.

    A case is the inflection into an adverb of some principal name; for example, 'justly' is inflected from 'justice,' [and]
25   therefore 'justly' is the case from 'justice.' Things which have issued and been drawn from the same thing in different ways are called conjugates; for example, 'just [thing]' and 'just [man]' from 'justice.' These are said to be conjoined (*conjugata*) with each other and with 'justice' itself.
30   /1192C/ Arguments are readily obtained from all these. For if what is [done] justly is good, what is just is also good; and if a just [man] is good, justice is also good. These things follow on the basis of a similarity to the principal name.

    [These] Topics are called intermediate because if there is a
35   question about justice and arguments are drawn from case or from conjugates, they seem to be drawn neither directly (*proprie*) nor indirectly (*conjuncte*) from the substance itself nor from things posited without but rather from the cases of the things themselves, that is, with a certain small change, from
40   the very things introduced (*deductis*). And so these Topics are

1192C rightly placed intermediate between those that are from the things themselves and those that are from without.

There remains the Topic *from division*, which is handled in this way. Every division arises either by negation or by parti-
5   tion. It arises by negation, for example, when someone proclaims 'Every animal either has feet /1192D/ or does not have feet.' It arises by partition if someone makes a division [of this sort]: 'Every man is either healthy or sick.' A universal division arises from [a division] of a genus into species, a whole
10   into parts, an utterance into its appropriate significations, an accident into subjects, a subject into accidents, or an accident into accidents. I explained the principles (*rationes*) of all these things more thoroughly in the book I wrote on division, and so fitting examples for the understanding of all these things
15   should be looked for there. Argumentations by means of division arise sometimes from the separation that results from negation, sometimes from the separation that results from partition. Those who use these divisions either argue by direct reasoning or else derive something impossible and absurd and
20   so adopt again what /1193A/ they had given up. Anyone will understand these things more easily if he has worked at the *Prior Analytics*.

But for present purposes, examples of this sort will provide understanding for these things. Suppose there is a question
25   whether there is any beginning of time. One who wants to deny this will certainly confirm by reasoning that there is in no way a beginning, and he will show this by direct reasoning in the following way. Time either has a beginning or it does not. Since the world is eternal (let this be granted temporarily
30   for the sake of the argument) and the world could not exist without time, time is also eternal. But what is eternal lacks a beginning. Therefore, time does not have a beginning.

If someone wants to show the same thing by means of an impossibility, he will speak in this way. Time either has a
35   beginning or it does not. But if time has a beginning, /1193B/ it was not always. But time has a beginning; therefore, there was once when time was not. But 'was' is an indication (*significatio*) of time; therefore, there was a time when time was not—and this cannot be. Therefore, there is no start of time. For
40   suppose that it took a start from anything; then something ab-

1193B surd and impossible occurs: that there was a time when time
was not. And so there is a return to the other part, that it lacks
a beginning.

When any arguments are acquired by means of the division
5   from negation, because there is a division into affirmation and
negation, it cannot be that both [parts] are. And so if one is
taken away, the other remains; when one is posited, the remaining one is removed. And this Topic *from division* is called
intermediate between those that are generally drawn from the
10   thing itself and those that are taken from without. /1193C/ For
when there is a question whether there is any beginning of
time, we assume that there is a beginning; and from this by
means of an appropriate consequence, a syllogism [conclud-
ing] to something impossible and false arises about the very
15   thing at issue. When this conclusion has been reached, there
is a return to the former [part], which must be true, since what
is opposite to it results in something impossible and absurd.
And so since the syllogism generally arises from the very thing
at issue, the Topic is drawn, as it were, from the things them-
20   selves; since, however, it does not remain in that but returns
to the opposite, it is, as it were, taken from without. For that
reason, this Topic *from division* is placed intermediate between
the two.

But those taken from partition are of two kinds. For some-
25   times the things divided can exist at the same time, for example, if we divide an utterance into its significations, they
can all exist at the same time, as when we say that 'I embrace'
/1193D/ signifies something done or something experienced,
and it can signify both of these at the same time. Sometimes,
30   just as in [division] from negation, the things divided cannot
exist at the same time; for example, he is either healthy or
sick.

Reasoning arises in the first sort of division sometimes because what is asked about is present or not present in all
35   things and sometimes because it is present or not present in
something which is present or not in other things. We will not
labor too long to explain these things if Aristotle's *Prior Analytics* or *Topics* has provided the careful reader with information. Suppose there is a question whether a dog is a sub-
40   stance. The one conversing makes this division: 'dog' is the

1193D name of an animal capable of barking or a marine animal or a
celestial star; and he shows one by one that an animal capable
of barking is a substance /1194A/ and that a marine animal and
a star can be put under *substance*. Then he has shown that a
5   dog is a substance, and he will appear to have drawn the
arguments from the things put forth in the question.

But a syllogism is taken from things that are without, that is,
from opposites—for example, in the following syllogisms: he
is either healthy or sick, but he is healthy, therefore he is not
10   sick; but he is not healthy, therefore he is sick; but he is sick,
therefore he is not healthy; but he is not sick, therefore he is
healthy.

So this whole Topic *from division* is held to be intermediate
between the two. If it consists of negation, in one way it is
15   taken from the things themselves but in another way it comes
from things that are external. If arguments are drawn from
partition, they provide an abundance now from the things
themselves, now from things that are external.

/1194B/ Such seems to be the division of the Topics accord-
20   ing to the Greek, Themistius, a most thorough and clear
writer, who recounts all these things to facilitate understanding.

And so I ought to recount the division of the Topics briefly
in order to demonstrate that there is nothing left out of it
25   which may not be shown to be included within it. Whatever is
in doubt in any question will be made certain by arguments
taken from the things that make up the question or drawn
from without or discovered on the border, as it were, of these.
And nothing else can be found outside this delimitation (*dif-*
30   *finitionem*).

If the argument is taken from the things themselves, it must
be taken from their substance, from the things that follow
from the substance, from the things that are inseparable accidents—those that adhere and /1194C/ cannot be or generally
35   are not separated or disjoined from their substance.

Those which are drawn from their substance consist in description, definition, or, in addition, explanation of the name.
Those that follow from the substance as if connected to it are
of this sort: they give help concerning the things being inves-

1194C tigated by means of a Topic from genus, differentia, complete
thing, species, or parts; and similarly, causes—efficient or material, forms, or end—or effects, destructions, uses, quantities,
time or modes. But what is properly called inseparable or ad-
5   hering accident will be numbered among associated accidents.
And besides these nothing can be found that can inhere in
anything.

    With these things laid down in this way, let us consider
now those Topics which /1194D/ we just now were declaring to
10   be taken from without. For those taken from without are not *external*
so separate and disjoined that they do not in some way, from a
certain region, as it were, look toward the things asked about.
For both similarities and opposites are without doubt referred
to the things they are similar or opposite to, although they
15   rightly and properly seem placed without. They are these:
similarity, opposition, greater, lesser, judgment. Similarity
contains sometimes similarity to a thing, sometimes the relationship (*ratio*) of proportion, for all things contain similarity.
Opposites consist of contraries, privations, relations, and
20   negations. Comparison of what is greater to what is lesser is a
certain dissimilarity of similar things; for among things similar per se, difference produces greater and /1195A/ lesser. What
is different in every quality and every relationship (*ratio*) will
in no way be able to be compared. Arguments from judgment
25   provide a witness, as it were, and are Topics which are not according to the art [of Topics]; they are altogether separate and
seek nothing other than opinion and general report. The Topic
from transumption consists now in equality, now in comparison of greater or lesser; for there is a transumption of argu-
30   ments and reasons (*rationes*) either to what is similar or to
what is greater or lesser.

    The Topics which we said before were mixed arise from
cases, conjugates, or division. In all these, consequences and
opposites (*repugnantia*) are preserved.

35   Arguments drawn from definition, genus, differentia, or
causes /1195B/ most of all provide force and order to demonstrative syllogisms; the remaining arguments, to syllogisms
which have the appearance of truth and are dialectical. The
Topics which have most of all to do with the substance of the

1195B things /1196A/ asked about in the question have to do with predicative and simple syllogisms; the remaining Topics, with hypothetical and conditional syllogisms.

5 Since the Topics have been set forth and made thoroughly clear as much by definition as by the light of examples, it seems that we ought to say in what way these Topics are the differentiae of maximal propositions, and that briefly, for the matter needs no long debate. All maximal propositions, contain a definition, description, explanation of a name, whole, 10 parts, genus, species, or the other things by which maximal propositions differ among themselves. For they differ not insofar as they are maximal but insofar as one is from definition, one from genus, and others come from other Topics; by these they are rightly said to differ, and these are said to be their 15 differentiae.

Since Themistius's division /1196B/ has been made clear, let us now turn to Cicero's division.

BOOK III

It ought not to be at all surprising to people of an attentive nature that we treat the differentiae of Topics variously and in different ways since it is plain that any one thing can often be divided by many differentiae and into different schemes (*figuras*) of division. Because not one but many differentiae often comprise individual things, there must be a diversity of divisions in accordance with the variety of differentiae. For example, we collect sometimes these differentiae of number: some [numbers] are even and others odd; but sometimes these: /1195C/ some [numbers] are prime and incomposite and others are secondary and composite. The discipline (*disciplinae tenor*) of geometry shows that triangles also may be divided in many ways, though in all cases one should watch that nothing is left out in any form of division and nothing superfluous and beyond what is necessary is added.

Consequently, should anyone be surprised if we gave the differentiae of Topics according to Themistius before and now produce different differentiae according to Cicero? When Cicero's division has been briefly put forth and explained by appropriate examples, then I will relate in what way it differs from or agrees with the preceding division [of Topics] and also in what way one includes the other.

Cicero maintained that all of logic (*logicam facultatem*), which he called the careful science of discourse (*ratio disserendi*), has two /1195D/ parts, one of discovering, the other of judging. Topics he defined as the foundations of argument, namely, things from which arguments are produced; and an argument he defined as a reason producing belief regarding something which is in doubt. He made a division of all the Topics in this way.

99

1195D   Of the Topics in which arguments are included, he says, some inhere in the matter at issue (*ipso de quo agitur*); others are taken from without. So he produced two species of Topics, for he maintained that some inhere in the terms of the ques-

5   tions and others are taken from without.

He divides those that inhere in the things asked about by a division of this sort: [those that inhere] in the thing [asked about are taken] sometimes, he says, from the whole, sometimes from the parts of the whole, sometimes from a sign

10   (*nota*), and sometimes from things which are in some way related to the thing asked about. He calls those extrinsic /1196B/ which are distant and thoroughly separated [from the thing asked about]. Besides these, he divided into appropriate parts the Topic drawn from things which are in some way

15   related to what is asked about, in this way: some are conjugates, he says, some are from genus, some from kind (*forma*), some from similarity, some from differentia, some from a contrary, some from conjoined things, some from antecedents, some from consequents, some from incompatibles (*repugnan-*

20   *tibus*), some from causes, some from effects, some from comparison of greater or lesser or equal things.

/1196C/ We must touch on the nature of all these things briefly and give examples for them.

The first of the Topics which inhere in the matter at issue

25   [Cicero] said is *from the whole*. The whole of any thing consists in the definition, for every definition is adequated to the thing which it defines, because if anything is a whole (and nothing can be complete unless it is a whole), then it must be a whole also in definition, that is, in the definition which contains the

30   whole substance of the thing it defines.

A definition is discourse which indicates the essence (*esse*) of any thing. An argument is drawn from definition in this way. Suppose there is a question whether trees also are animals. I might say: an animal is an animate substance capable

35   of perceiving; a tree is not an animate substance capable of perceiving. I might conclude: trees, therefore, are not animals. The question has to do with genus. The maximal /1196D/ proposition: whatever the definition is absent from, the thing defined is also absent from. The Topic: *from definition*.

40   Parts are those things whose coming together produces the

1196D whole. Those things which divide the whole are also called parts, but these are commonly called species or kinds. An argument is taken from parts in this way.

5 [An argument arises] from the parts whose conjunction composes the whole in this way. Suppose there is uncertainty about whether the soul is corporeal. We will divide the soul into three parts, as it were, because it manifests [itself as] vegetative, perceptive, or intellective. But to be alive (*vegetare*), perceive, or understand is not corporeal. And since no

10 part of the soul is corporeal, we have shown that the soul altogether is not corporeal. The question has to do with genus, that is, whether soul /1197A/ is subordinated to body as a genus; the argument is an argument from parts. The maximal proposition: whatever things the parts are absent from, the

15 whole is also absent from. The Topic: *from parts making up the whole.*

Similarly [an argument arises] from the parts which divide the whole in this way. Suppose there is a question whether the soul moves spatially. I might say that there are three spe-

20 cies of spatial motion: increase, decrease, and change (*permutatio*). But the soul does not increase or decrease, nor does it go from one place to another. Therefore, it does not move. The question has to do with accident. The maximal proposition is the same as above. The Topic: *from parts dividing the whole.*

25 There is an argument from a sign whenever belief regarding something which is in doubt is sought from the explanation of the name. For example, suppose there is doubt whether philosophy is good. We will say: philosophy is the love of wisdom, but this is good; /1197B/ therefore, philosophy is good.

30 So here we have not defined the thing but we have expounded the name by a definition. The question has to do with genus. The maximal proposition: a thing is clarified by the explanation of its name. The Topic: *from designation (notatio).*

Conjugates are things which are derived from the same

35 name, as 'just,' and 'justly' from 'justice.' From these an argument is taken in this way. Suppose there is a question whether to laugh is to rejoice. We will say: if laughter is joy, to laugh is also to rejoice. The question has to do with accident. The maximal proposition: the nature of conjugates is the same.

40 The Topic: *from conjugates.*

sign

1197B   Genus is what is predicated of more than one differing in species in respect of what they are (*in eo quod quid*). An argument is drawn from genus in this way. Suppose there is a question whether the soul is a measure (*numerus*) moving it-
5   self, as Xenocrates would have it. We will say: a soul is a substance, but a measure is not a substance; therefore, /1197C/ a soul is not a measure. The question has to do with definition. The Topic: *from genus*. The maximal proposition: things whose genera are different are themselves also different.
10   Kind is what is predicated of more than one differing in number in respect of what they are. An argument arises from kind in this way. Suppose there is a question whether color is in a subject. We will show that it is [so] from the fact that white or black are in a subject, that is to say, going from species to
15   genus. The question has to do with genus; for to be or not to be in a subject indicates an accident or a substance, and these are the primary genera of things. The maximal proposition: the attributes (*proprietates*) of genera are observed in [their] kinds. The Topic: *from kind*.
20   Similarity is the same quality in differing things. An argument is thought to arise from similarity in this way. Suppose there is a question whether rulers of states should be acquired by lot rather than by choice. /1197D/ It might be denied, since even for a ship a skilled ruler is selected not by lot but by
25   choice. A ship is similar to a state, a pilot to a magistrate. The question has to do with accident. The Topic: *from a similar*. The maximal proposition: regarding similars, the judgment is one and the same.
Similarly, from differentia. For example, suppose there is a
30   question whether a king and a tyrant are the same. We will say not at all; for in a king there is reverence (*pietas*), justice, and clemency, but in a tyrant all is otherwise. The question has to do with definition. The Topic: *from differentia*. The maximal proposition: regarding differing things, the judgment is
35   not one and the same.
The things which Cicero calls contraries are divided into four sorts: adverse contraries, such as white and black; privative contraries, such as justice and injustice; relative contraries, such as master and servant; or negative contraries,
40   such as living and /1198A/ not living. From all these, argu-

1198A ments are taken in these ways. From adverse contraries: if
health is good, sickness is bad. From privative contraries: if
we flee injustice, we should pursue justice. From relative contraries: whoever wants to be a father should have a child.
5 From negative contraries: you do not accuse me of having
done what you defend me for not having done [, do you]? The
questions have to do with accidents. The maximal proposition: contraries cannot agree with each other when they are
adverse, privative, or negative; and when they are relative,
10 they cannot occur without each other. The Topic: *from contraries* (which might better be called 'opposites').

Associated things are those which have a common boundary *associated*
(*finitimum locum*) so that in time sometimes they go before, as *things*
meeting (*congressio*) before love, sometimes they go with the
15 thing with which they are associated, as the noise of footsteps
with walking, and sometimes they follow, as mental agitation
follows a horrible crime. These things are not /1198B/ necessary *necessary*
even though they happen often. For he who has met [some-
one] has not always loved; and he who has not met [some per-
20 son] has fallen in love at first sight [with that person]. It is possible that there be no noise of footsteps when someone is
walking; and there can be a noise of footsteps when someone
is not walking, if he remains in the same place and moves his
feet. Someone can be agitated who has done nothing horrible;
25 and it can be the case that someone who has done something
horrible is not agitated.

From these an argument will be drawn when we maintain
that someone loves because he had previously met [the person
he loves], or that someone walked in a place since the noise of
30 footsteps was heard, or that someone whom we see agitated
had committed a horrible crime. In these cases, the questions
have to do with accidents. The Topic: *from associated things.*
The maximal proposition: things which are associated with
other things are judged on the basis of those things (*ex ad-
35 junctis adjuncta perpendi*).

Antecedents are things from which something else /1198C/
must immediately follow once the antecedents have been asserted, as when we say: if it is a man, it is an animal. In these
things neither the formula (*ratio*) nor the necessity of the
40 things varies with time, but, as was said, the antecedent fol-

child

1198C lows immediately from the consequent. This whole Topic is
made up of a condition. Once the condition is posited, if the
antecedent is, the consequent must also be. For example, if
she has borne a child, she has lain with a man. The antecedent
5   is that [she] has borne a child; the consequent is that [she] has
lain with a man. There is no question [in such a case] concerning what is earlier and what is later in time. Often these vary
in such a way that what is later in time appears to be the antecedent in the proposition; for example, having borne a child is
10   later than having lain with [a man]. Nevertheless, if she has
borne a child, then, of course, she has lain with a man; and
when the former [that she has borne a child] precedes and is
asserted first, the latter [that she has lain with a man] is necessarily /1198D/ understood. Sometimes [antecedent and con-
15   sequent] are simultaneous; for example, if the sun is risen, it
is day. Sometimes the antecedent is earlier and the consequent
later; for example, if he is arrogant, he is hateful; for one
comes to be hateful from arrogance.

From an antecedent an argument is taken [in this way]. If
20   she has borne a child, then she has lain with a man. I take the
antecedent: but she has borne a child; I conclude the consequent: therefore, she has lain with a man. From consequents
in this way. I take the consequent: but she has not lain with a
man; I conclude the antecedent: therefore, she has not borne a
25   child. The question has to do with accident. The Topic: *from
antecedents and consequents*. The maximal propositions: once
the antecedent has been asserted, the consequent follows;
once the consequent is taken away, the antecedent is taken
away.

30   Incompatibles are /1199A/ consequents of contraries. For example, sleeping and waking are contraries, and snoring is associated with sleepers. So snoring and waking are incompatibles. An argument arises from incompatibles in this way: Do
you say that he who snores is awake? The question has to do
35   with accident; it is an argument from incompatibles. The maximal proposition: incompatibles cannot occur together.

An efficient cause is what precedes and produces a thing; it
does not always precede in time but rather in natural order
(*proprietate naturae*), as the sun [precedes] the day. An argu-
40   ment is taken from efficient cause in this way. Why do you

1199A doubt whether it is day when you perceive that the sun is in the sky? The question has to do with accident, for it is an accident of the atmosphere that it is day, that is, that it is light on account of the sun. It is an argument from efficient causes. The maximal proposition: where the cause is, the effect cannot be absent.

An effect is that which a cause produces. An argument /1199B/ is taken from an effect in this way: Do you doubt whether he desired (amasse) her whom he carried off by force? The question has to do with accident; it is an argument from effects. The maximal proposition: where the effect is, the cause cannot be absent—just as desire (amor) was not absent, and desire was the cause of his carrying her off by force, which is the effect.

Comparison of the greater occurs when the lesser is compared to the greater. From this Topic an argument is taken in this way: If he who fought against his country in war nevertheless merited pardon from the citizens, why should not he who was driven into exile for instigating insurrection also merit pardon? The question has to do with accident; it is an argument from comparison of the greater. The maximal proposition: what holds good in the greater thing holds good in the lesser.

Comparison of the lesser occurs when a greater thing is compared to a lesser. An argument is taken from comparison of the lesser in this way: /1199C/ If Scipio, a private person, killed Gaius Gracchus, who was an unremarkable troubler of the state of the republic, why should the consuls not take vengeance on Catiline, who is eager to ravage the world with carnage and conflagration? The question has to do with accident; it is an argument from comparison of the lesser. The maximal proposition: what holds good in the lesser thing holds good in the greater.

Equals are things which are of the same quantity, and equality is always similarity of quantity. An argument arises from equality in this way: If someone wants to praise Demosthenes, why does he censure Cicero? The question has to do with accident; it is an argument from comparison of equals. The maximal proposition: regarding equals, the judgment is one and the same.

probable

1199C   There remains the Topic which he said is taken from without. This depends on judgment and authority and is only
readily believable, containing nothing necessary. That is readily believable which appears to be so to everyone or to most
5   people /1199D/ or to the learned and wise—and among these,
to the illustrious and preeminent or to those who have at-
tained to skill in any art, such as the doctor in the field of medicine or the geometer in the field of geometry. From this Topic
there is an argument of this sort. Suppose I say: it is difficult to
10   wage war against the Carthaginians, since P. Scipio Cornelius
Africanus said so, and he had frequent experience of it. This
Topic is said to be from without since it is not taken from the
subject or predicate term but comes from judgment posited extrinsically. It is also called unskilled and lacking in art since
15   the orator does not produce the argument from his [Topic] by
himself but uses evidence [already] worked up and put forth.
    Since the differentiae have been presented by which Cicero
distinguishes among /1200A/ maximal propositions (which we
said are Topics), it seems to me that the division divided
20   above ought to be treated briefly so that things which appear
similar to one another will be separated from each other by a
fitting reason (*ratio*).
    The Topic from the whole seems similar to that from a sign,
because both consist in a definition, for explanation of the
25   name is a certain definition of the name. But the difference between them is very great, because the Topic from the whole
defines the thing, but that from a sign does not define the
thing but explains the name. And the thing and the name are
different, for the latter signifies, the former is signified.
30   Again, the Topic from enumeration of parts seems similar to
the Topic from kind. It is the case both that a kind is a part
and that whoever divides the genus enumerates parts; nor can
an argument from kind arise unless [the kind] is divided from
the genus, for a kind /1200B/ can be obtained only by division
35   [of a genus]. But here too the difference is great. Enumeration
of parts—whether the parts are [integral] parts or [parts which
are] species—must divide all the parts and take them all
together in order to have belief for the argumentation, so that
the genus may be demonstrated from the species and the

1200B whole from the parts. But in the case of [the Topic from] kind, any one kind suffices to prove what is said of the genus.

Again, the Topic from a contrary and [that] from incompatibles seem to be similar, but they are different, because contraries are prima facie opposed to each other, but incompatibles are shown to be opposed to each other by their connection with contraries. For example, sleeping and waking are contrary to each other as they stand; but snoring is incompatible with waking because snoring is connected with sleep.

Associated things and antecedents and consequents /1200C/ are neighbors, as it were. But there is some distance among them because in associated things there is no necessity, but in antecedents and consequents there is the greatest necessity. In associated things, times are immeasurably important, for what is associated [with something] generally precedes [that] thing or occurs at one and the same time with it or follows later. With regard to antecedents, there are none of these things; but apart from the consideration (*ratio*) of time, as soon as the antecedent has been, the consequent must be; and if the consequent has not been, the antecedent must be taken away.

Enough has been said about Cicero's Topics. Now let us return to Themistius's division so that we may briefly set forth how the divisions divided above can agree with each other.

First, let us compare in general the differentiae of the whole division. Themistius's division above taught that some Topics inhere in the terms /1200D/ about which the question is raised, some are taken from without, and some are used intermediate between both of these. So here we understand a threefold division. Cicero's division sets out the Topics in a twofold division. He maintains that some inhere in the matter at issue and some are taken from without. All the Topics which Themistius maintained are intermediate [Cicero] conjoined and added to those which are comprised in the terms of the matter at issue. In general such is the difference between the divisions; and it will become clearer if we discuss the particulars.

In the first division, Themistius maintained that those Topics which are posited in the terms asked about in the question are sometimes in the substance and sometimes in the consequents of the substance. *Definition, description,* /1201A/

1201A and *explanation of the name* are in the substance. *Genus, whole,*
species, part, efficient cause, matter, form, effect, destruction, end,
use, and *associated accidents* are consequents of the substance.
He separated those taken from without into those of *judgment,*
5 *similarity, comparison of quantity, opposition, proportion,* and
transumption. Those he maintained are intermediate consist in
oblique forms, conjugates, and *division.*

Cicero maintained that those Topics that are in what is
asked about are *from a whole, the parts of the whole, a sign,* or
10 *things that are in some way related to that which is asked about.*
Related things are multifariously divided, and *judgment* alone
is separated [as coming] from without. Many of those things
which in /1201B/ Themistius's division are put forth as consequents of the substance and similarly the intermediate
15 Topics [Cicero] numbered among the related things.

In so varied a division it is inevitable that the two [divi-
sions] will not match each other part for part, but this can happen in all things that are divided in many ways. For example,
suppose someone divides the kinds of triangles in this way.
20 Some kinds of triangles are equilateral, others have only two
sides equal, and others are put together out of sides that are all
unequal. Again, there might be this division. Someone might
say that some have a right /1202A/ angle (and these are called
orthogonal); others, he might say, are contained by three acute
25 angles (and these are oxygonal); others are extended in an ob-
tuse angle (and these are ambligonal). So it is inevitable that
the two [divisions] match each other by different considerations *(ratio)* of parts. What is orthogonal is always contained
either by two equal sides or by three unequal sides. What is
30 ambligonal is contained either by two equal sides or by three
unequal sides. What is oxygonal is contained by three equal
sides or by two unequal sides. Again, what is equilateral is
always oxygonal. What is contained by two equal sides can be
orthogonal, ambligonal, or oxygonal. What is contained by
35 three unequal sides /1202B/ must be orthogonal or ambligonal.

According to this method, let us begin from the beginning
the whole division of Cicero and Themistius together, and let
us show how each in turn includes the other. In all these
things, one ought to remember both the examples and expla-
40 nation *(intelligentiae)* set forth above. So let us arrange Themis-

1202B tius's whole division and put down after it Cicero's division so that the things that are to be said, by being more evidently presented to the eyes, may become clear to the mind. [See diagram I.]

5 /1203A/ Since these things have been delineated in this way, we will now explain in what way Cicero's division matches Themistius's division.

The Topic which Cicero called *from the whole,* Themistius maintained is *from substance;* for both consist in definition, 10 whether it be substantial or a description.

The Topic which Cicero's *Topica* claimed is *from the enumeration of parts* is the same as that which is called *from division,* one of the intermediates in Themistius's division. For when we try to show that something is or is not, if we obtain belief 15 from an enumeration of the parts, we must necessarily do so on the basis of division; and division, whether of species or of parts, will have gone before. Although Themistius included the Topic *from division* among the intermediate Topics, Cicero puts it in the treatment of genus. For when Cicero talks about 20 genus, he speaks /1203B/ in this way: "The argumentation taken from genus, when the parts are sought from the whole, is properly treated in this way. If fraud occurs when one thing is done and something else is pretended, it is possible to enumerate the ways in which this happens and then include in 25 some one of those ways that which you contend is fraud. This genus of argument generally seems particularly solid."

Cicero's Topic *from designation* is Themistius's Topic *from explanation of the name.*

The Topic *from conjugates* is common to them both; Themis-30 tius included it among the intermediate Topics.

Cicero had a Topic *from genus;* Themistius, *from the whole.*

Cicero's Topic *from kind,* that is, from a part [is] Themistius's Topic *from species.*

The Topic *from similarity* is common to them both, except 35 that Cicero includes *proportion* under it.

Cicero's Topic *from differentia* can be understood either as the Topic *from the whole* in Themistius's division or as the Topic *from a part;* /1203C/ *from the whole* if the differentia from which the argument is taken is constitutive, and *from a part* if 40 it is divisive.

Diagram I.
(referred to in 1202B, as given in *PL* text)
Themistius's Division

Topics

Intrinsic

1. From substance
2. From definition
3. From description
4. From explanation of the name
5. From consequents [of the substance]
6. From whole or genus
7. From parts or species
8. From efficient [causes]
9. From matter
10. From form
11. From end
12. From effects
13. From destructions
    From uses
14. From associated accidents

Extrinsic

1. From judgment
2. From similars
3. From the greater
4. From the lesser
5. From opposites
   either contraries
   or relatives or
   according to pri-
   vation and
   possession or by
   means of affirma-
   tion and negation
6. From proportion
7. From transumption

Intermediate

From cases
From conjugates
From division

Cicero's Division

Topics

Intrinsic

From the whole
From parts
From a sign
From conjugates
From genus
From kind
From similarity
From differentia
From a contrary
From associated things

From antecedents
From consequents
From incompatibles
From causes
From effects
From comparison
   either of greater
   things or of lesser
   things or of equal things

Extrinsic

From authority

1204A /1204A/ The Topic *from contraries* is the same [for both]; in Themistius's division it is called *'from opposites'* and established extrinsically.

The Topic *from associated things* (*adjunctis*) is what is called
5 *from associated* (*communiter*) *accidents* in Themistius's division and is named among the consequents of substance.

The Topic *from antecedents and consequents* is distributed in many ways. Both definition and description can be both antecedent and consequent to a thing; similarly, explanation of the
10 name. Similarly, species is antecedent and genus is consequent. Also, an efficient cause is antecedent, and the effect is consequent. An effect is consequent to the material cause. Also, associated accidents, if they are inseparable, must be consequent [to their subject]. Conjugates also are antecedent
15 or consequent to one another. And so this Topic [*from antecedents and consequents*] is entangled in many; and it is diverse from all the others not so much in what it is (*rebus*) as in how it is treated (*tractatione*), for the condition of a consequence /1204B/ makes [it] another Topic although the condition of the
20 consequence is asserted in regard to a definition, description, kind, cause, or the others.

Incompatibles are reckoned among opposites. Effective things are similar to efficient or material causes. Effects are similar to the Topic Themistius put forth as *from the end*, for
25 the effect of causes is an end.

The Topic *from comparison of the greater or the lesser* is the same [for both]; with Themistius it is put among the extrinsic Topics *from the greater and the lesser.*

The Topic *from the comparison of equals* should be considered
30 to be among those which are drawn from similars, for it was said that similarity in quantity is equality.

There remains the Topic, common to them both, which is included among [those] from without and which Cicero, as well as Themistius, maintained is *from judgment.*

35 Cicero's division /1204C/ could include the preceding division of Themistius in this way, which can be seen in the delineation below. [See diagram II, p. 76.]

/1203D/ Cicero's whole division of Topics appears included in Themistius's division in the diagram of the delineation
40 above.

1204C   *Diagram II.*
                        (referred to in 1204C, as given in *PL* text)

Ciceronian division	*Themistius's division*
From the whole	From substance
From enumeration of parts	From division
From designation	From explanation of the name
From conjugates	From conjugates
From genus	From genus or from whole
From kind	From part or species
From similarity	From a similar
From differentia	From the whole or from a part
From a contrary	From opposites
From associated (*adjunctis*) things	From associated (*communiter*) accidents
From antecedents	From definition, description, explanation, species, cause, matter, associated accidents, or conjugates
From consequents	
From incompatibles	From opposites
From efficient things	From causes
From effects	From the end
From comparison of greater things	From the greater
of lesser things	From the lesser
of equal things	From similars
From authority	From judgment

Now we must reduce Themistius's division to Cicero's division; the greater part of it agrees with Cicero's division, as the preceding delineation shows. If what remains of Themistius's division /1204D/ is laid alongside the order of Cicero's division, we show briefly and easily how each division in turn is reduced to the other.

In the delineation above, of Themistius's Topics these match the neighboring division of Cicero. Cicero: *from the whole;* Themistius: *from substance. From the enumeration of parts,* Cicero; *from division,* Themistius. /1205A/ *From designation,* Cicero; *from explanation of the name,* Themistius. *From conjugates* is common to them both. *From genus,* Cicero; *from the whole,* Themistius. *From kind,* Cicero; *from a part,* that is, *from species,* Themistius. *From similarity* is common. *From differentia,* Cicero; *from the whole* or *from a part,* Themistius. *From contraries,*

5

10

15

1205A Cicero; the same, according to Themistius, is *from opposites.*
From associated things (adjunctis), Cicero; Themistius presented
the same thing, *from associated (communiter) accidents. From antecedents and consequents*—these are mingled with many. *From*
5 *incompatibles,* Cicero; Themistius calls the same thing *'from opposites.' From effective things,* Cicero; *from causes,* Themistius.
From effects, Cicero; *from the end,* Themistius. *From comparison
of the greater and of the lesser,* Cicero; Themistius's *from the
greater and from the lesser* are the same. From *comparison of*
10 *equals,* Cicero; *from similars,* Themistius.

Since Cicero's whole division /1205B/ fits some parts of Themistius's division, it cannot be the case that the parts of Themistius's division are not immediately reduced to the appropriate parts of Cicero's division. So if there is anything
15 remaining in Themistius's division which does not seem attributed [to something in Cicero's division] in the diagram
above, we will be able to match it to the full division of Cicero, for the divisions are mutually and reciprocally conjoined.

/1206A/ The following Topics of Themistius remain: *from*
20 *uses, effects, destructions, proportion,* and *transumption.*

If the use is always a producer of something, [the Topic]
from uses should be matched to Cicero's Topic which is called
'from effective things.' If the use itself is produced, it should be
assigned to Cicero's Topic which is called *'from effects.'*

25 If the effect produces something, [the Topic] *from effects* is
[the Topic] *from efficient causes.* If the effect shows something
complete and entire, it is the Topic which Cicero called *'from
effects.'*

[The Topic] *from destructions* can be called *'from effective
30 things';* for since every generation produces something (that is,
it forms a substance), destruction itself in turn also produces a
certain thing, namely, it strips off and removes the substantial
form, as death produces the dissolution of the body.

From proportion is the same as that which Cicero called *'from
35 similars,'* /1206B/ for in many, many things proportion is a similarity.

If transumption is to something greater, the Topic is *from
comparison of the greater;* if it is to something lesser, the Topic
is *from comparison of the lesser;* and if it is to something equal,
40 the Topic is *from comparison of equals.*

1206B   *Diagram III.*
                      (referred to in 1206B, as given in *PL* text)

Themistius's [division]   Cicero's [division]

From uses	If the use produces something	From efficient things
	If the use is produced	From effects
From effects	If the effect produces something	From efficient things
	If the effect is produced	From effects
From destructions		From efficient things
From proportion		From similars
From transumption	If it is to [something] greater	From comparison of greater things
	If it is to [something] lesser	Of lesser things
	If it is to [something] equal	Of equal things

For all the things that were [yet] to be reduced, the diagram
(*exemplum*) of the delineation suffices. [See Diagram III.]

/1205B/ We have set forth as much about the dialectical
Topics as the nature (*ratio*) of the proposed work requires.
5   Now, it seems, we must say something about the rhetorical
Topics: what they are or in what way /1206B/ they seem to differ from the dialectical Topics. Let us reserve the whole space
of the fourth book for a full consideration of this.

BOOK IV

If anyone carefully examines and considers the title of [this]
work, since we wrote 'De topicis differentiis,' he will be bound
to expect from us not only that we give the differentiae [which
distinguish] the dialectical Topics from one another, or even
that we give the differentiae [which distinguish] the rhetorical
Topics [from one another], but much more that we separate
the dialectical from the rhetorical Topics. And we consider that
we can undertake this more effectively if we begin the discussion with the very nature of the disciplines (*facultatum*). For
when the similarity and dissimilarity of dialectic and rhetoric
have been shown, we must draw the likenesses and differences of the Topics which serve the disciplines from the
forms of the disciplines themselves.

The dialectical discipline examines the thesis only; a thesis
is a question not involved in circumstances. The rhetorical
[discipline], on the other hand, investigates /1205D/ and discusses hypotheses, that is, questions hedged in by a multitude
of circumstances. Circumstances are who, what, where, when,
why, how, by what means.

Again, if dialectic ever does admit circumstances, such as
some deed or person, into the disputation, it does not do so
for their own sake (*principaliter*), but it transfers the whole
force of the circumstance to the thesis it is discussing. But if
rhetoric takes up a thesis, /1206C/ it draws it into the hypothesis. Each investigates its own material but takes up that of the
other so that the matter depends on the discipline more suited
to it.

Again, dialectic is restricted to question and answer. Rhetoric, on the other hand, goes through the subject proposed in

1206C unbroken discourse. Similarly, dialectic uses complete syllogisms. Rhetoric is content with the brevity of enthymemes.

This too produces a differentia, namely, that the rhetorician has as judge someone other than his opponent, someone who
5   decides between them. But for the dialectician, the one who is the opponent also gives the decision because a reply [which is], as it were, a decision is elicited from the opponent by the cunning of the questioning.

So every difference between these [disciplines] consists in
10   matter, use, or end. In matter, because thesis and hypothesis are the matter put under the two of them. /1206D/ In use, because one disputes by question, the other by unbroken discourse, or because one delights in complete syllogisms, the other in enthymemes. In end, because one attempts to per-
15   suade a judge, the other attempts to wrest what it wants from the opponent.

With these things considered beforehand, we will enumerate a little later both rhetorical questions which are posited in issues (constitutionibus) /1207A/ and Topics of the appropriate
20   kind. For the immediate present, it seems to me that we must examine the whole discipline quite briefly, [and this is] a great and difficult task. The internal complication of the rhetorical art is so great that it cannot be easily examined; and it can scarcely even be understood by [one] hearing [it explained],
25   still less is it easily understood by [one] discovering [it for himself]. We have received no tradition from the ancient authors on this subject, for they taught the particulars but did not work at the whole at all. Let us undertake this missing part of [their] teaching as best we can. Accordingly, we will talk
30   about the genus of the art, [its] species, matter, parts, instrument, parts of the instrument, work, function of the speaker, the end—and after that, about questions and Topics.

So let us take the beginning of the discussion from what is to be observed [about the subject] in general.
35   The genus of rhetoric /1207B/ is discipline. [Its] species are [these] three: judicial, epideictic, and deliberative.

It is clear that the genus is what we said it is. The species are those we mentioned above because the whole discipline of rhetoric is in them. It is complete in the judicial genus of

1207B cases, likewise in the epideictic or the deliberative. But these are the genera of cases; for all cases, whether special or individual, fall under one of these three genera. For example, special cases, such as that of an offense against the sovereignty of

5 the people or that of extortion by a provincial governor, fall under the judicial genus. Under deliberative, every case that involves planning (*consultatio*): for example, in special cases, if you treat of war or peace, in individual cases, if you treat of the war or peace of Pyrrhus. Similarly in epideictic [cases],

10 every one that has to do with praise or censure is put under the epideictic genus: for example, in a special case, the praise of a brave /1207C/ man, in an individual case, the praise of Scipio.

The matter of this discipline is every subject proposed for a
15 speech. But, for the most part, it is a political question.

The species of rhetoric come into this [matter, namely, the political question] and take [the] matter to themselves as if they were forms of a certain sort; and in a threefold way they constitute the form [of rhetoric], as will be clear later, so that

20 the political question, which heretofore was without form as far as the species go, accepts bounds and becomes subject to one or another of the species of rhetoric. For example, a political question heretofore without form becomes a political question established in the judicial genus when it has accepted

25 from the judicial genus the bounds [which are] the just. When it has taken the advantageous or the proper from the deliberative genus, then it will become a political question established in the deliberative genus of cases. If it has taken the good from the epideictic genus, then it is an epideictic /1207D/ political

30 question. The species come from rhetoric into the matter, because no discipline can work on its matter except insofar as it employs its parts. For if all its parts were absent, rhetoric itself would also be absent. But since it has been said that the species of rhetoric are the genera of cases, they are so in this way.

35 Of all the actions (*negotiorum*) involved in the political question, the genus is judicial when they have been bounded by the just; and of all those involved in the political question, the genus is deliberative when they have been bounded by the proper or the advantageous; and also of all those involved in

1207D the political question, the genus is epideictic when they have
been bounded by the proper only or by the good. But this suffices for these things.

/1208A/ Now we must give our attention to the parts of rhet-
5   oric. There are five parts of rhetoric: discovery, arrangement,
expression, memorization, delivery. They are called parts because if an orator lacks any of these, the discipline is incomplete, and because it is right to call those things which
make the oratorical discipline a whole the parts of that dis-
10   cipline.

Since these are the parts of the rhetorical discipline and
make the rhetorical discipline whole, it must be that where
rhetoric is whole (namely, in the appropriate species), the
parts themselves also follow. So, all the parts of rhetoric will
15   be in the species of rhetoric. And therefore they are also employed in the political actions to be discussed, which are given
form by the aforementioned species of rhetoric. So, discovery,
arrangement, expression, /1208B/ memorization, and delivery
are equally suitable for a judicial, deliberative, or epideictic
20   action.

Since almost every discipline uses an instrument to do what
it is able to do, there will also be an instrument for the rhetorical discipline. This is discourse; and it is used partly in the political genus and partly not. But we are talking now about dis-
25   course which involves a question or which is suitable for the
purpose of untangling a question. Discourse used in the political genus runs along without a break; but that which is not
used in political cases unfolds in questions and answers. The
first is called rhetorical; the second, dialectical. The latter dif-
30   fers from the former, first because the former examines a political hypothesis [but] the latter, a thesis; [and] then because the
former is carried on by unbroken discourse [but] the latter, by
interrupted discourse, and because rhetorical discourse has a
judge in addition /1208C/ to an opponent, but dialectical dis-
35   course uses the same person as both judge and opponent.

This rhetorical discourse has six parts: the prooemium,
which is the exordium, the narrative, the partition, the confirmation, the refutation, the peroration; and these are the parts
of the instrument of the rhetorical discipline. Since rhetoric is
40   in all its species, [these] will be in all the species. Nor will they

1208C be in [the species more] than they will assist the things that are carried on by means of those same [species]. So, the series of prooemium, narrative, and the rest must be in the judicial genus of cases, and [these things] must be in the epideictic
5 and deliberative genera as well.

The work of the rhetorical discipline is to teach and to move; but this is accomplished by just those same six instruments, that is, the parts of discourse.

Since the parts of rhetoric are parts of a discipline, /1208D/
10 they are themselves also disciplines. Therefore, they themselves also take a share in the use of the parts of discourse as instruments; and in order that the parts of the instrument may function by the parts of rhetoric (his operentur), it will be in the parts of the instrument (eisdem inerit). For unless the five afore-
15 mentioned parts of rhetoric are in exordia, so that the orator discovers, arranges, expresses, memorizes, and delivers, the orator accomplishes nothing. And in the same way, unless all the remaining parts of the instrument have all the parts of rhetoric, they are futile.
20 The practitioner of this discipline is the orator, whose function is to speak appropriately for persuasion.

The end is sometimes within the orator himself and some-times within another. [When it is] within the orator himself, it is to have spoken well, that is, to have spoken in a way appro-
25 priate for persuasion; [when it is] within another, it is to have persuaded. For it is not the case that if they hinder the orator in such a way that he persuades the less as a result, the end has not been achieved, when his function has been per-formed. /1209A/ The end which was near and related to the
30 function is achieved when the function has been performed; the end which is external, however, often is not achieved. But rhetoric, which has striven for its end, is not thereby deprived of [its] honor.

These things are mixed in such a way that rhetoric is in [its]
35 species, and the species are in the cases. The parts of cases are called 'issues' (status); one may call these also by other names, sometimes 'points in dispute' (constitutiones), sometimes 'questions' (quaestiones).

Issues are divided as the nature of things is divided. But let
40 us describe the differentiae of questions [that is, issues] from

1209A the beginning. Since rhetorical questions are all involved with circumstances, either they involve debate over some document or they take the beginning (*exordium*) of the dispute from outside the document, from the thing itself.

5   Those that have to do with a document can arise in five ways. First, when /1209B/ one man argues from the words of a writer; another, from the writer's meaning. This is called 'what is written and what is intended.' In another way, if laws disagree among themselves by a certain opposition, and [two

10   men each] argue from an opposed part, the documents produce a controversy. This is called 'an issue from opposed laws.' Third, when the document about which there is some dispute contains an ambiguous meaning. This is called by the [corresponding] name 'ambiguity.' Fourthly, when from what

15   is written, something different which is not written is understood. This is called 'reasoning' or 'syllogism,' because it is found by reasoning and a consequence of a syllogism. Fifthly, when a word is written whose force and nature is not easily made clear unless it is discovered by definition. This is called

20   'limit' or 'circumscribing.'

To differentiate all these things is a part not of our task but of the rhetorician's; /1209C/ for we put these things forth to be examined by the learned, not to teach the ignorant, although we have discussed their differentiae in passing in the com-

25   mentaries on the *Topics*.

The differentiae of the issues external to documents and put forth in dispute about things themselves are divided according to the diversity of the nature of the things themselves, for in every rhetorical question what is in doubt is whether it is,

30   what kind of thing (*quid*) it is, what qualities it has, and in addition, whether judgment can be lawfully or morally administered.

If the deed or matter which is alleged is denied by the opponent, the question is whether it is. This is called 'a conjectural

35   issue.' If it is established that the deed occurred but what it is (*quid sit*) is not known, the issue is called 'definitional' since the import of the deed must be shown by definition. If it is established that [the deed] occurred and that it fits the definition of the matter /1209D/ but there is some question about the

40   qualities of the deed, then because there is doubt about what

1209D genus it ought to be put under, [the issue] is called 'generic qualitative.' In this question, an account (*ratio*) of quality, quantity, and comparison is employed.

5 Since the question is about genus, this [last] issue must be divided into many parts according to the nature of genus. Every generic question—when one asks about the genus, quality, and quantity of a deed—is divided into two parts. One asks about the quality of what is under discussion either with respect to the past or with respect to the present or fu-

10 ture. If with respect to the past, the issue is called 'juridical.' If it contains a question of present or future time, the issue is called 'legal (*negotialis*).'

A juridical inquiry considers what is past; it is divided into two parts. /1210A/ Either the force of the defense is in the deed

15 itself, and the quality is called 'absolute'; or the force of the defense is assumed from without, and the issue is called 'assumptive.'

The latter is distributed into four parts; the crime is acknowledged, removed, transferred, or, finally, compared.

20 The crime is acknowledged when one introduces no defense of the deed but asks for pardon. This can happen in two ways: if you entreat or if you justify. You entreat when you produce no excuse. You justify when the blame for the deed is ascribed to things which cannot be withstood or prevented but are not

25 part of the character (for that falls under another issue). These things are ignorance, chance events, and necessity.

The crime is removed when it is shifted from him who is accused to someone else. Removal of the crime can occur in two ways: /1210B/ if the responsibility or the deed is removed. The

30 responsibility is removed when it is argued that something was done by someone else's power. The deed is removed when it is shown that someone else either could have or ought to have done it—these things are of most use if the indictment brought against us is of this sort, that we have not done what

35 we ought to have done.

The crime is transferred when it is argued that the misdeed was justly committed against someone since the one against whom it was committed was often unjust and deserved to suffer what it is charged [that the defendant did].

40 A comparison occurs when the deed which the opponent

1210B argues was committed is defended [as having been done] for the sake of what is better or more advantageous.

There are appropriate differentiae of all these and also very minute divisions; the books of the rhetoricians, written to 5 teach and explain these things, contain them more thoroughly. /1210C/ For us, it is enough to have taken these things from Cicero, for the whole plan of the work hurries on to something else, all of which we must now examine.

Cicero shows that issues are parts of cases in the passage in 10 which he argues against Hermagoras: "if they cannot rightly be thought parts of a genus of cases, still less will they rightly be thought parts of a part of a case. But every issue is part of a case"—indicating that issues are parts of cases.

Hence there is considerable question about the way in 15 which issues were considered to be parts of a case. If they are parts in the way species are parts, how can it be that there are many issues in one case? For species cannot mingle with each other, but many issues enter into a case. Therefore, issues are not parts of cases as species. /1210D/ There is this also: no 20 species aids the substance of another species opposed to it, but one issue strengthens belief for another. Nor can it be that they are parts of cases as parts of a whole, for there can be no whole and complete thing composed of one part, and in a case one issue is enough to constitute the case.

25 The road to reason therefore shows us what to say.

An issue (constitutio) is not said to be part of a case which comes into dispute and which is constituted by an issue (status), especially since an issue (status) added to a case which is already established by one issue (constitutio) is not a principal 30 issue but an accidental one. And in one action there occur as many disputes as issues, and as many cases as disputes. Although one action may contain these, nevertheless the cases do not mingle /1211A/ but are different from each other. For example, someone sees a young man coming out of a brothel 35 and a little later sees his wife coming out of the same place, and he accuses the young man of adultery. What is involved here is one action but two cases: one conjectural if he denies that he did it, the other definitional if he says that copulation in a brothel cannot be thought adultery. But the conjectural

1211A issue is not a part of this dispute if he denies [that he did it],
nor is the definitional issue a part if [his defense is] in defining; for [either way] the issue contains the whole case. I am
using 'case' not generally but [only] as a dispute formed by
5   some issue.

But issues are parts of a case in general in this way. If the
whole case were conjectural and no other issue were found,
the issue would not be part of the conjectural case, but the
case itself would without doubt be conjectural. But since
10   /1211B/ all cases are comprised partly by what is conjectural,
partly not, partly by quality, partly by transference, an issue is
part not of the case which it informs by comprising it but
rather of the case in general which it divides. Separating from
such a case as a kind of part, any one issue produces its own
15   [case]. So issues are parts which are species of a case in general but not of a case which any one issue has informed and
comprised.

So the genus of rhetoric is discipline. There are three species
of rhetoric: judicial, epideictic, and deliberative. The matter
20   [of rhetoric] is the political question, which is called a case. The
parts of this matter are issues. The parts of rhetoric are discovery, arrangement, expression, memorization, and delivery.
[Its] instrument is discourse. The parts of the instrument are
exordium, narration, partition, confirmation, refutation, and
25   peroration. [Its] work is /1211C/ to teach and to move. The one
who does this work is the orator. [Its] function is to speak
well. [Its] end is sometimes to have spoken well, sometimes to
persuade.

All of rhetoric is in [its] species. The species inform all the
30   matter in such a way that they in turn appropriate all the matter for themselves; and this can be understood from the fact
that the individual species contain all the parts of the matter,
for you will find four issues in the judicial [species], and you
can find the same four in the epideictic and deliberative [spe-
35   cies]. And so, if the individual species have all the parts of a
case in general, which is a political question, and the case itself is all the parts, then it is shown that the species in turn appropriate the whole case (that is, the political question) in the
same way as an utterance simultaneously comes to the ears of

1211C many, complete and with its parts (namely, the syllables); for
the whole case /1211D/ with its parts simultaneously goes
through to the different species.

5 When the species have come into the matter, that is, into the
political question, and have obtained it with its parts, they
bring with themselves also the rhetorical discipline itself. So
the parts of rhetoric too will be in the individual issues. Once
the matter has been produced, it brings with it its instrument;
so it brings with it discourse, and discourse brings with it its
10 own parts. And so in the issues to be discussed there will be
exordium, narration, and the rest.

When the instrument has come into the political question, it
also brings with it at the same time its work; so in every issue
there will be teaching and persuading. These cannot occur by
15 themselves; there must be someone who moves them like a
craftsman or builder. This is the orator. When he /1212A/ has
come to a case, he produces his function. Therefore, in every
genus of cases there will be [someone who] speaks well. And
in every issue, he will produce the end also: sometimes, to
20 have spoken well in every issue; sometimes, to have persuaded.

We have now dealt with the particulars in general. Later, if
it is convenient, we will also discuss them separately. And
that is enough about these things.

25 Now we must examine discovery. For previously we gave
the dialectical Topics, and now we are bringing the rhetorical
Topics to light; and these must come from the attributes of the
person and the action.

The person is the one brought to trial, some deed or speech
30 of whose is censured. The action is the person's deed or
speech for which he is brought to trial. Every division of
Topics is comprised in these two. For unless the things that
give occasion for censure /1212B/ verge on the altogether inex-
cusable, they also provide an abundance of defense; for every
35 accusation and every defense are established from the same
Topics. If a person is brought to trial and no deed or speech [of
his] is censured, there can be no case. Nor can any deed or
speech be brought into a trial if there is no person. And so
every account (*ratio*) of trials involves these two, namely, per-
40 son and action.

1212B   As was said, the person is the one who is brought to trial; the action is the person's deed or speech, for which he, the defendant, is judged. Therefore, the person and the action cannot supply arguments, for the question is about them, and the
5   things brought into question cannot produce belief for what is in question. But an argument was a reason /1212C/ producing belief regarding what is in doubt. The attributes of persons and actions, on the other hand, do produce belief regarding an action. And if a person sometimes does produce belief regard-
10   ing an action—for example, if someone believes that Catiline plotted against the republic because Catiline is a person marked by the baseness of vices—then it is not insofar as he is a person and brought to trial that he produces belief regarding the action but rather insofar as he has a certain nature, from
15   the attributes of the person.

        To show the order of [these] things more clearly, I think circumstances must be discussed. Circumstances are things which, by coming together, produce the substance of the issue (*quaestio*). For unless there is someone who did [something]
20   and something which he did, and a reason why he did it, and a place and time in which he did it, and manner and means (*facultates*) [in and by which he did it], there will be no case.

        Cicero divides these circumstances in two. The circumstance /1212D/ "who [did it]" he puts among the attributes of the per-
25   son. The other circumstances, according to him, consist in the attributes of the action.

        The first of the circumstances, which is "who" and attributed to the person, he divides into eleven parts: name (for example, 'Verres'); nature (for example, foreigner); mode of
30   life (for example, friend of nobles); fortune (for example, rich); studies (for example, geometrician); luck (for example, exile); feelings (for example, loving); disposition (for example, wise); purpose; deeds; and words (deeds and words other than the deed and speech now brought into the trial).

35   The remaining circumstances—what, why, how, where, when, with what means—he puts among the attributes of the action.

        "What" and "why" he says are connected with the action itself. "Why" is comprised in the reason, according to him, for
40   the reason /1213A/ for any deed is that on account of which it

1213A was done. He divides "what" into four parts: the gist of the deed, for example, the killing of a parent (from this the Topic of amplification is most often taken); before the deed, for example, he seized a sword in a state of excitement; while [the
5   deed] occurs, [for example], he struck violently; after the deed, [for example], he hid in a secret place. All these things are deeds; nevertheless, since they pertain to the performed action in question, they are not the deeds which are counted among the attributes of the person. For those deeds which are posited
10   outside the action at issue and which form the person provide belief regarding the action which the accusation deals with; but the deeds connected with the action itself pertain to the very action in question.

     Cicero puts the last four circumstances among the perform-
15   ing of the action, which is /1213B/ the second part of the attributes of actions. The circumstance "when" he divides into time, for example, he carried it out by night, and opportunity, for example, when everyone was sleeping. The circumstance "where" he calls place, for example, he carried it out in the
20   bedroom. Of the circumstances, "how" is the method, for example, he carried it out secretly. He calls the means the circumstance "with what aid," for example, with a large band of men. Even if the differences among these Topics are clear from the nature of the circumstances, we will show more goodwill if
25   we present the differentiae among them more abundantly.

     Cicero maintained that some of the circumstances are connected with the action itself and others are connected with the performing of the action. Among those connected with the action itself he numbered the Topic which he called "while it oc-
30   curs"; from the signification /1213C/ of the expression, this Topic "while it occurs" seems to be the same Topic as that which is in the performing of the action. But such is not the case, because the former "while it occurs" is what is committed at the time while the crime is being perpetrated, for ex-
35   ample, he struck. In the performing of the action there are things which contain what is done before the deed which was performed, while that deed occurs, and after that deed; for in all of these there is a question about time, place, opportunity, method, and means. Again, the "while it occurs" is the deed
40   by which the action is accomplished. So the things which are

1213C in the performing of the action are not deeds but adherents to the deed, for no one would agree that time, opportunity, place, method, and means are deeds, but they are equally adherents to any deed whatever, as was said. And this is not
5 in any way altered because in a certain relationship (relatio) they are subsumed under the action which was performed.

Similarly, the things which are in the performing /1213D/ of the action can be without the things which are connected with the action. The place, time, opportunity, method, and means
10 of any deed can be understood even if no one does the deed, which could occur in that place or time or opportunity or by that method or those means. So the things which are in the performing of the action can be without the things which are connected with the action itself; but the latter cannot be with-
15 out the former, for there cannot be a deed without place, time, opportunity, method, and means.

Those things which consist in the attributes of the person and the action /1214A/ [are] like those among the dialectical Topics which inhere in the very things asked about. The re-
20 mainder, however, which either are associated with the action or follow from the action performed, are (in Themistius's divi- sion) partly like those among the dialectical Topics which fol- low from the substance of the thing, partly like those from without, and partly like those used as intermediates—or (in
25 Cicero's division) like those numbered among the related things or those posited from without. They are associated with the action and equally produce belief regarding the question, being related in a certain way to what is in question and hav- ing regard to the action at issue.

30 Seven circumstances are numbered among the attributes of the person or the action. When these begin to be compared and to come into a relationship, as it were, then if [what is being compared] is held up to that which contains or to that which is contained, it is either species or genus; [of whatever
35 it is held up to]; if it is held up to /1214B/ what is far different from it, it is a contrary, and if it is held up to its own goal and end, it is a result. In the same way, they are compared to things that are greater, lesser, and equal. The Topics which are considered in relation to something are altogether of this sort,
40 for greater and less than, or similar to, or equally great as, or

1214B different from are accidents of the circumstances which are
numbered among the attributes of the person and the action,
so that when these circumstances are compared to others, an
argument about the speech or deed brought into the trial
5   arises from them.

They are different from the preceding Topics, because the
preceding Topics either contained deeds or adhered to deeds
in such a way that they could not be separated, as place, time,
and the rest, which do not desert the action performed. But
10   those things that are associated with the action do not adhere
to the /1214C/ action itself but are accidents of the circumstances, and they provide an argument only when they enter
into comparison. The arguments, however, are taken not from
contrariety but from a contrary, and not from similarity but
15   from a similar, so that the argument seems to be taken not
from a relationship [such as contrariety] but from things associated with the action [such as contraries]. Those things are
associated with the action which are related to the very action
at issue.

20   Consequence is the fourth part of the attributes of the action. It is not in the things which do not leave the substance of
things nor is it derived from comparison, but it precedes or
even follows the thing performed. And this whole Topic is ex-
trinisc. In this Topic one asks first by what name it is fitting to
25   call what has been done; and here one takes pains not with
/1214D/ the thing but with the word. Then one asks who the
doers of this deed are and who approve of its having been
thought up and are emulators of it. This whole [Topic] comes
together from judgment and from a kind of witness which is
30   extrinsic in order to aid the argument. Then one asks also
what is the law, custom, agreement, judgment, opinion (*sententia*), and theory (*artificium*) for the thing [in question]. Then
one asks if the kind of thing involved generally befalls the
mass of men or whether it happens contrary to custom and
35   rarely; [also] whether men in these matters are accustomed to
agree to and defend this by [giving it] their authority; and [so
on with] other things which in the same way generally follow
some deed either immediately or after a time, which are extrinsic /1215A/ and must tend more to opinion than to the very
40   nature of the things.

1215A   So one can divide the attributes of actions into the following four. In part, they are connected with the action itself and, as was said above, these are deeds. In part, they are in the performing of the action; and, as we showed previously, these are

5   not deeds but the adherents to deeds. In part, they are associated with the action. And these, as was said, partly are put forth in a relationship and partly follow from the action performed; belief regarding these is taken from without. And enough has been said about rhetorical Topics.

10   Now we must explain the similarity and the difference between these and dialectical Topics. When I have shown this sufficiently and appropriately, then the plan of the work proposed will be completed.

First of all, according to Themistius, among the dialectical

15   Topics there are some which inhere in the very things in question, some which /1215B/ are taken from without, and some which are placed intermediate between these two. So also among the rhetorical Topics, some are in the persons and the action which are in contention, some are from without, such

20   as those which follow from the action performed, and some are intermediate.

Of the circumstances, those which are thought to rest in the performing of the action are the closest to the action. Those which are associated with the action are also placed among the

25   intermediate Topics since they are tied to the action at issue by a certain relationship. Or, someone might say that the attributes of the person or the things connected with the action itself or those considered to be in the performing of the action are similar to the dialectical Topics which are drawn from the

30   very things asked about in the question; the things following from the action /1215C/ he might consider extrinsic, and the things associated with the action he might designate as intermediate between those two.

It is similar to Cicero's division in this way. The things con-

35   nected with the action itself or those which are considered to be in the performing of the action inhere in the things in question. The things associated with the action are placed within [Cicero's Topic of] related things. The things that follow from the action performed are taken from without. Or,

40   someone might think that the things connected with the action

1215C [are like those of Cicero's Topics which] inhere in the things themselves, that those which are in the performing of the action or are associated with the action are [like Cicero's Topic of] related things, and that those which follow from the action

5   performed are from without.

The likenesses are already clear, because almost the same Topics are used in both disciplines, such as genus, part, similarity, contrary, and greater and lesser. /1215D/ Enough has been said about likenesses.

10   The differences are that dialectical Topics are suited also for theses, but rhetorical Topics are suited for hypotheses only, that is, they are arrogated to questions informed by circumstances. For as the disciplines are distinguished from one another by the universality [of the one] and the particularity [of

15   the other], so also their Topics differ in range and /1216A/ restriction, because the range of dialectical Topics is greater. Since they are independent of circumstances, which produce individual cases, they are useful not only for theses but also for arguments put forth in hypotheses, whose Topics, com-

20   posed of circumstances, they include and range over.

So the rhetorician always proceeds from dialectical Topics, but the dialectician can be content with his own Topics. For since a rhetorician draws cases from circumstances, he takes arguments from the same circumstances; but these must be

25   confirmed by the universal and simple, namely, the dialectical [Topics]. The dialectician, on the other hand, is prior and has no need of anything posterior, unless on occasion there happens to be a question about a person, as when a dialectician happens to prove his thesis by a case involving circumstances,

30   then only /1216B/ does he use rhetorical Topics.

So in dialectical Topics, arguments are taken from, say, the genus, that is, from the very nature of genus. But in rhetorical Topics, arguments are taken from the particular genus which is the genus at issue; they are not taken from the nature of

35   genus, but from the generic thing, from the thing that is the genus. But in order to proceed, the argument (*ratio*) depends on the fact that the nature of genus is known beforehand. For example, suppose there is a question whether someone was drunk. If we want to refute [the charge], we will say that he

40   was not since he had never before been dissipated. Therefore,

1216B since dissipation is, as it were, a genus of drunkenness, and since there was no dissipation, there certainly was no drunkenness. But this depends on something else. For the fact that there could be no drunkenness since there was no dissipation
5 is shown from the nature of genus, and this the dialectical argument (*ratio*) provides. For where the genus is absent, there /1216C/ the species must also be absent, since the genus does not leave the species.

And in the same way for similars and contraries. In these
10 things there is a very great difference between rhetorical and dialectical Topics. Dialectic discovers arguments from qualities themselves; rhetoric, from things taking on a quality. So the dialectician [discovers arguments] from genus, that is, from the nature of genus; the rhetorician, from the thing that is the
15 genus. The dialectician [discovers arguments] from similarity; the rhetorician, from a similar, that is, from the thing which takes on similarity. In the same way, the former [discovers arguments] from contrariety; the latter, from a contrary.

Now that all the things which we proposed above have been
20 explained, I think we ought to add this. Cicero's *Topica*, which he published for C. Trebatius, who was skilled at law, does not examine how one can dispute about these things themselves but how arguments of the rhetorical discipline /1216D/ may be produced, which we explained more thoroughly in the
25 commentaries we wrote on Cicero's *Topica*. How one disputes about them with dialectical arguments (*rationibus*) we explained in the commentaries we wrote on Aristotle's *Topics*, translated by us.

NOTES

NOTES TO BOOK I

[Each note is keyed first to a line in the *PL* edition and then to a page, line, and word in my translation.]

1. 1173C1 (29.1); "*disserendi.*" The use of the phrase '*ratio disserendi*' as a designation for logic and the idea of logic as the science of discourse became important in later medieval philosophy. For use of the phrase '*ratio disserendi*,' see L. M. de Rijk, ed., *Logica Modernorum*, 2 vols. (Assen, 1962, 1967), I, 191.7ff., 282.10–12, 265.5; II, pt. II. 31.5–18, 147.3. See also Abelard, *Scritti di logica,* ed. Mario dal Pra (Rome-Milan, 1954), pp. 209ff. See also Norman Kretzmann, "History of Semantics," *The Encyclopedia of Philosophy,* ed. Paul Edwards (New York, 1967), VII, 358–406, esp. 370–371.

2. 1173C1 (29.2); "Peripatetics." Bonitz's *Index* indicates that Aristotle did not use the noun 'λογική' for all of logic; cf. also Innocentius M. Bocheński, *Ancient Formal Logic* (Amsterdam, 1951), p. 25. The origin and history of 'λογική' as a word for logic are not clear. Carl Prantl, *Geschichte der Logik im Abendlande* (Leipzig, 1855–1860), I, 535, says that both Alexander of Aphrodisias and Cicero use 'λογική' as an established term for logic.

3. 1173C3 (29.3); "judging." The characterization of logic as *ratio disserendi* and the division of logic into these two parts is almost certainly taken from Cicero; cf. *Topica* II.6. The objects of discovering and judging are arguments, as will emerge in the course of this treatise; see also Cicero's *Topica* II.7–8.

4. 1173C5 (29.5); "analytical." Boethius is here attempting to introduce a Latin term (*resolutoria*) analogous to the Greek technical term.

5. 1173C6 (29.5–6); "*facultatem.*" According to Lewis and Short, '*facultas*' comes from the Latin for 'easy' and 'easily,' '*facilis,*' '*facul*'; see also the entry in Merguet's *Lexikon*. Its uses divide into two main groups: *facultas* in things that are done, and *facultas* in material things. When applied in the area of actions, the basic idea of ease becomes skill or proficiency; in the area of material things, it becomes wealth or abundance. The closest English word in range of meaning is 'competence,' I think; I have also translated the word as 'capability' and 'discipline' in some passages.

6. 1173C7 (29.7); "*localis.*" Boethius's word here is the adjective formed

from 'locus,' the Latin word for the Greek 'τόπος'. 'Locus' is the standard Latin term for Topic, and Boethius is trying to introduce the adjectival form of the word as a technical term also.

7. 1173C8 (29.8); "elsewhere." Perhaps Boethius is referring to his previously written books on the categorical and hypothetical syllogisms where he examines matters pertaining to judging arguments. See *Introductio ad syllogismos categoricos, PL,* LXIV, 761–794; *De syllogismo categorico, ibid.,* 793–832; and *De syllogismo hypothetico,* ed. and tr. Luca Obertello (Brescia, 1969), pp. 204–390; *PL* 831–876.

8. 1173C10 (29.9); "Topics." Boethius's word is 'loci.' 'Locus' is a standard technical term not only in Cicero and Boethius but also throughout later medieval philosophy. The equivalent Greek term is frequently translated 'Topic,' and in current secondary literature 'Topic' is the most commonly used English word for 'locus' as well. The complicated concept of a Topic will emerge in the course of the treatise.

9. 1173C10 (29.10); "differentiae." 'Differentia' here is a technical term which it would be misleading to translate simply as 'difference.' It is one of the five Porphyrian predicables (see Porphyry, *Isagoge,* ed. Adolf Busse, *CAG* (Berlin 1887), IV, pt. i. 8ff.); and Aristotle, too, discusses it (see, for example, *Top.* 101b18–19, 139a28–29). For Boethius's discussion of differentia in this treatise, see 1178B5–C4. Cf. also Boethius, *In Isagogen,* ed. Samuel Brandt (Leipzig, 1906), pp. 239ff. (*PL* 115Bff.). See also the chapters on differentia below.

10. 1173C11 (29.10); "syllogisms." The purpose of the Topics is discovering arguments, and for Boethius arguments are primarily syllogisms (cf. 1184D7–1185A3). But not all Topics are equally well suited to discover all kinds of syllogisms. Boethius divides syllogisms in two ways: first, some are demonstrative and others dialectical; second, some are predicative and other conditional. In 1195A13–1196A3, Boethius explains briefly which Topics are suited for which kinds of syllogism.

11. 1173C14 (29.13–14); "*Topica.*" Cicero's *Topica* is very different from Aristotle's *Topics,* which is the ultimate Greek source; see the Introduction for explanation and reference to secondary sources. Exactly how and by whom the tradition was changed between Aristotle and Cicero is not clear; see the chapter "Between Aristotle and Boethius" below. The Greek side of the tradition to which Boethius refers is taken from Themistius (see, for example, 1194A15ff.), whose understanding of the Topics is closer to Cicero's than Cicero's is to Aristotle's. The two divisions of Topics, Cicero's and Themistius's, are laid out in Books II and III of this treatise.

12. 1173D6 (29.19); "definitions." It is not immediately clear from the text that Boethius does go on to give definitions of the individual Topics; though he does give a general definition for the sort of Topic at issue (1185A4ff.), he never explicitly gives a definition for a particular Topic. But perhaps Boethius has something of this sort in mind. A definition is a genus plus differentiae. Now Boethius seems to think of the genus for Topics in general as *maximal proposition* (for an explanation of this technical term, see 1185A4ff.), and then in discussing particular Topics he

gives differentiae of maximal propositions. The genus plus one of these differentiae, then, constitute a definition of a Topic; so once Boethius has given a differentia, he has in effect also given the definition, and it would be redundant to spell out the definition explicitly, too. Boethius says that he is giving definitions *and* differentiae because the differentiae involved have a technical function of their own, other than serving as part of a definition; they turn out to be a second sort of Topic.

13. 1173D6 (29.21); "arise." Boethius here seems to be distinguishing the Topics in his treatise from all other Topics. 'Locus' (Topic) is also the Latin word for place or spatial location; and the study of *locus* is important in ancient physics (the Greek analogue 'τόπος' occurs frequently in Aristotle's *Physics*). But, perhaps more important, *locus* also plays a crucial role in the ancient art of memorization (see, for example, Frances Yates, *The Art of Memory* [London, 1966], and Richard Sorabji, *Aristotle on Memory* [London, 1972]; also the Introduction above). There they are literally places, generally in some architecturally complex building, which aid the orator in discovering or calling to mind what he has memorized. Because these places are also Topics (*loci*) that are useful in discovering, it may be these which Boethius means to exclude when he says that he is going to consider only "those Topics from which arguments arise."

14. 1173D11 (29.25); "commentary." The commentary Boethius refers to here is his *In Ciceronis Topica*. It is not extant in its entirety; the last part of the sixth Book and the whole of the seventh are missing.

15. 1173D15 (29.30); "rhetorical Topics." Dialectical Topics occupy Books II and III of this treatise; rhetorical Topics are discussed in Book IV. In this paragraph, Boethius seems to imply that all Topics are either dialectical or rhetorical. But sophistical Topics are common among later medieval logicians. For instance, William of Sherwood devotes a large part of one chapter in his introductory logic text to sophistical Topics (*Introduction to Logic*, ed. Grabmann, pp. 85–104; tr. Norman Kretzmann [Minneapolis, 1966], pp. 134–167). They are also discussed in *Summa Sophisticorum Elencorum*, *Log. Mod.* I, 286, 397; *Dialectica Monacensis*, *Log. Mod.* II, pt. II, 558; and *Excerpta Nurimbergensia*, *Log. Mod.* II, pt. II, 130ff. Furthermore, Aristotle mentions sophistical Topics in *Soph. El.* 165a4–6 and 166b20–21. Boethius might have ruled them out as genuine Topics because a Topic is the foundation of an argument and sophistical arguments for Boethius are not really arguments (see 1181A4–11).

16. 1174C5 (30.9); "oratio." In Boethius's translation of Aristotle's *De Int.*, 'oratio' is used consistently as the translation for 'λόγος', and Boethius's definition of 'oratio' is the definition given for 'λόγος' in *De Int.* 16b26: *oratio* is a significant utterance, parts of which in separation are significant, not as affirmations but as words (*dictio*, φάσις). An *oratio*, then, is a certain linguistic entity that can be as small as a pair of words and as large as a complex sentence. Though an *oratio* is said to be a kind of utterance in the definition above, Boethius also says that it can be spoken, written, or thought; see *In Perihermeneias*, ed. Carolus Meiser (Leipzig, 1880), II, 29.16ff. (*PL* 407A8ff.) and 42.15ff. (*PL* 413D12ff.).

17. 1174C10 (30.14–15); "arguments." Though it is possible, according

to Boethius's definition of argument (1174D1ff.), that a single premise or proposition is an argument, it is disturbing that Boethius says 'arguments' in his definition of conclusion here, because he knows of and uses conclusions derived from only one premise (cf., for example, 1198D5–8). Perhaps he is thinking of the Topics (maximal propositions) as premises involved directly or indirectly in all (dialectical) arguments, so that even arguments with only one premise are really dependent on that premise plus some Topic. If so, and if he is thinking of each premise as an argument, it would be true to say that a conclusion is a proposition proved by arguments.

18. 1174D9 (30.32); "argument." This definition of 'Topic' is taken from Cicero; see *Topica* ii.8. What a Topic is will emerge more clearly later in the treatise; see in particular 1185A3–1186B12 where Topics are discussed generally and in more detail.

19. 1174D13 (30.37); "said." I am not certain what in the preceding lines Boethius is referring to. There are two good reasons for thinking that it is Topics that will be laid out in species, parts, and schemes. First, Boethius is talking about making a division, and his concern in these first pargraphs as well as in the treatise as a whole is with divisions of Topics. Second, 'scheme' (*figura*) is used only rarely in the treatise; and when it occurs, it refers to the two different schemes of division of Topics that Cicero and Themistius give. So it is plausible that Boethius's reference here ("as we said") is to 1173C9–11 or 1173D5–7 or both. In the first of those places, Boethius says he will explain what the Topics are and what their differentiae are; in the second, he says he will collect definitions, examples, and differentiae of the Topics. The species of anything is what is defined, and the definition of a thing consists in its genus and differentiae. So perhaps when Boethius says he is going to give definitions and differentiae of Topics, he means approximately the same thing as when he says he will show the species of Topics. The phrase "as we said" comes after "species and parts" and before "schemes" in the Latin. Boethius may mean only species and parts to have been previously mentioned. And possibly 'species and parts' is a pleonastic construction—species are a sort of part, according to Boethius (1188C9–13)—so that Boethius in fact is referring only to a prior promise to give the species of Topics.

20. 1174D15 (30.38); "said." Boethius's previous definition is in 1174C5–6.

21. 1175A12 (31.15); "these." Boethius is making an ordered division. Propositions consist of affirmations and negations, and affirmations and negations are universal, particular, indefinite, or singular. The word 'these' here refers to universal, particular, indefinite, and singular affirmations and negations: propositions that are universal, particular, indefinite, or singular affirmations or negations constitute predicative or conditional propositions.

22. 1175B9 (31.27); "names." What Boethius says here is misleading; by 'terms' he means not only single words but also whole phrases or expressions, as becomes clear in 1175D4ff. Boethius also frequently gives the im-

pression that he is thinking of the subject and predicate as things rather than as words; cf., for example, 1177D10ff.

23. 1175B9 (31.28); "together." Boethius says that grammarians treat of eight parts of discourse (*oratio*) but that philosophers, whose whole concern in this connection is with signification, consider verbs and names the only parts of discourse because they alone have full signification (*Intro.* 766A13–B4; see also *In Perihermeneias,* ed. Meiser, II, 14.28ff.; *PL* 399B5ff.). The other parts of discourse are assimilated to the noun or the verb (*Intro.* 766B6–C12); they are not parts of a proposition but supplements to the parts, and their function is to bind the parts together (*Intro.* 796D2ff.). The copula is not a part either. Rather it designates the quality of the proposition; that is, it signifies whether the proposition is affirmative or negative (*Intro.* 769A5ff.). I am indebted to Gabriel Nuchelmans, *Theories of the Proposition* (Amsterdam, 1973), p. 124, for these references.

24. 1175B14 (31.32); "*major.*" Boethius's examples, including the one in the next lines, elucidate his meaning of 'greater' and 'lesser.' His point seems to be that a predicate is greater than its subject if it applies to more things than the subject.

25. 1175C2 (31.35); "substances." Cf. *In Isag.,* ed. Brandt, p. 184.19–22 (*PL* 93A11–14). Boethius is probably referring to the celestial spheres, which were thought by some to be moved by intelligent souls. For a presentation of ancient and medieval theories about the souls of the spheres, see Harry A. Wolfson, "The Problem of the Souls of the Spheres, from the Byzantine Commentaries on Aristotle through the Arabs and St. Thomas to Kepler," *Dumbarton Oaks Papers,* 16, (1962), 65–93.

26. 1175C12 (32.3); "term." As is made clear by the rest of the paragraph, Boethius does not mean that a sentence can have two subjects and no predicate. His point is that each such term may equally well be predicated of the other, as is not the case when the predicate is greater than the subject.

27. 1175D3 (32.10); "greater." Cf. Porphyry, *Isagoge, CAG,* p. 7.4ff. It seems clear that Boethius here means something like is predicated correctly or truly of the greater; otherwise, he could not rule out false propositions, and what he says would be an obviously false empirical claim. And in the discussion of the same point in *ICT* 278.34–37 (*PL* 1050A6–11), he uses the phrase "no one *truly* says" (emphasis added). In the preceding paragraph (1175C1–3), Boethius seems to imply that a predicate is greater than its subject in case it applies to more *kinds* of things than the subject does: " 'man' is less than 'just,' for justice can be not only in man but also in corporeal and divine substances.'' If his claim is that the predicate must apply to an equal or greater number of species than the subject does, it is easy to come up with counterinstances. For example, 'Some animal is a man' is a true affirmative particular proposition, but the predicate 'man' applies to fewer species than the subject 'animal.' Boethius may mean his claim to be not about species but about individuals: a predicate must apply to an equal or greater number of individual things than the subject does. But for this claim, too, it is easy to find counterexamples.

For example, 'Some number is a prime less than 4' is a true affirmative particular proposition in which the predicate 'prime less than 4' applies to fewer individual numbers than the subject 'number.' There is, however, a way in which to read Boethius's claim that does make it true. If the subject of the sentence is taken to include the quantifier, then the subject of 'Some number is a prime less than 4' is not 'number' but 'some number.' The most we can say about 'some number' taken out of context is that it applies to at least one number. If we take it in the context of some true proposition such as the one above, then, of course, it applies to at least as many but not more individuals than the predicate (since if in context 'some number' applies to, say, the numbers 1 through 4 and the predicate applies only to 1 through 3, then the proposition 'Some number is a prime less than 4' would be false). So for particular propositions, the subject, understood in the way I have suggested, applies either to one thing or else to as many things as or fewer things than the predicate does; either way it does not apply to more things than the predicate does. As for the three other kinds of propositions Boethius recognizes, the subject of a singular proposition will apply to only one thing; and so in no true singular proposition will the subject apply to more things than the predicate does. (Boethius, I think, would not agree to the view that some predicates apply to nothing at all.) Indefinite propositions are equivalent either to particular propositions or to universal propositions; and universal propositions are the easy case for Boethius's claim. Whether the interpretation of Boethius's claim that I have been developing and defending is in fact what he meant is not clear; neither in *De top. diff.* nor in *ICT* does he explain or argue for the claim.

28. 1176A4 (32.24); "justice." The sentence in the example here appears to be a sentence in which the terms are equal, because the similarity in question is identified with justice. Sentences in which the terms are equal are legitimate instances of predication for Boethius (see 1175C9–D3). But because the terms are equal, the example is not strictly parallel to the other sentences in this paragraph; and it is analogous more to 'Man is a risible thing' than to 'Man is just.'

29. 1176A9 (32.28); "*interpretatione.*" For information on editions of Boethius's commentaries on *De int.*, see Bibliography.

30. 1176A11 (32.30); "propositions." For Boethius's view of the conjunction 'if' and the reason for his not mentioning it as a part of conditional propositions, see note 23 and the references cited there.

31. 1176A12 (32.32); "consequent." Boethius divides hypothetical propositions into implications and disjunctions. According to Boethius, the order of speaking determines the antecedent and the consequent in disjunctions; whichever of the disjuncts is spoken first is the antecedent. But in implications, the antecedent is whatever predicative proposition has the conjunction 'if' attached to it; and, of course, the if-clause is generally first in the order of speaking as well. See *De syll. hyp.*, ed. Obertello, p. 220.1–9 (*PL* 835D12–836A7).

32. 1176B9 (33.5); "syllogisms." Discussion of composite or conjoined conditionals takes up much of Boethius's treatise on hypothetical syl-

logisms; for discussion of the variety of composite conditionals, see *De syll. hyp.*, ed. Obertello, p. 226.1ff. (*PL* 837B4ff.) and p. 244.1ff. (*PL* 841C14ff.). A conjoined conditional is one containing at least one conditional as a part so that those conditionals having a conditional for the antecedent, the consequent, or both, are conjoined or composite conditionals.

33. 1176B11 (33.7); "propositions." Boethius is giving a simplified or summary view here, which is all he needs for his purposes in this treatise. In *De syll. hyp.* ed. Obertello, p. 226.1ff. (*PL* 841C14ff.), he recognizes one hundred sorts of simple conditional propositions, including modal propositions.

34. 1176C6 (33.19); "these." For discussion of this sort of proposition and the role it plays in demonstration, see, for example, Aristotle, *An. Pos.*, 71b20–72a8.

35. 1176C13 (33.24); "demonstrated." In other words, maximal propositions prove secondary propositions, which are not indemonstrable.

36. 1176D14 (34.2); "proposition." What Boethius considers in relation to the proposition are these: quality (affirmative, negative), quantity (universal, etc.), division into predicative and conditional parts of predicative propositions, parts of conditional propositions, division of conditional propositions into simple and conjoined conditionals, division of simple conditionals into four kinds, and division of propositions into propositions known per se and secondary propositions. If we take into account Boethius's view of the question as a proposition in the interrogative mood, then it is clear that all these classifications of propositions, including the final one, can be used to classify questions as well.

37. 1177A1 (34.3); "composite." Here and elsewhere in the following paragraphs, 'simple' is used interchangeably with 'predicative' (and 'categorical'); 'composite' is used interchangeably with 'conditional' (and 'hypothetical'), as well as being a synonym for 'conjoined' in 'conjoined conditional proposition.'

38. 1177A12 (34.15); "propositions." See 1175B7ff. and 1176A9–13.

39. 1177B3 (34.20); "conjoined." Boethius includes disjunctions among conditionals (see, for example, *De syll. hyp.*, ed. Obertello, p. 216.13–14; *PL* 834C8–10). When he is distinguishing implications from disjunctions, he refers to implication as '*conjunctio*' (see, for example, *De syll. hyp.*, ed. Obertello, p. 212.47–54; *PL* 833D8–834A2). So 'conjoined' here is probably no more than 'conditional' in our sense of the word.

40. 1177B7–9 (34.27); "term." It becomes clear in 1177D13ff. that when Boethius speaks of the predicate inhering in the subject term, he is not thinking of the subject and predicate as linguistic entities; instead, by 'subject' and 'predicate' (or even 'subject term' and 'predicate term'), he at least sometimes means the thing that is signified rather than the linguistic entity that signifies. Here he means that the doubt in predicative questions is engendered because we are not sure whether what is signified by the word or expression in the predicate inheres in what is signified by the word or expression in the subject.

41. 1177C5 (34.38); "doubt." Cf. 1174C5–14.

42. 1177C7 (34.40); "question." See note 36.

43. 1177C8 (35.1); "question." The distinction that follows can be found in Cicero, who also attributes it to the Greeks (as Boethius is about to do); see *Topica* XXI.79–80. Aristotle says that, strictly defined, 'θέσις' refers to a conception contrary to accepted opinion but that "now practically all dialectical problems [that is, questions] are called theses" (*Top.* 104b34–36). Aristotle's use of 'hypothesis' in the *Topics* seems unrelated to the sense of the word given here (cf. *Top.* 108b8 and 119b35).

44. 1177D8 (35.17); "later." See 1209A6ff.

45. 1177D11 (35.20); "inheres." See note 40.

46. 1177D12 (35.20); "subject." Cf. Aristotle, *Top.* 103b1–19.

47. 1177D14 (35.22); "asserted." Reading *contendetur* for *contenditur*.

48. 1177D14 (35.23); "substance." Here Boethius begins to lay out his criteria for the four predicables: genus, definition, property, and accident. When Aristotle defines the four predicables (see *Top.* 101b37–102b26), he uses some form of 'τὸ τί ἦν εἶναι' a phrase which is regularly translated as 'essence' and which seems to be the same criterion as Boethius's 'predicated of the substance' (*substantialiter*, or *de substantia praedicabitur*).

49. 1178A5 (35.28); "greater." See note 27.

50. 1178A10 (35.33); "man." Boethius is aware of a clear and important distinction between genus and species (see *In Isag.*, ed. Brandt, p. 203.16ff.; *PL* 101A7ff.). It seems, then, that he ought to say genus *or* species is greater than its subject and predicated of the substance of the subject—unless he thinks that species is equal to, not greater than, its subject, but then species ought to be included in what he says in the following lines about definition. Furthermore, differentia, too, is predicated of the substance of its subject and is greater than its subject (*In Isag.*, ed. Brandt, p. 265.21ff.; *PL* 127A11). Why Boethius leaves differentia and species out of his account in this passage is not clear. He may simply have decided to adopt Aristotelian rather than Porphyrian predicables (cf. note 52 below) for his work in this treatise, but if so, the reasons for his choice are obscure.

51. 1178B2 (35.40); "property." Properties are accidents that have a special relationship to their subject (cf. Porphyry, *Isagoge, CAG*, p. 12.12ff.); that is, they are predicated convertibly of the subject because they belong to only one species and every member of that species always has the characteristic in question. Aristotle adds that an accident that is not technically a property can sometimes be a property in a certain context; for example, when only one person is sitting, sitting may be a property of that person. But properties of this sort, he says, are not properties absolutely but only in a certain respect (see *Top.* 102b20–26). See also the chapters on differentia below.

52. 1178B4 (36.2); "property." These four—genus, accident, definition, and property—are the four Aristotelian predicables (cf., for example, Aristotle, *Top.* 101b37–102b26). Porphyry's *Isagoge*, which Boethius commented on, is entirely devoted to a discussion of the predicables, and Porphyry discusses five predicables—genus, species, differentia, property, and accident. Boethius sometimes uses all six predicables (see, for

example, 1179A5–7). But when he is laying out the predicables as basic concepts important for the study of Topics, he uses just the Aristotelian four. In his discussion of differentia immediately following, Boethius makes some attempt to show how Porphyry's five can be reduced to Aristotle's four, though he does not deal explicitly with species. And it may be that he uses the Aristotelian four instead of the Porphyrian five for the sake of simplicity because he thinks Aristotle's four are sufficient to generate the remaining two.

53. 1178B5 (36.3); "differentia." See note 9.

54. 1178B6 (36.4); "not." See note 25.

55. 1178B11–12 (36.10); "divisive." When a differentia is thought of as composing a species, it is a constitutive differentia. When it is thought of as dividing a genus into its species, it is a divisive differentia. The species *man,* for example, can be analyzed into the genus *animal* plus the differentiae *rational* and *mortal.* Considered as composing the species *man, rational* is a constitutive differentia. But considered as separating the genus *animal* into two species, that of rational animals and that of irrational animals, it is a divisive differentia. See the chapters on differentia below.

56. 1178C2 (36.14–15); "differentia." See the chapters on differentia below for a thorough discussion of Boethius's views of differentia.

57. 1178C4 (36.17); "genus." See the chapter "Differentia" for an explanation of the difficulties in this paragraph.

58. 1178C8 (36.21); "accidents." Cf. Aristotle, *Top.* 102b14–20.

59. 1178C12 (36.26); "definition." Cf. Aristotle, *Top.* 103a6–39.

60. 1178C15 (36.31); "question." Reading *quaestionis* for *quaestiones.* The Basel 1570 edition reads *quaestionis* (p. 860).

61. 1178D6 (36.35); "affirmation." Boethius here is confining himself to simple conditionals; cf. notes 32 and 33.

62. 1179A1 (37.4–5); "affirmation." In this division and the other three that are to follow (the divisions of the conditional question made up of two negations, of an affirmation and a negation, and of a negation and an affirmation), Boethius is doing something like this. The questions that are being divided into their subdivisions may be thought of as composed of an interrogative part ('is it the case that') followed by a proposition. The proposition in all these cases is a simple conditional proposition; but for Boethius's purposes here, it should be thought of not as a conditional, whose truth or falsity is to be evaluated by way of answer to the question, but rather as an argument with one premise and a conclusion. The answer to the question must be based on a judgment about whether the antecedent is true and whether the consequent follows from the antecedent, that is, whether the one-premise argument is sound. In the four divisions that follow Boethius gives varieties of one-premise arguments that are sound for each type of simple conditional question. His purpose, then, is less to divide the kinds of simple conditional question into appropriate and exhaustive subdivisions than to show which of these questions should be answered in the affirmative and what side of a simple conditional question can be defended by a sound argument.

63. 1179A3 (37.6); "questions." Boethius means that he is going to di-

vide questions composed of two affirmations into various sorts and that this subdivision of the question falls in some way within the division he made of predicative questions. The best candidate for a division of predicative questions is the division of theses (predicative dialectical questions) in 1177D9ff. into four different kinds of questions, depending on which of the four predicables they involve. The subdivision of conditional questions at issue here falls within that subdivision of predicative dialectical questions because some of the varieties of conditional questions are also questions about predicables. But Boethius's point is misleading. The varieties of conditional question at issue here have to do not as much with the predicables themselves as with certain relationships among the predicables.

64. 1179A5 (37.7); "before." See 1178A6–B4.

65. 1179A10 (37.12); "definition." What Boethius says here can be shown usefully in a chart.

| | follows from | | | | | inseparable |
	species	genus	differentia	definition	property	accident
Species				X	X	
Genus	X					
Differentia	X			X	X	
Definition	X					X
Property	X			X		
Inseparable accident	X					

None of the other predicables appears to follow from genus, differentia, or inseparable accident. Genus and inseparable accident both belong to more than one species; given only the fact that something belongs to a particular genus or has a particular inseparable accident, one is not in a position to pick out its species. And differentia, definition, and property are tied to the species; if one cannot pick out the species, one cannot pick out those three either. Furthermore, inseparable accidents may belong to species in different genera—black, for example, is an inseparable accident of crows and ebony—so one cannot always pick out the genus given the inseparable accident. Nor can one pick out the inseparable accident given the genus because inseparable accidents are inseparable from a particular species and one cannot pick out a species given the genus. Hence, it seems right that none of the others follows from genus or inseparable accident.

Understanding the case of differentia is harder. If the differentia is the differentia for a lowest species, and if one knows that it is so, then one is in a position to pick out the species given the differentia (see the chapter "Differentia," however); and, according to Boethius, the remaining predicables follow from the species. For example, given the characteristic *mortal* and the knowledge that it is being used as a differentia for a lowest species, we are in a position to pick out a species, namely, *man* (*mortal rational animal*). On the other hand, if one is simply given an attribute and does not know that it happens to be a differentia, it seems possible to pick out at least one of the genera in the Porphyrian hierarchy. If we know that something is mortal, we are in a position to know that it is in the genus *animate substance* since inanimate things do not die. And furthermore, Boethius says (1178B9ff.) that questions about differentia reduce to questions about genus; so we ought to be able to know the genus, at least, from the differentia. But Boethius implies that nothing follows from the differentia.

The case of definition and property is similarly troublesome. A property belongs to only one species, and a definition is the formula or analysis for a particular species. So given the property or definition, one can legitimately pick out the species, as Boethius says; and given the species, the remaining predicables follow. Why, then, does Boethius say that only two of the remaining predicables follow in each case? One possible answer is that a predicable such as species follows directly from the definition or the property but that other predicables follow directly from the species and only indirectly from the definition or the property and so are not listed as following from the definition or the property. But definition consists of genus plus differentiae (for example, *mortal rational animal*), and hence one can know the genus (*animal*) as well as the differentiae (*mortal* and *rational*) directly from the definition. Yet only differentia is listed as following from definition. As for property, it is hard to see why Boethius would maintain that, given the property, we are in a position to pick out, for example, the definition but not the genus, which is a constituent of the definition. If given the property *risible,* we are in a position to pick out *mortal rational animal,* surely we are also in a position to pick out *animal.*

66. 1179B2 (37.18); "risible." There seems to be a textual error here. Boethius gives eleven cases of one predicable following from another and matching examples for them; in order, the eleven cases are

(1) species → genus	(7) definition → species
(2) species → differentia	(8) property → differentia
(3) species → definition	(9) property → definition
(4) species → property	(10) definition → differentia
(5) species → inseparable accident	(11) definition → property
(6) property → species	

For (10) we ought to have an example of a differentia following from a definition (see the chart in the preceding note); but the last example, covering both (10) and (11), involves *risible* and *two-footed,* both of which are properties. I suggest emending '*risibile*' to '*rationale*,' since *rational* is a differentia, and the abbreviations for the two words might easily have been confused by a scribe or editor. The Basel 1570 and the Paris 1537 editions, as well as the Orleans ms., all read *risibile,* the same reading the *Patrologia* gives.

67. 1179B2 (37.18); "two-footed." On two-footedness being a property, see, for example, Aristotle, *Top.* 102a27–29 and 140b32–34.

68. 1179B6 (37.24); "day." There is perhaps some textual error in this second example. Though it is the example of a cause following from an effect, it looks very little different from the example of an effect following from a cause. Furthermore, it is very hard to see how the existence of light could be a cause for the appearance of the sun, but that is how the example would have to be taken if it is an example of a cause following from an effect. It is possible, however, to translate *'lucet'* not as the idiom 'it is day' but, rather, literally as 'it shines,' and *'videtur'* not as the idiom for 'it appears' but, again, literally as 'it is seen.' Then the first example would be that the presence of the sun is the cause of its shining, and the second example would be that its shining is the cause of its being seen. I am indebted to Norman Kretzmann for this suggestion.

69. 1179B10 (37.30); "justly." Cf. Aristotle, *Top.* 106b30. Boethius's use of the adverb and copula may reflect the Greek habit of using an adverb with the neuter definite article in place of an adjective; if so, then the phrase here ought to be not 'what is done justly' but 'that which is just.'

70. 1179B10 (37.30); "good." Boethius here deviates from his normal pattern in these paragraphs. All his other examples have been of the form 'If it is *A*, then it is *B*.' But here his examples are 'If *A* is good, then *B* is good.' His point in this section is not clear. He begins by saying that the oblique form follows from the principal name, and the examples make it seem as if one can be substituted for the other as the subject of a predicative proposition. But surely it is not the case that for every true predicative proposition that has the principal name as its subject there is a corresponding true predicative proposition with a phrase containing the oblique form as subject. For instance, one of Boethius's own examples can be reversed to give a predicative proposition with 'justice' as the subject: "Justice is Socrates's similarity to the celestial divine substances" (1176A3–4), and here the phrase 'what is done justly' cannot be substituted for 'justice.' Does Boethius then mean to restrict his point to propositions with the predicate 'is good'? I can find no satisfactory explanation for the peculiarities of this paragraph.

71. 1179C5 (37.35); "namely." To sum up as Boethius does seems misleading. What is at issue here is not, say, genus or differentia but rather whether what is in the consequent (and that might be a genus or a differentia) follows from the antecedent.

72. 1179C6 (37.37); "name." Boethius omits from the list a pair one would have expected him to include: accidents and their subject. Perhaps he expects the initial mention of accident to refer both to an accident's relationship to other predicables and to an accident's relationship to its subject.

73. 1179D1 (38.7); "either." What Boethius gives here is just the principle of *modus tollendo tollens*. What he wants as cases and examples here are simply the contrapositives of those he gave in the preceding division. The chart for this division is analogous to that for the preceding division.

follows from denial of

Denial of	species	genus	differentia	definition	property	inseparable accident
Species	X	X	X	X	X	
Genus						
Differentia						
Definition		X				
Property		X		X		
Inseparable accident						

74. 1180A9 (38.28); "night." The choice of day and night as examples of contraries that lack an intermediate seems infelicitous; evening and dawning come readily to mind as intermediates. What Boethius wants here are contraries that are in fact contradictories, such as perceptible and imperceptible or conceivable and inconceivable.

75. 1180A13 (38.33); "theory." Boethius is beginning all over again to classify the question. The new classification here is based not on the grammatical or logical structure of the question, as the preceding classification is, but on the subject matter of the question.

76. 1180B2 (38.37); "happiness." Cf. Aristotle, *Top.* 105b20.

77. 1180B6 (39.3); "not." Boethius's point here is that, with the exception of composite questions, every predicative dialectical question has an 'or not' understood as attaching to it. Given any such question, according to Boethius, there are two propositions that could be defended in answer, and one of them is a negation of the other.

78. 1180C1 (39.13–14); "arguments." See 1174C10 and note 17.

79. 1180C2 (39.15); "proposition." see note 36.

80. 1180C6 (39.20); "question." Cf. Aristotle, *An. Pos.* 71b19–72a5.

81. 1180C10 (39.25); "necessary." See the definition Boethius gives of 'necessary' in 1180D6–7. His use of 'necessary' in this connection probably stems ultimately from Aristotle (see *An. Pos.* 74b5ff.). For Boethius, necessary arguments are demonstrative arguments; and by 'necessary' in this section, he seems to mean not much more than true and legitimately used in demonstrative arguments. In both cases when he is explaining what is not necessary (1180D11ff. and 1181A4ff.), he treats 'not necessary' as equivalent to 'not true.'

82. 1181C10 (41.11); "something." Boethius defines argument not as something of a particular form—a certain number of premises and terms in a particular order—but as a reason having a certain effect on its perceiver. Because he defines argument in psychological rather than logical or formal terms, he can exclude arguments of the fourth sort, such as that in his example above (1181A6–7), without explaining what fallacy is involved in the rejected arguments. One of the peculiarities entailed by Boethius's definition is that the same things are arguments and not arguments, depending on who is perceiving them.

83. 1181D5 (41.22); "not." Because at least one of the purposes of both

the dialectician and the orator is to persuade; cf., for example, 1206C7–12 and 1208D10–1209A4.

84. 1182A12 (41.36); "sophistical." According to Boethius, then, when sophists are being sophistical they are not readily believable or believed (see 1181A4–11)—a thought to which "agreement is not spontaneously and willingly given."

85. 1182A14 (41.38); "truth." Compare what Aristotle says the purpose of the Topics is (*Top.* 100a18–24). Boethius's statement shows how far the study of the Topics has been removed from the context of oral disputation, the dialectical match (see the chapter on Aristotle below).

86. 1182C6 (42.20); "reader." Boethius seems inconsistent here. If sophistical arguments produce no belief and hence are not really arguments (1181A4–11, 1182A10–12), there ought not to be any exercise for the reader in separating sophistical Topics or sophistical arguments from the others; those that are sophistical ought to leap off the page.

NOTES TO BOOK II

1. 1181D10 (43.4); *"topicis."* See note 5 in Introduction.

2. 1183A9 (43.17); "argumentation." At first, it appears odd that Boethius divides the two Books as he does. The subsequent discussion of argumentation seems to belong in the first Book with the rest of the introductory material. But the purpose of the whole treatise is to provide a method for finding "argumentations," and the theory of topics involves argumentation directly in a way in which it does not involve the things discussed in Book I (cf. 1185A5ff.). With the discussion of argumentation, therefore, Boethius is moving into the heart of the theory of Topics, as becomes clear in the following pages. The discussion of proposition, question, conclusion, and argument, on the other hand, is propaedeutic for the theory of Topics in Book II because proposition, conclusion, and argument are constituents of argumentation (cf. *ICT* 277.5–12; *PL* 1048B13–C8).

3. 1183A10(43.17); "unfolding." What Boethius means by 'unfolding' is not clear. He explicitly distinguishes argument and conclusion (1180C1); but syllogism, which is one kind of argumentation, is discourse in which something is concluded by means of other things (1183A10–15). So argument does not include a conclusion, but argumentation does; and yet argumentation is, on Boethius's view, only a certain unfolding of an argument. Hence, it may be that by 'unfolding' Boethius means also to include deriving the conclusion from the reason in the premises.

4. 1183A10(43.18); "argument." This is the same definition of argumentation as that given in 1174D8–9. Boethius tends to use 'argument' to refer to the content of an argumentation, but he explains that 'argument' and 'argumentation' may also be used interchangeably (see *ICT* 282.1–12; *PL* 1053B3–C4).

5. 1183A15 (43.23); "to." Boethius here is giving Aristotle's definition of 'syllogism'; see *An. Pr.* 24b18–22 and *Top.* 100a25–27. The breadth of

Boethius's definition should be noted. Nothing in his definition immediately commits him to use 'syllogism' to refer only to one of the valid syllogistic moods of the *Prior Analytics* or even to all argumentation of that form, valid or not; and Boethius should not be held to a narrow interpretation of the word. That he is using 'syllogism' in a broader sense than '(valid) Aristotelian syllogism' is clear from some of the examples which he considers syllogisms and which do not fall under any one of the moods of the syllogism (cf., for example, 1185A1–3 and 1185B11–C3).

6. 1183B2 (43.26); "full." See *De syllogismo categorico* 821A7–822C14. One of the things Boethius says there about the syllogism he seems not to adhere to strictly in this treatise. Arguments of only one premise, according to *De syll. cat.*, are not true syllogisms; to be a true syllogism, an argument must have at least two premises. But in *De top. diff.* Boethius not infrequently gives one-premise arguments that he seems to consider syllogistic; see, for example, three of the four arguments in 1189B10–C2.

7. 1183B6 (43.29); "substance."[2] As Boethius must have known, though his definition of the syllogism is Aristotle's, the form of his syllogisms differs somewhat from that of the syllogisms Aristotle gives, which are almost always formulated as one conditional proposition rather than three predicative ones. The syllogism Boethius gives here is in the first mood of the first figure (Barbara). Aristotle gives Barbara in this way (*An. Pr.* 25b37ff.): necessarily, if *A* is predicated of every *B* and *B* is predicated of every *C*, *A* is predicated of every *C*. In *De syll. cat.*, Boethius tends to formalize the moods according to Aristotle's pattern but to give examples according to the pattern in his example here; cf., for example, 814B12–C5.

8. 1183B6 (43.30); "discourse." See note 16 on 'discourse' (*oratio*) in Book I.

9. 1183B13 (44.6); "produced." For Aristotle's understanding of this part of the definition of syllogism, see *An. Pr.* 24b20–22. What Boethius says here may be misleading, though less so perhaps than Aristotle's formulation given in note 7 above; it should probably be taken as no more than a stylistic variant of what he says in the original statement of the definition: "Something other than the things agreed to must result by means of the things agreed to." From 1183B2 through 1183C5 Boethius is giving an example of a syllogism and showing how it fits the definition of syllogism; he is not adding any further explanation of the nature of the syllogism.

10. 1183C12 (44.18); "condition." What Boethius says here may be misleading. He does not mean that every hypothetical syllogism contains only one condition; hypothetical syllogisms with only one hypothetical proposition he considers a special kind of hypothetical syllogism (see, for example, *De syll. hyp.*, ed. Obertello, p. 210.24–27; PL 833B10–14).

11. 1183C12 (44.18–19); "hypotheticals." Unlike predicative syllogisms, which must have only predicative propositions, hypothetical syllogisms need not be composed entirely of hypothetical propositions, as the example here shows. In *De syll. hyp.*, ed. Obertello, p. 210.24–27 (PL 833B10–14), Boethius classifies arguments with one hypothetical and one

predicative premise and a predicative conclusion as hypothetical syllogisms.

12. 1183D2 (44.25); "particulars." The Latin word for 'particulars' is the same word Boethius uses to describe propositions of a certain quantity: propositions are universal, particular, indefinite, or singular (1175A2–4). But the premises in the immediately following example of an induction are not particulars in this sense of the word. If they were, they would read 'Some pilot to govern ships is chosen not by lot, etc.'; and such premises would not establish the universal. It may be that in connection with induction 'particular' and 'universal' are relative terms: *A* is a particular relative to *B* if *B* is higher than *A* on a Porphyrian tree; Socrates and Plato are particulars relative to the species *pilot,* and the species *pilot* and *charioteer* are particulars relative to the genus *ruler.*

13. 1183D3 (44.25); "universals." Boethius's definition of induction is Aristotle's, and even his example of induction is very similar to the example of induction Aristotle gives when he defines induction in the *Topics*; see *Top.* 105a13–16, and cf. also *An. Pr.* 68b15–29 and *An. Pos.* 71a5–9.

14. 1184A3 (44.39); "art." This second universal, meant only to recall the first, not only is different from the first but also is an improper conclusion to the induction given. One could give what would be a legitimate induction in Boethius's view and also would support the second universal: "for ruling horses, the charioteer should be chosen according to his possession of the art in question, etc." But the induction that is given supports only the first universal.

15. 1184A7 (45.3); "lot." In this sort of argument, it is as if the initial recounting of instances established a tacit universal, of which the conclusion is a further, derived instance.

16. 1184A8 (45.5); "syllogism." Aristotle makes the same remark about induction; see *Top.* 105a16ff. Aristotle's idea seems to be that induction is more closely related to sense perception than the syllogism is and that therefore induction is more readily believable; cf. *An. Pos.* 81a38–b9.

17. 1184A11 (45.6); "particulars." 'Particulars' and 'universals' here should not be taken as referring to propositions of those quantities. If they are so taken, Boethius will seem to be suggesting that every syllogism has universals in the premises and a particular as the conclusion. But, of course, two of the basic moods of the syllogism (Barbara and Celarent) have universals as conclusions, and some moods have one premise that is not universal. Furthermore Boethius would just have provided a counterexample in 1183B4–6. Instead, 'particulars' and 'universals' should be understood as they were understood in the discussion of induction; see note 12 above.

18. 1184B3 (45.13); "follow." Boethius's example here might seem not to be a good one for his case because it appears to fail as a result of an equivocation on 'know,' which is used in different senses in the premises and in the conclusion. In the former, it is used in the sense of 'know' in 'know how to'; and in the latter, in the sense of 'know' in 'know that.' The knowledge at issue in the premises is the knowledge of a skill, but that in

the conclusion is theoretical or abstract knowledge. But perhaps Boethius is thinking of the fallacy in the induction in this way. In an induction, a number of similar things are brought together (cf. Aristotle, *Top.* 108b9–12), and one of the ways an induction is open to error is that what makes the cases similar may be misperceived; one may hit on something other than the true cause of the similarity. Such an error might be what is supposed to mar this induction. The universal is tacitly and wrongly understood to be something of this sort: whoever knows about something has skill at doing the thing he knows about. If so, then the similarity among the cases in the premises is misperceived, and the universal tacitly derived is false; and consequently, the particular in the example's conclusion, which follows from that universal, is wrongly supposed to be similar to the cases in the premises.

19. 1185A1 (46.13); "translated." Since an enthymeme is an imperfect syllogism and an example is an incomplete induction, Boethius's point here hinges on whether induction is drawn from and depends on syllogism. The Aristotelian passage Boethius is referring to is perhaps *An. Pr.* 68b15–37. Aristotle explains induction as being (like syllogism) a certain process of relating extreme and middle terms. He concludes by contrasting syllogism and induction, saying that syllogism is by nature primary and more knowable. Example is also treated as an argument depending on certain relations among three terms; see *An. Pr.* 68b38–69a19.

20. 1185A4 (46.16); "is." Cf. note 8, Book I.

21. 1184A5 (46.17); "it." See Cicero, *Topica* II.8.

22. 1185A8 (46.21); "proposition." This second kind of Topic is taken up and discussed in 1186A7ff.

23. 1185A11 (46.25); "propositions." Cf. the earlier discussion of such propositions in 1176C6–D7; cf. also *ICT* 279.33–281.1 (*PL* 1051A5–1052B5). Boethius says in *ICT* that as there are greater and lesser terms, so there are greater (*maior*) and lesser (*minor*) propositions in a syllogism; the greater proposition is that which contains the greater two of the three terms in the syllogism. A maximal (*maxima*) proposition is a greatest proposition, one that is greater than all its secondary propositions, in the sense that at least one and perhaps both of its terms are of greater extension than one or both of the terms of any of its secondary propositions. The two crucial characteristics of a maximal proposition are that it is most general and that it is known per se or is self-evidently true (*ICT* 280.12–14; *PL* 1051C7–10); because of these two characteristics, maximal propositions are useful in dialectical argument (see the chapter on Boethius below).

24. 1185B1 (46.29); "found." Cf., for example, Aristotle, *An. Pos.* 71b20–72a8.

25. 1185B5 (46.34); "arguments." Cf. *ICT* 281.35–41 (*PL* 1053A6–13); for the function of maximal propositions, see the chapter on Boethius below.

26. 1185B13 (47.2); "good."[1] The consulate was never longer than a year, and Boethius seems to be implying that evil reigns of kings are cut short by rebellion. For the conclusion of this argument to be acceptable, the condition "when both are good" must attach to it as well. Perhaps the

condition should be taken not as part of the first premise but as a presupposition for the whole argument.

27. 11845C3 (47.7); "time." The maximal proposition is, of course, not true as it stands, but Boethius perhaps expects an intelligent reader to understand a *ceteris paribus* phrase.

28. 1185D5 (47.23); "man." From the following considerations we can see how the definitions of wise man and envious man differ. The definition of anything consists in genus plus differentiae. The definition of envious man, then, consists in a genus—*man*—plus differentia(e)—*who pines at others' good*. The species *wise man* falls under the same genus as *envious man,* namely, *man;* but the differentia of *envious man* given above does not apply to wise men, and so the definitions of the two species must be different. See also the chapter on Boethius below.

29. 1186A2 (47.34); "body." In the *Physics* (210a14–24), Aristotle discusses a number of different ways in which one thing may be said to be *in* another; and Boethius here may want to pick out a particular kind of containing. He may be specifying that it is a body's *quantity* that is contained in order to indicate that a place contains a body as far as the physical dimensions of the body are concerned and not as far as, say, the essence of the body is concerned, or by being a whole of which the body is a part.

30. 1186A8 (47.40); "Topics." These two accounts of what a Topic is correspond to two different methods for finding arguments. The first account and corresponding theory are Aristotle's, or what Boethius takes to be Aristotle's (see *ICT* 282.44–283.4; *PL* 1054B2–8). The second is the one Boethius works on at length in this treatise. For a discussion of the two theories, see the chapter on Boethius below.

31. 1186A9 (48.1); "question." For an elucidation of Boethius's point here, see 1186D6ff.

32. 1186A13 (48.4); "themselves." In other words, the genus *maximal proposition* is divided by various differentiae into different species of maximal propositions, depending on the subject matter of the maximal propositions. See the chapter "Differentia and the Porphyrian Tree" below for a discussion of the way Boethius divides the genus into its various species of maximal propositions.

33. 1186B1 (48.6); "Topics." Cf. *ICT* 281.3–30; *PL* 1052B8–D14, where Boethius explains that as the maximal propositions are Topics for the secondary propositions that fall under them, so the Differentiae are Topics for the maximal propositions of which they are the Differentiae because they contain their maximal propositions within their scope: "And as these [maximal propositions] were said to be Topics of the remaining propositions because they contain them within their scope, so these Differentiae of the maximal and universal propositions themselves will appear to be Topics (even if not truly, nevertheless metaphorically) since [maximal propositions] were reduced to them by an appropriate principle. . . . They are divisive differentiae, and they are in the place of a genus . . . to the maximal propositions themselves." Cf. also *ICT* 281.35–282.1 (*PL* 1053A6–B3).

34. 1186B2 (48.8); "differentiae." The reason for what Boethius says here is that differentiae constitute species and the substance of anything is its species.

35. 1186B6 (48.12); "man." Boethius's example here seems misleading. Rationality is more universal than man at least partly because it belongs to more than one species, to the gods as well as to man. The differentia of a maximal proposition, on the other hand, seems to be more universal only in the sense that it belongs to more than one maximal proposition, to all the individual maximal propositions in the species it constitutes, and not in the sense that it belongs to more than one species of maximal proposition.

36. 1186B10 (48.15); "fewer." 'More universal' should be taken to mean something like 'more general' or 'more abstract.' Boethius is probably thinking of the Porphyrian tree here: as one moves down toward the lowest species, the tree becomes broader. The Porphyrian tree begins with one highest genus, *substance*, which is the most universal thing in the hierarchy. It is divided into two, less universal, subaltern genera. On the next lower level, there are four subaltern genera, less universal than the two higher genera from which they come, and so on down the remaining levels of the tree. See also the chapter "Differentia and the Porphyrian Tree" below.

37. 1186B12 (48.17); "science." The theory of Topics that Boethius is about to lay out, then, is neater and more elegant than the theory that depends on Topics that are maximal propositions. It is important that the theory is neater, and that the higher-order Topics are more easily memorized and retained. The purpose of the art of Topics is to offer a method for finding arguments readily and easily. The less cumbersome the method, the more effectively the art of Topics will achieve its aim.

38. 1186C4 (48.24); "definition." Cf. 1177D10–1178B4.

39. 1186C13 (48.31); "accident." At first glance, it seems odd to single out accident in this way. Surely it is also true that whatever inheres but does not inhere as accident, property, or definition inheres as genus; and so on for the remaining two predicables. But Boethius's procedure is not as strange as it seems. First, the three predicables other than accident seem easier to specify than does accident. A property belongs to only one species; if the attribute in question belongs to more than one species, it is not a property. Definition consists of genus plus differentiae. And genus is the category into which a thing falls in virtue of its essence. But accident, on the other hand, is described simply as what can belong or not belong to something. Second, a thing has one definition, one genus, and a limited number of properties; a thing's accidents, however, seem theoretically innumerable. So if one wants to determine which of the predicables a given predicate is, it is not a bad rule to see first whether the predicate is a genus, definition, or property of its subject. If it is none of these but does inhere in the subject, it is an accident of the subject. Cf. also Aristotle, *Top.* 102b4–14. For Boethius's other description of accident, see 1178A10–12. Boethius says that the other description is to be preferred to

the one discussed here in his commentary *In Isag.* (ed. Samuel Brandt [Leipzig, 1906], p. 283.4–14; *PL* 134A9–B6) where he raises the same question I raised here.

40. 1186D1 (48.37); "*currentibus.*" The phrase "to those going through these things in detail" is hard to explain. Perhaps Boethius's point is something like this: those who are learning about these things piecemeal, rather than having a thorough foundation in the associated sciences, will be aided by an example.

41. 1186D6 (48.40); "example." Boethius means that there will be one example for each Differentia but that a single example will be an example of a question, argument, and maximal proposition, as well as of a Differentia. Cf. 1187A6–B1; similar examples occur frequently in this Book and the next.

42. 1186D10 (49.4); "two." These three groups of Topics—intrinsic, extrinsic, and intermediate—are the three main kinds of Topics for this division, which Boethius later identifies as Themistius's division (1194B1ff.). What Boethius means by intrinsic, extrinsic, and intermediate Topics will emerge in the rest of this Book; see also the chapter on Boethius below.

43. 1186D12 (49.6); "question." What Boethius means by "drawn from the terms [that is, the subject and predicate] . . . is the question" is something of this sort. Take a maximal proposition Boethius has given us: "Things whose definitions are different are themselves also different" (1185D2–3). This maximal proposition falls into the group of maximal propositions that have to do with definitions; so its Differentia is *from definition* or *definition.* If the maximal proposition is about definition, then definition will play a part in the argument aided by the maximal proposition; otherwise the maximal proposition would not be relevant to its argument. And if the conclusion is to contain the two terms of the question, then the question's subject or predicate will be defined in the argument. Because the Topic is *definition,* and definition of the question's terms plays a part in the argument, the Topic is related to the terms in the question, and, hence, the Topic is intrinsic. Extrinsic Topics or Differentiae are not directly related to the terms in the question, and intermediate Topics are in one way directly related to the terms and in another way not.

44. 1186D14 (49.8); "substance." From what Boethius says later (1188A7ff.), we can see that by "things which follow from their substance" he means things we can specify if we know the substance of something: either things that are in some way part of the substance, such as genus, or things that are in some way regularly associated with or dependent on the substance, such as the efficient cause of a thing.

45. 1187A1 (49.10); "alone." Boethius is using "definition" here more broadly than he generally does; cf. 1187B13ff.

46. 1187A3 (49.11–12); "definition." For Boethius's earlier treatment of definition, see 1177D10–1178A15.

47. 1187A8 (49.17); "perceiving." *Animate substance capable of perceiving* is the definition of animal. The genus is *substance; animate* and *capable of perceiving* are the differentiae. The true definition of tree, on Boethius's

view, includes the differentia *animate* but not the differentia *capable of perceiving*.

48. 1187A10 (49.19); "genus." According to Boethius, what is at issue in any predicative question is whether the predicate inheres in the subject; and if it does, there is a further doubt about whether it does so as genus, property, definition, or accident (1186C1–10). Any predicative question, then, is a question involving one of the four predicables. Two considerations show us that the predicable at issue in this question is genus. First, if animal does inhere in tree, it is more universal than tree; it belongs to many things other than trees. Second, animal inheres in the substance of whatever it inheres in. Whatever is an animal has animal as part of its essence; it cannot sometimes be an animal and sometimes not. Hence, since a predicate that is more universal than its subject and predicated of the subject's substance is the genus of the subject (1178A8–11), animal will be the genus of tree if it inheres in tree at all.

49. 1187A14 (49.24); "Topic." The phrase 'higher differentia' (*superior differentia*) is puzzling. Perhaps Boethius is thinking of the Porphyrian tree: a differentia is more universal than the species it constitutes, and so it occurs higher up on the tree.

50. 1187B9 (49.33); "*perceiving*." The maximal proposition in this case is a proposition about definition, and the definition of one of the question's terms is part of the argument. So the maximal proposition might be thought of as drawn from definition, namely, from the definition of one of the terms in the question. And since the definition of anything pertains to that thing's substance, the maximal proposition is drawn from the substance of one of the terms in the question.

51. 1187C4 (50.3); "property." For the relationship between accidents and property, see note 51, Book I.

52. 1187C5 (50.4–5); "*differentiis*." Boethius is beginning his exposition of the Topics that are Differentiae, and he is now discussing the Topics taken from substance. But description, introduced here because it sometimes takes the place of a definition, may or may not pertain to the substance of the thing described. If it is a description composed of differentiae without a corresponding genus, it will involve the substance (since differentiae are part of a thing's substance); but if it is made up of accidents that comprise a property, it will not pertain to the substance (because neither accidents nor properties are part of a thing's substance).

53. 1187C6 (50.6); "definitions." Although one would expect 'descriptions' rather than 'definitions' here, the parallel passage in 1187D10 is evidence that Boethius did intend 'definitions' here.

54. 1187C9 (50.10); "shows." Reading *demonstrat* for *demonstrant*. The Paris 1537 edition has *demonstrat* (p. 28), and the Orleans ms. has *monstrat* (p. 67).

55. 1187C14 (50.13); "genus." Cf. note 48 above.

56. 1187C15 (50.14); "accident." What is given in this first premise is a description rather than a definition of substance because a definition consists in genus plus differentiae, but all the first premise gives as genus is "that which." No true definition of substance can be given because *sub-*

stance is a highest genus and, consequently, there is no higher genus to which it belongs.

57. 1187D3 (50.16); "above." See 1187A12–14.

58. 1187D9 (50.21); "Now." See 1187C6–11.

59. 1188A2 (50.31); "argument." Boethius does not fill out his discussion of this argument as he did the preceding two; he does not specify the maximal proposition, the Differentia, or the predicable the question has to do with. The Differentia, it seems plain enough, is *explanation of the name*. As for the maximal proposition, when Boethius considers the corresponding Ciceronian Topic in Book III, he gives a very similar argument; and the maximal proposition there is "A thing is clarified by the explanation of its name" (1197B3–4). In *ICT* he gives the following maximal proposition for the Differentia *explanation of the name:* "The interpretation of the name is equivalent to the name" (291.26–27; *PL* 1063A9–11).

60. 1188A2 (50.32); *"Hortensius."* Cicero's *Hortensius* is no longer extant.

61. 1188A13 (51.2); "causes." [1] Efficient, material, formal, and final cause (or end) are the four Aristotelian causes. Cf., for example *Physics* 194b16ff.

62. 1188A14 (51.3); "end." Boethius's idea seems to be that if a thing is a substance of a certain sort, then there is something that is its whole, parts, efficient cause, material cause, formal cause, or final cause. And if one knows the substance or the definition of a thing (cf. 1187A2–3), then one is in a position to specify that thing's whole, parts, or causes. Cf. Boethius's understanding of a conditional such as "if it is a man, it is an animal" in *De syll. hyp.*, ed. Obertello, p. 210.14–17 (*PL* 833A13–B1).

63. 1188A15 (51.5); "elsewhere." Reading *aliquo* for *aliquid*. What passage Boethius is referring to is not clear.

64. 1188B2 (51.6); "be." The omission of formal cause here is no doubt a scribal or editorial error or else an (unimportant) oversight on Boethius's part.

65. 1188B5 (51.11); *"accidentibus."* Boethius later explains associated accidents as accidents that cannot, or generally do not, leave their subject; see 1190B3–5.

66. 1188B14 (51.20); "justice." Cf. the similar example in 1178C10–15, which is said to be a question having to do with definition, not accident. In the earlier example, Boethius is comparing two characteristics—being advantageous and being virtuous (*honestum*)—in order to determine if they are the same; and hence he considers whether or not they have the same definition. Here he is considering a characteristic—being advantageous—and something the characteristic is supposed to be an attribute of, namely, justice; what is at issue is the relationship between that characteristic and its putative subject. Hence, in this example, being advantageous is a candidate only for the role of accident.

67. 1188B15 (51.22); "species." The maximal proposition Boethius gives here is hard to translate clearly and faithfully. Boethius means something like this: The species is constituted by its genus and differentiae, and so everything that pertains to the genus as genus will also pertain to each one of its species. The point of the maximal proposition is not that what-

ever can be said of the genus can be said of the species, but rather that the essence of the genus and the accidents adhering to that essence are also part of the species.

68. 1188C6 (51.29); "accident." In other words, what is at issue in the question is whether being ruled by providence is an accident belonging to human affairs. If being ruled by providence belongs at all to human affairs, it belongs as an accident. It is clearly not the genus (and hence not the definition) of human affairs; the genus of human affairs is *affair (res)*, just as the genus of rational animals is *animal*. According to the first premise, providence rules many things other than human affairs if it does rule those; hence being ruled by providence cannot be a property of human affairs. And, according to Boethius's rule, what belongs but not as definition, genus, or property is accident (1186C10–13); so being ruled by providence, if it characterizes human affairs in any way at all, is an accident of them.

69. 1188C7 (51.29); "also." This maximal proposition looks as if it sanctions the fallacy of division, and the argument in the corresponding example looks as if it exemplifies the fallacy of division. Perhaps the argument and the maximal proposition are meant to be sophistical, thrown in to exercise the reader (see Boethius's warning 1182C4–6).

70. 1188C8 (51.30); "highest." Cf. note 49. My tentative explanation of 'higher Topic' is not applicable here, and I have no good explanation for Boethius's puzzling locution "highest Topic."

71. 1188D2 (51.38); "virtue." Cf. Aristotle's definition of virtue, *Nicomachean Ethics* 1106a21–24. For Boethius's criteria for definition, see 1177C10–1178A15.

72. 1188D6 (52.4); "genus." These four are the four Greek cardinal virtues. For Aristotle, at least, it seems as if these four do not exhaust the genus *virtue* (cf. *Nicomachean Ethics,* Book III, chap. 6, to Book VI), but the maximal proposition for this argument seems to require that the characteristic that inheres in the parts belongs to all the parts of the whole in question.

73. 1188D8 (52.6); "whole." This maximal proposition seems to sanction the fallacy of composition, as the preceding maximal proposition seemed to sanction the fallacy of division; cf. note 69.

74. 1189A3 (52.15); "therefore." It is not clear why Boethius gives a hypothetical syllogism of this sort instead of continuing in the pattern of categorical syllogisms (whether expressed as one conditional proposition or not). He could easily have given a predicative argument here. The second premise of this hypothetical syllogism and the appropriate maximal proposition would yield the conclusion he wants.

75. 1189A4 (52.16); "advantageous." Boethius does not give a maximal proposition for this argument, but the context and his "similarly" at the start of the paragraph strongly suggest that the maximal proposition in this case is the same as that in the preceding example: what inheres in the individual parts must inhere in the whole. For the role of the maximal proposition in this argument, see the chapter on Boethius below. For a discussion of the connection between Topics and conditional proposi-

tions, developed in the study of *consequentiae* in later medieval philosophy, see the Introduction.

76. 1189A9 (52.22); "liberty." In other words, we might have a question such as 'Was Epictetus set free?'; if we can show that he was emancipated in a will, for example, we can conclude that he was set free. Emancipation by will is not a part of granting liberty in the same way driving out disease is a part of the art of medicine. Driving out disease and the rest are parts that together constitute the art of medicine, and medicine is not complete in any one of those parts. No one part is sufficient but each part is necessary for the complete art of medicine. Granting liberty, on the other hand, is completely accomplished by emancipation in a will or by any one of the rest of the acts described as parts. No one part is necessary but each is sufficient for the complete granting of liberty. With parts such as these, it is clear that one part is sufficient to establish the argumentation.

77. 1189A13 (52.26); "part." Boethius seems to be discussing different kinds of wholes and parts in this and the immediately preceding example. In the first example, what is at issue is a whole that is completely present if only one of its parts is present; in the second example, the whole is absent if only one of its parts is absent. In the first case, the existence of one part is a sufficient condition for the existence of the whole; but in the second case, the existence of all the parts is a necessary condition for the existence of the whole.

78. 1189A13 (52.27–28); "substances." Presumably, then, the preceding examples of whole and parts have all been wholes and parts of substances. The examples so far have been these:

Whole		*Part*
virtue	(1188B12ff.)	justice
world	(1188C4ff.)	men
virtue	(1188D3ff.)	justice, courage, temperance, and wisdom
medicine	(1188D14ff.)	driving out disease, curing wounds, and ministering to health
granting liberty	(1188A5ff.)	emancipation by will, enrollment in census, and manumission staff
house	(1189A9ff.)	roof, walls, foundation

Of all these, the only one that is immediately apparent as a substance is house. Substance can, of course, also be incorporeal or immaterial; and possibly Boethius is thinking of virtue, the art of medicine, and granting liberty as immaterial substances, but such a view seems highly implausible. In his commentary on Aristotle's *Categories*, for example, Boethius discusses and seems to assent to Aristotle's view that virtue belongs to the highest genus *quality* (241A1ff., especially 242B12), and hence not to the highest genus *substance*. But perhaps the difficulty here is to be solved by thinking of Boethius's opening remark about substances as nothing more than an offhand allusion to the preceding example of house.

79. 1189B8 (52.36); "whole." Reading *totum* for *notum*. The Basel 1570 edition (p. 867), the Paris 1537 edition (p. 31), and the Orleans ms. (p. 68) all read *totum*.

80. 1189B12 (53.1); "moved."[2] Again, different kinds of parts seem at issue here and in the preceding example. The order of the argument here, from the part to the whole, would not work in the preceding example; it would be absurd to argue that because something is now, it is always. The two examples, though, are alike in an important way. What is offered in the first clause, whether it is a part or a whole, entails what is wanted in the conclusion. "Always" entails "now," and "moved in some way" entails "moved." Something similar can be said of the two examples that follow. Cf. also Aristotle's discussion of the different notions of a whole, *Met.* 1023b26–36.

81. 1189C1 (53.6); "Romans." Augustine refers to an ambiguous prophecy about Pyrrhus. According to the *City of God* III.xvii, Apollo prophesied, "I say, Pyrrhus, that you the Romans can conquer," a prophecy that could be construed as true regardless of whether Pyrrhus won or lost. Pyrrhus won initially, though at heavy cost to his own side, and then was defeated in battle by the Romans and withdrew from the campaign.

82. 1189C2 (53.7); "here." All four arguments suggested in this paragraph are simple hypothetical syllogisms of the sort given in full in the second example: a conditional first premise, a predicative second premise, and a predicative conclusion. The first, second, and fourth arguments are examples of *modus ponendo ponens*, with an instantiation of a universal in the second example; and the third is *modus tollendo tollens*. The form of the first, second, and fourth arguments is the same as that of the Stoics' first undemonstrated argument; the form of the third, that of the Stoics' second undemonstrated argument (cf. *De syll. hyp.*, ed. Obertello, p. 258.63–260.6; *PL* 845A13–C3 and ed. Obertello, p. 266.1–7; *PL* 846D7–14; also Benson Mates, *Stoic Logic* (Berkeley, 1953), pp. 69–70). Except for the second, the arguments are not given in full, presumably because the second premise and conclusion wanted are clear. The function of an appropriate maximal proposition in each of these arguments seems to be to support the initial conditional.

83. 1189C9 (53.16); "justice." Reading *justitiam* for *justitia*. The Basel 1570 edition (p. 868), the Paris 1537 edition (p. 32), and the Orleans ms. (p. 69) all read *justitiam*.

84. 1189C15 (53.20); "causes." Two things are wrong with this 'for' clause. First, though it is a general description about causes, it is offered as an explanation of why this Topic is from a particular *kind* of cause, namely, efficient cause; but a general observation about causes is useless as an explanation of why this Topic is from efficient—rather than material, formal, or final—causes. Second, as a general observation about causes, it is false. Only efficient causes act as causes (in the Aristotelian sense) by producing or effecting something; the other three causes perform their functions in different ways, as Boethius explains in various parts of this section on causes. Furthermore, the Latin word translated 'effects' is *'efficit,'* which is cognate with 'efficient.' So I suggest reading the

sentence as 'for the *efficient* cause of anything produces the thing it causes.'

85. 1189D7 (53.28); "effected." What Boethius says here seems odd. Why single out the first two kinds of causes and say that they are equally causes of what is effected? Surely the remaining two kinds of causes are also and equally causes. I think what Boethius means here is not that they are equally the causes of the thing that is being effected or produced—as causes of the thing in question they are neither more nor less causes than the other two kinds of cause—but rather that they are equally causes of that thing's being effected or produced.

86. 1189D12 (53.34); "good." Boethius's maximal proposition should not be taken as equivalent to the saying that the end justifies the means or as open to the objection that the road to hell is paved with good intentions. "End" here should be understood in the Aristotelian sense of 'telos': that which arises naturally from something as that thing's completion or perfection or that which is the natural and final outgrowth or outcome of something.

87. 1190A3 (53.38); "allowed." The argument goes something like this:

(1) One cannot do what his natural form does not allow.
(2) Daedalus's natural form does not include wings.
(3) Therefore, Daedalus's natural form does not allow flying.
(4) Therefore, Daedalus cannot fly.

In order for the inference from (2) to (3) to have a hope of succeeding, 'natural form' has to be taken simplistically—the shape of the body, the number and sort of limbs, and so on. But then the generalization in (1) is false; men, for example, can do many things with the aid of tools and machines that they could not do solely in virtue of their natural form. If, on the other hand, 'natural form' is taken in a sophisticated way, so that natural form includes things such as men's brains and their capacity to solve problems and use tools, then (1) might be thought true. In that case, however, the inference from (2) to (3) is invalid. The more plausible way to take the argument, I think, is to see the inference from (2) to (3) as valid. In that case, (1)—the maximal proposition—is false, and hence is not really a maximal proposition at all. Furthermore, the conclusion of this argument is, of course, false; Daedalus flew with wings he had made. This argument and its maximal proposition are excellent candidates for "sophistical Topics (and arguments) introduced to exercise the reader."

88. 1190A5 (53.40); "good."[2] The argument suggested here and in the following five examples is very similar to the argument given in the example for the Topic *from the end* (see 1189D9–11). The function of the maximal proposition in each case (see 1190A13–B3) is to support the conditional, and the conditional is part of a hypothetical syllogism with one conditional and two predicative propositions.

89. 1190B8 (54.16); "repentance." The argument is made from an associated accident of the predicate because a bad deed's having been done is an accident that cannot or generally does not leave repentance—that is, if repentance occurs, then generally or always a bad deed has been done. The thrust of the argument is that the associated accident (the doing of a

bad deed) does not inhere in a wise man; but since subjects do not occur without their associated accidents, if the associated accident is not in the wise man, neither is its subject, repentance.

90. 1190B11 (54.19); "either." The maximal proposition seems false. For example, animality follows from rationality but inheres in many things (namely, all the irrational animals) that rationality does not inhere in.

91. 1190B15 (54.23); "questions." Extrinsic Topics are Topics that are altogether or primarily about things other than the substance or attributes of what is subject or predicate in the question. Their nature and the sense in which they are extrinsic is better seen in the examples that follow.

92. 1190C4 (54.26); "sort." For Boethius's discussion of the similar Ciceronian Topic, see 1199C12ff. and *ICT* 386.8ff. (*PL* 1166D13ff).

93. 1190C6 (54.29); "arts." Cf. Aristotle, *Top.* 100b21–23.

94. 1190D11 (55.8); "*itself*." There seems to be no method for deciding what is more and what is less; the decision appears to result only from an appeal to intuition.

95. 1191A7 (55.20); "suppose." This parenthetical remark presents editorial problems. The Paris 1537 edition lacks it altogether. As the *PL* edition gives it, it seems to be a scribal comment that has wandered into the text; if the reference in "he says elsewhere" is not to some other passage of Boethius, it is completely mysterious. The Orleans ms. has '*animal*' instead of '*alias*,' making the line read "and suppose the definition of man is that one which says *two-legged animal capable of walking*." The reading of the Orleans ms. seems to me the neatest and the most sensible.

96. 1191A9 (55.23); "*animal*." Boethius here seems to suggest that a thing can have two different definitions, but such a suggestion is inconsistent with what he has said earlier about definition. In 1187A2–3 he says that "definition shows the substance, and the whole demonstration of the substance is the definition." Every thing has only one substance; and since a thing's definition shows the whole substance, there cannot be two different definitions of the same thing.

97. 1191A15 (55.29); "Topics." Boethius's commentary on the *Topics* is not extant.

98. 1191B4 (55.34); "city." Cf. 1183D3ff.

99. 1191C1 (56.6); "categories." See Aristotle, *Cat.* 11b17–14a25.

100. 1191C4 (56.9); "virtue." in other words, whether virtue is the only thing that is praised and everything that is praised is virtue.

101. 1191C6 (56.12); "contraries." Boethius's concisely stated maximal proposition ought to be taken in this way, I think. Suppose A and B are contraries and X and Y are contraries. Then if X inheres in A, Y inheres in B, and vice versa; and the contrapositive: if Y does not inhere in B, X does not inhere in A, and vice versa. Furthermore, the mode of inhering should be the same. If X inheres in A as a genus, then Y inheres in B as a genus, and so on.

102. 1191C15 (56.21); "present." Reading *adesse* for *abesse*. The Paris 1537 edition (p. 36) and the Orleans ms. (p. 70) read *adesse*.

103. 1191D8 (56.30); "other." Boethius's argument goes something like this:

(1) Being procreated is a property of a child.

(2) A father is related to his children as procreator to procreated.

(3) Therefore, being a procreator is a property of a father.

The maximal proposition needed is something of this sort. If A and B are relatives and X and Y are relatives, then if X inheres in A as genus, property, definition, or accident, Y inheres in B in the same way. The maximal proposition Boethius gives looks inappropriate. It seems designed to support a conclusion that some property (*being a procreator*) is a relative (of *being procreated*), but what is wanted is a conclusion that a relative (*being a procreator*) is a property (of fathers).

104. 1191D10 (56.33); "animal." As the text now stands, Boethius is saying that animal and inanimate are opposites; but on his own view they are not opposites, though they are incompatible. Animal is sensitive animate corporeal substance; what is opposite to inanimate is simply animate. It is possible that "animal" here is a textual error for 'animate.'

105. 1191D13 (56.36); "opposites."[2] Here, as in the preceding case, Boethius's maximal proposition seems inappropriate to the argument. The argument goes something like this:

(1) What is animal (animate?) and what is inanimate are opposites.

(2) Being moved and not being moved are opposites.

(3) Not being moved is not a property of what is inanimate.

(4) Therefore, being moved is not a property of what is animate.

The maximal proposition needed here is the same as the one needed for the preceding argument, except that where the first one had 'relatives' this one should have 'opposites.' But the maximal proposition Boethius gives is different and seems unsuitable for much the same reason as in the preceding case: it supports the conclusion that a property is an opposite, but what is wanted is a conclusion that an opposite (*being moved*) is a property (of animals).

106. 1192B6 (57.19); "philosopher." Boethius gives no maximal proposition for either case of transumption. The maximal proposition would presumably give the justification for drawing a conclusion about one case from an argument about another case, and it is not clear what such justification would be. Circero does not include this Topic in his list of Topics; and when Boethius compares the Themistian Topics to the Ciceronian ones, he assimilates the Topic *from transumption* to the Topics *from comparison* (from greater, lesser, and equal); see 1206B2ff. So perhaps the maximal propositions for transumption should be thought of as similar to those for comparison from the greater.

107. 1192D5 (58.11); "subjects." In the *Liber de divisione* (ed. Pozzi, p. 109; *PL* 878A12ff.), Boethius gives examples for this and the following two groups involving accident. Of an accident into subjects: of all the things wished for, some are in the soul and some in bodies. Of a subject into accidents: of all men, some are black, some white, and some intermediate colors. Of an accident into accidents: of all white things, some are hard and some are fluid.

108. 1192D6 (58.12); "accidents." Since every division must be a case of negation or partition, a universal division must be one or the other also. Perhaps Boethius means it to be one kind of partition.

109. 1192D7 (58.13); "division." See *Liber de divisione, PL* 875D–892A.

110. 1193A2 (58.22); "*Analytics.*" Cf. *An. Pr.* 61a17–33 and ff.

111. 1193A13 (58.32); "beginning." The statement that begins this argument, that time either has a beginning or does not have a beginning, in no way serves to establish the conclusion; but only in that statement is division by negation brought into the argument. It is hard to see, then, how the argument is taken from division by negation; it seems as if the argument could have been made and the conclusion could have been established without division by negation at all.

112. 1193B5 (58.39); "time." The argument here seems to be this:

(1) [Suppose] time has a beginning.
(2) Therefore, there was once when time was not.
(3) 'Was' is an indication of time.
(4) Therefore, there was a time when time was not [—which is impossible].
(5) Therefore, time does not have a beginning.

As Boethius gives the argument, it opens with the statement that time either has a beginning or it does not; but that statement need not come into the argument at all. The argument depends on division by negation only insofar as it is a *reductio ad absurdum;* and in every such *reductio,* there is some statement that is supposed and then finally denied. In the explanation in the following paragraph, it seems as if Boethius is thinking of the disjunction as a first premise of the argument. He thinks of the argument as if it went in this way: the first premise is 'Either *p* or *q*,' and the *reductio* establishes that '*p*' is not true, so '*q*' must be true. But the '*q*' of Boethius's disjunction happens to be nothing but 'not *p*'; and 'not *p*' is what the *reductio* itself establishes.

113. 1193B13 (59.8); "removed." It has been hard to see in exactly what way division by negation is a means for producing the arguments; the explanation may be something of this sort. Perhaps Boethius is thinking of *division by negation* as the Differentia of a maximal proposition such as the law of noncontradiction. That law does give "force from without" to the arguments here and functions more apparently than otherwise in an argument that is a *reductio ad absurdum.*

114. 1193C10 (59.21); "without." Boethius has in mind something like this: The question at issue is derived, say, from an affirmative proposition. That affirmative proposition is taken as a premise, and from it an absurdity is deduced. So a negative proposition, the denial of the supposition, is concluded. The affirmative proposition is the very thing at issue; the negative proposition is something extrinsic to the very thing at issue. If this is in fact what Boethius means, then the Topic *from division by negation* is useful only for arguments that support a negative answer to the question at issue. There seems to be no reason, however, why this Topic should not be useful for supporting both negative and affirmative answers and still be intermediate. To support an affirmative answer, the argument would have to begin with what is extrinsic and end up with the very things at issue.

115. 1193D2 (59.29); "time." 'I embrace' in Latin is a passive form that may be taken in either a passive or an active sense. What Boethius says

here is ambiguous. On the one hand, it can mean that in some statements 'I embrace' is to be understood as signifying both something done and something experienced. Or, on the other hand, it can mean that all the appropriate significations of 'I embrace' belong to the expression 'I embrace' at the same time, even though in a given statement only one of the significations is intended. If the second interpretation is the right one, Boethius is thinking of 'I embrace' out of context, in isolation; it then has all its significations together, and we need a use of it in some context to eliminate any of them. Boethius's discussion of this sort of division and his examples in *Liber de divisione* tend to support the second interpretation (ed. Pozzi, p. 108; *PL* 877D7–878A1).

116. 1193D8 (59.36); "things." As the following discussion shows, these two ways in which "reasoning arises" correspond to the two kinds of partition laid out just above.

117. 1193D14 (60.2); "animal." Reading *animal latrabile* for *canem latrabilem*.

118. 1194A5 (60.8); "syllogisms." As far as division by partition is concerned, the following examples seem to be cases of a subject's being divided into accidents; cf. 1192D1–6. All the examples Boethius gives in *Liber de divisione* of partition involving accidents depend fundamentally on contrariety (see 878A12–B10); and contrariety is essential also to the arguments given here. It should be noted, though, that Boethius can have the disjunction he wants as first premise ("he is either healthy or sick") only for contraries that admit of no intermediary; and this kind of partition is partition in which the parts cannot all exist together. If the maximal proposition for division by negation is the law of noncontradiction, perhaps the maximal proposition for this kind of division by partition is the law of excluded middle.

119. 1194A15 (60.18); "external." The two kinds of arguments mentioned here correspond to the two kinds of partition. Partition in which the parts can all exist together produces arguments from the things put forth in the question (1193A3–4); partition in which the parts cannot all exist together produces arguments from things that are without (1194A8–10). But the case of division by negation is different. One and the same argument that depends on a *reductio ad absurdum* is said to be drawn in one way from the things themselves, in another way from extrinsic things (1193C7–10).

120. 1194B3 (60.21–22); "understanding." Themistius's work on the Topics is no longer extant, but paraphrases and summaries of at least some of it are preserved in Averroes's commentary on Aristotle's *Topics;* see the Bibliography for the full reference to Averroes.

121. 1194C6 (61.1); "differentia." In the original list (1188A11ff.), differentia is not included. Perhaps Boethius includes it here under the aegis of genus since he holds that questions about differentia are equivalent to questions about genus (1178C2–4).

122. 1194C12 (61.7); "anything." Boethius's comment here seems untrue. A variety of separable accidents, for example, are omitted from his list, although they do inhere. The color of something, for instance, is an

accident of that thing and so inheres in it; but it fits in none of the listed groups.

123. 1194D10 (61.16); "similarity." Boethius explains proportion as similarity of relation; see 1191B6–8.

124. 1195B2 (61.38); "dialectical." For an explanation of this passage, see the chapter on Boethius below.

Maximal Propositions (explicitly given) and Differentiae
(asterisk indicates conditional)

	Differentia	Maximal Proposition
1185B13		Goods that last a longer time are of more worth than those that last a short time.
1185D2		Things whose definitions are different are themselves also different.
1187A13, D2	Definition (Description)	That to which the definition (description) of the genus does not belong is not a species [of the genus defined].
1188B15	Whole (genus)	Whatever is present to the genus is present to the species.
1188C7	Whole (complete thing)	What suits the whole fits the parts also.
1188D7	Parts (species)	What inheres in the individual parts must inhere in the whole.
1189C13	Efficient causes	Those things whose efficient causes are natural are themselves also natural.
1189D2	Matter	Where the matter is lacking, what is made from the matter is also lacking.
1189D11	The end	That whose end is good is itself good.
1190A1	The form	A thing was capable only of what its natural form allowed.
1190A14	Effects, Destructions, Uses	That whose production is good is itself also good and vice versa, etc.
1190B9	Associated accidents	What follows from something that does not inhere in a thing cannot inhere in that thing either.
1190C9	Judgment	What seems true to everyone or the many or wise should not be gainsaid.
*1190D2	Similars	If something inheres in a way similar [to the thing asked about] and it is not a property, neither can the thing asked about be a property.
*1191A1	The greater	If what seems the more to inhere does not inhere, neither will that inhere which will seem the less to inhere.

Maximal Propositions (explicitly given) and Differentiae
(asterisk indicates conditional) (*Continued*)

	Differentia	Maximal Proposition
*1191A10	The lesser	If what seems the less to inhere inheres, then what will seem the more to inhere will inhere.
1191B9	Proportion	What occurs in one thing must occur in what is proportional to that thing.
1191C6	Contraries	Contraries are suited to contraries.
1191C15	Possession and privation	Where the privation can be present, the possession is not a property.
1191D7	Relatives	Properties of opposites that are related to each other are themselves also related to each other.
1191D12	Affirmation and negation	The properties of opposites must be opposites.

Distribution of Differentiae by Predicable in Question

	Genus	Accident	Definition	Property
1187A10	Definition			
1187D8	Description			
1188B13		Genus		
1188C6		Whole		
1188D1			Parts (species)	
1188D14		Parts (integral)		
1189C11		Efficient causes		
1190B9		Associated accidents		
1190C9		Judgment		
1190D1				Similars
1191A1			The greater	
1191A9			The lesser	
1191B8		Proportion		
1191C5				Contraries
1191C14				Privation and possession
1191D6				Relatives
1191D11				Affirmation and negation

NOTES BOOK III

1. 1195B10 (63.7); "differentiae." For a dicussion of Boethius's point about differentiae, see the chapter "Differentia and the Porphyrian Tree" below.

2. 1195C10 (63.18); "Cicero." In the discussion that follows, much of what Boethius says is paralleled by his commentary on Cicero's *Topica*. I

will cite parallel passages only when the relevant passage in *ICT* is of major importance in clarifying what Boethius says here.

3. 1195D2 (63.26); "judging." See Cicero, *Topica* II.6–8. Cf. also 1173C1–9.

4. 1195D3 (63.27); "produced." Cf 1185A4ff.

5. 1195D4 (63.29); "doubt." Cf. 1174D1–9 and 1180C4–12.

6. 1195D6 (64.1); "included." Cf. 1173D5.

7. 1196B4 (64.15); "related." Reading *affectis* for *effectis*.

8. 1196B11 (64.21); "things." Among the Topics Cicero gives as intrinsic are some that in Themistius's division are intermediate or extrinsic (cf. 1190B12–C3 and 1192B8–10). For very brief arguments that these Topics are intrinsic, see *ICT* 296.15ff. (*PL* 1068A1ff.). Boethius gives some explanation for the divergence of Cicero's and Themistius's divisions in 1200C14–1202B4.

9. 1196C4 (64.26); "definition."[1] Boethius seems to be simply following Cicero and using "whole" differently from the way he uses it in Book II; cf. 1188B7–9.

10. 1196C10 (64.32); "thing." In *ICT* 287.38 (*PL* 1059B2–3), Boethius says a definition is an expression (*oratio*) that signifies the substance of any thing; so 'being' (*esse*) here probably should be taken in the sense of 'essence' or 'substance.'

11. 1196C15 (64.37); "genus." Cf. 1187A6–12.

12. 1196D2 (64.39); "from."[1] Boethius gives a different maximal proposition for this same argument in 1187A12–14, but the difference between the two maximal propositions is less than it appears to be at first glance. The first maximal proposition is "That to which the definition of the genus does not belong is not a species of the genus defined"; in other words, if the definition of a genus does not inhere in a thing, the genus does not inhere in that thing either. The second maximal proposition, then, seems to differ from the first only in being more general. The first says about the definition of something that is a genus what the second says about the definition of anything. If this interpretation of the maximal propositions is correct, then one of two things is true. Either the first maximal proposition may be derived from the second, even though Boethius has given the impression that a maximal proposition has nothing more basic than itself by means of which it may be demonstrated (1185A8–B1); or Boethius is mistaken, and the first maximal proposition is not a maximal proposition at all since it is demonstrable.

13. 1196D12 (65.9); "corporeal." The premise Boethius ought to have here is one to the effect that none of the soul's parts is corporeal (that is, material or bodily); but he has instead a premise that none of the soul's activities is corporeal, which makes the argument look fallacious. No activity considered as an activity is corporeal, whether or not the source of the activity is corporeal.

14. 1197A3 (65.15); "from."[1] Putting the maximal proposition as Boethius does is odd. Subjects are not generally said to be absent from their attributes; rather, attributes are said to be absent from their subjects. Furthermore, if the maximal proposition is to apply to the argument, it

must be taken in this way: If the parts (of the soul) are absent from something (corporeality), the whole (soul) is also absent from that thing (corporeality). Understood in this way, however, it looks very much like the maximal proposition for parts in Book II (1188D7–8) and seems to sanction the fallacy of composition.

15. 1197A11 (65.24); *"whole."* Parts making up the whole are integral parts; parts dividing the whole are parts that are species.

16. 1197B3 (65.31); "genus." One would expect Boethius to say that the question has to do not with genus but with accident. Goodness is not a genus of anything; it is found in all ten highest genera (the ten categories) but is not a genus in its own right in any of them (cf., for example, Aristotle, *Nicomachean Ethics* 1096a19–29).

17. 1197B4 (65.33); "name." In *ICT*, Boethius gives the following as a maximal proposition for this Topic: the explanation of the name is equivalent to the name (291.27; *PL* 1063A10–11). The point of these maximal propositions seems to be that the explanation of the name signifies the thing named as much as does the name itself, so that what can be said about the thing by using the explanation of the name can also be said about the thing by using the name.

18. 1197B12 (66.2); *"quid."* Cf. Porphyry, *Isagoge,* ed. Adolf Busse, *CAG* (Berlin, 1887), IV, pt. i, pp. 2.15ff.; also Boethius, *In Isag.,* ed. Samuel Brandt (Leipzig, 1906), p. 180.4ff (*PL* 91A8ff.). For Boethius's earlier comments on genus in this treatise, see 1177D10–1178A10.

19. 1197B14 (66.5); *"it."* Xenocrates (fourth century B.C.) was the third head of the Academy, after Plato and Speusippus. This view of the soul is attributed to him by Plutarch, *Moralia* 1012D (see also 1013E); cf. also Aristotle, *De Anima* 404b29–30 and 408b32–33, *An. Pos.* 91a37–b1, and *Top.* 140b2–3.

20. 1197B15 (66.5–6); "substance." An affirmative answer to the question at issue yields the view that measure (which is not a substance) is the genus of soul; so it might seem as if the first premise here almost begs the question. But as the maximal proposition for this argument helps make clear, Boethius is considering only whether measure is the proximate genus of soul. To make his argument, he looks at what is higher than both in the Porphyrian tree and considers whether both measure and soul can be put under the same higher genus, namely, substance. If they do not both fall within the scope of the same higher genus, one cannot be the proximate genus of the other. For explanations of the technical terminology involving predicables, see the two chapters on differentia below.

21. 1197C5 (66.11); "are." Cf. Porphyry, *Isagoge, CAG,* p. 4.9ff.; also Boethius, *In Isag.,* ed. Brandt, p. 203.16ff. (*PL* 101A7ff.).

22. 1197C8 (66.15); "genus."[1] That is, from the species *white* and *black* to the genus *color.*

23. 1197C9 (66.15); "genus."[2] In other words, what is in doubt is whether *what is in a subject* is a genus of color.

24. 1197C11 (66.17); "things." Boethius means here something like this: Anything that is in a subject is an accident; everything else (anything that is not in a subject) is a substance. So the question about color is a ques-

tion whether color is a substance or an accident. Substance is the first of the ten categories (or highest genera), and the other nine categories are varieties of accident (cf., for example, *In Isag.*, ed. Brandt, p. 14.8–16; *PL* 14A12–B8; cf. also Aristotle, *Cat.* 3a7–28); so the question whether color is in a subject is a question whether color is under the genus *substance* or under one of the other nine highest genera.

25. 1197C12 (66.19); "kinds." The point of the maximal proposition is that by observing the kinds of a particular genus we can perceive the characteristics of their genus, much as we perceive the characteristics of a species by observing the individuals that fall under that species. It is possible that black and white are supposed to exhaust the genus *color*. The ancients seem to have taken black and white as the primary colors; W. K. C. Guthrie (*A History of Greek Philosophy*, II [Cambridge, 1962–1969], 445, n. 1) says that Aristotle in *De sensu* 440a20 criticizes an explanation of the view that the two primary colors are black and white, but that he himself retained such a view.

26. 1197C13 (66.20); "things." Cf. what Boethius says about similarity in 1190D3–7. He seems to believe that there can be similarity having to do with quantity as well as similarity having to do with quality but that the word 'similarity' is most properly used of sameness of quality.

27. 1197D3 (66.25); "magistrate." All Boethius needs for his argument here, especially given the maximal proposition involved, is the similarity between pilot and magistrate, but the similarity between ship and state helps make the relevant similarity between pilot and magistrate clearer.

28. 1197D5 (66.27); "judgment." The Latin *'judicium,'* like its English counterpart 'judgment,' seems to range in meaning from 'the correct and appropriate verdict on something' to 'the opinion people have of something.' Boethius intends the maximal proposition to be read in this way, I think: either, 'the correct and appropriate verdict on similars is the same'; or, 'the opinion people have of similars should be the same'.

29. 1197D6 (66.30); "same." Aristotle discusses questions having to do with the sameness of two things in *Top.* 103a6–39. There he says that two things can be the same in number, species, or genus. To see whether two things are the same in species, one sees whether the definition of the one fits the other also. It is probably for considerations such as these that Boethius in the next line describes this question as having to do with definition.

30. 1197D8 (66.32); "clemency." Presumably, then, these three are the differentiae of *king*; and *king* is divided from *tyrant* by three differentiae.

31. 1197D12 (66.37); "sorts." For the four kinds of opposites in the Themistian division, see 1191B11ff.

32. 1198A3 (67.2); "bad." Boethius gives neither the question nor the rest of the argument, presumably because he assumes the reader can supply both. The Topic given below is "Contraries cannot agree with each other when they are adverse," and it serves to justify the passage from antecedent to consequent in the conditional. What the maximal proposition means and how it serves to justify the conditional, however, are not clear. The conditional contains two pairs of contraries: health—sickness and

good—bad. Given the nature of contraries, it is plausible that the maximal proposition is equivalent to 'Contraries cannot be in the same thing (at the same time, etc.).' In that case, the contraries to which the maximal proposition applies are good and bad, which are attributes of health and sickness. But the maximal proposition so understood and the proposition in the antecedent ("health is good") yield only the conclusion that health is not bad and not the conclusion wanted, namely, that sickness is bad. It is also possible that the maximal proposition should be taken as 'Contraries cannot have the same attributes,' though taken in this way, it needs qualification since contraries do share some attributes (they sometimes have the same genus, for example; cf. Aristotle, *Cat.* 14a15–18). In this interpretation of the maximal proposition, the maximal proposition applies to the contraries health and sickness. But now the maximal proposition and the conditional's antecedent give only the conclusion that sickness is not good and not the conclusion that sickness is bad. Boethius wants and needs a maximal proposition having to do with the relations among the four elements of two pairs of contraries. The maximal proposition corresponding to the Themistian Topic *from contraries* is 'Contraries suit contraries' (1191C3–7); and it seems more appropriate here than the maximal proposition Boethius actually gives. For Aristotle's treatment of this particular example and of good and bad with respect to contraries, see *Cat.* 13b36–14a6.

33. 1198A4 (67.3); "justice." Boethius's thought seems to be that we not only flee injustice but are also right to do so. The maximal proposition given below serves to support the passage from antecedent to consequent in the conditional; the same difficulties arise here as in the preceding example.

34. 1198A5 (67.4); "child." The Topic for this conditional, given below, is "Relative opposites cannot occur without each other." Boethius does not mean to imply that relatives must exist simultaneously; children, of course, frequently live on after their father's death. Aristotle says a relative—*x*—is what it is in virtue of its being *x of* or more *x than* something else; for example, something is double only insofar as it is double of something else (cf. *Cat.* 6a36ff.). And Boethius's point seems to be simply that there can be no relation without at least two things that are related. Here, too, the maximal proposition supports the argument by justifying the passage from antecedent to consequent in the conditional.

35. 1198C2 (67.38); "animal." For Boethius's explanation of which things follow from which things, see 1179A1–1180A10.

36. 1198C5 (68.1); "consequent." The point seems to be that what is referred to in an antecedent can be temporally prior to, simultaneous with, or posterior to what is referred to in the consequent, just as one associated thing can be temporally prior to, simultaneous with, or posterior to the corresponding associated thing. In the case of associated things, attention must be paid to relative temporal positions; in the case of antecedents and consequents, however, relative temporal position does not have the same function or importance. For the difference between associated things and antecedents and consequents, see 1200B15–C9.

37. 1198D8 (68.20); "man." The conclusion is an affirmation or negation of the proposition from which the question is derived; so the question in this case is Has she lain with a man? The argument proceeds by presenting a conditional and making a hypothetical syllogism; as Boethius says (1198C5), this whole Topic consists in a condition. The appropriate maximal proposition given below is just the rule for *modus ponendo ponens* and *modus tollendo tollens*. It seems an odd maximal proposition to give here because one needs help, not in establishing the consequent of the conditional involved, but rather in finding the appropriate conditional in the first place.

38. 1199A6 (68.36); "together." 'In the same thing' should be understood here. Then the argument comes to this. Since snoring and waking are incompatibles and incompatibles cannot occur together in the same thing, if snoring "occurs in" a certain man, waking cannot "occur in" him at the same time.

39. 1199A7 (68.37); "thing." For the discussion of efficient cause in the Themistian division, see 1189C7–15.

40. 1199A9 (68.39); "day." That is, the fact of its being day is dependent on the presence of the sun, but not vice versa; and, therefore, the sun precedes the day "in natural order."

41. 1199A12 (69.4); "sun." The question, then, has to do with whether or not it is day. Boethius's way of dealing with this question is interesting. 'It is day' is a slightly veiled existential proposition, which, even more clearly in Latin than in English, has no predicate term. But Boethius divides all nonconditional propositions into four groups depending on the way the predicate inheres in the subject (cf., for example, 1177D8–1178B4), and it has not been clear just how a straightforward existential fits into the scheme. Here, where we have an existential proposition, Boethius treats it as if it were in fact predicative. What appears to be the subject, namely, *day* (or, possibly, *being day*), he takes as the predicate. He takes the subject to be *atmosphere,* which is understood but not expressed in the proposition. And the whole question is seen as a question whether day or being day inheres in the atmosphere as an accident.

42. 1199A15 (69.6); "absent." Boethius does not mean here that a cause and its effect must be in the same place. 'Where' should not be taken literally but as equivalent to 'when' or 'if.' Cf. Aristotle, *Physics* 195b16–21.

43. 1199A15 (69.7); "produces." For discussion of effects in the Themistian division, see 1190A3–B3.

44. 1199B4 (69.12); "absent." Cf. note 42. In *ICT* 307.31–32 (*PL* 1080B4–5), Boethius gives the maximal proposition for this Topic as "Causes cannot be separated from their effects."

45. 1199B6 (69.15); "greater." For the similar Topic in the Themistian division, see 1190D7–1191A4. The Themistian Topic, unlike the Ciceronian one, is an extrinsic Topic. Boethius discusses reasons why this Topic might be considered intrinsic in *ICT* 307.42–308.3 (*PL* 1080C12–D4).

46. 1199B7 (69.16); "greater." Both this comparison and the following comparison of the lesser seem to be cases involving argument a fortiori. The arguments given as examples for both kinds of comparison contain in

a premise some claim similar to that wanted as conclusion, and the claim adduced in the premise involves something greater or something less than some part of whatever is involved in the conclusion. But whether the claim in the premise involves something greater or lesser, it always consists in a case harder to establish than the one wanted as conclusion. Since it is accepted as premise, the conclusion, too, must be accepted; and so the conclusion is shown true a fortiori.

47. 1199B11 (69.20); "accident." The question is something such as Does an exiled instigator of insurrection merit pardon? If the question has to do with accident, then the accident must be *meriting pardon;* and the issue is whether meriting pardon inheres in an exiled instigator of insurrection.

48. 1199C4 (69.30); "conflagration." Boethius apparently means the antecedent of this conditional to be read as '. . . *rightly* killed Gaius Gracchus.' The example is a quotation from Cicero's *In Catil.* I.3. Marius Victorinus quotes it in his commentary on Cicero's *De inventione* (*Rhetores Latini Minores,* ed. Charles Halm, p. 227).

49. 1199C4 (69.30); "accident." Here the question seems to be 'Is it right to take vengeance on Catiline, who . . . ?' The accident then is *being a right action,* and the issue is whether or not it inheres in taking vengeance on Catiline.

50. 1199C10 (69.37); "Cicero." The argument is supposed to be from equality, presumably because Demosthenes and Cicero possess the oratorical art or oratorical excellence in the same degree. The question at issue here seems to be 'Is it right to censure Cicero?' ('insofar as he is an orator' should be taken as understood); and the issue is whether being right inheres as an accident in the action of censuring Cicero.

51. 1199C10 (69.38); "accident." The 'wants to' in the question about Demosthenes and Cicero should not be taken too literally; Boethius is not talking about someone who has never praised Demosthenes but has a nagging desire to do so. Something such as 'thinks it right to praise' is more nearly what Boethius has in mind here.

52. 1199C14 (70.3); "necessary." For a discussion of this Topic, see the chapter on Boethius below.

53. 1199C14 (70.4); "believable." The description of what is readily believable is taken from Aristotle; see *Top.* 100b21–23.

54. 1200A6 (70.24); "definition." What Boethius says here and his worry in this paragraph are more understandable if one remembers that in Book II explanation of a name is classified as a sort of definition (1187D9–1188A5). As Boethius indicates there, the explanation of a name is not a true definition, just as descriptions are not true definitions, but still it is enough like definition so that it is put in place of a genuine definition and is sometimes classified as definition.

55. 1200B1 (70.35); "genus." Boethius's point here is that whoever divides a genus enumerates parts because a genus is divided into species and species are parts. In order for there to be a species, there must be division of a genus because a species is just a subdivision of a genus; it is constituted by its genus and the differentia that divides that genus. In

order for there to be an argument from species, then, there must be enumeration of parts (the parts that are species), and so it seems as if *from species* and *from enumeration of parts* are the same.

56. 1200B8 (71.2); "genus." What Boethius says in this paragraph can easily lead to confusion. He is contrasting two Topics, *from enumeration of parts* and *from kind* (or species). But there are two sorts of parts, integral parts and species (1196D2–5). So he is contrasting the Topic *from enumeration of integral parts* and *from enumeration of species,* on the one hand, with the Topic *from kind,* on the other hand. Boethius says that in order to prove something about a genus, all the integral parts (that is, all the species) must figure in the argument (for an example of such an argument, see 1196D6–1197A4); but for arguments using the Topic *from kind,* one species alone is enough to prove something about a genus. In 1189A4ff., Boethius discusses cases in which one part (integral parts as well as species) establishes the argument, and what he says here seems directly to contradict that passage. Furthermore, arguments from kind or species are given in 1197C3–12 and 1188D2ff.; and in both cases, more than one species is involved in the argument. The solution to these difficulties may be simply terminological. It may be that Boethius wants to call 'enumeration of parts' just those cases in which all the parts must be involved in the argument and 'kind' just those cases for which one part is sufficient (though more than one may be used in the argument).

57. 1200C9 (71.20); "away." There are two differences between associated things and antecedents and consquents. First, one associated thing may be deduced from another only probably or for the most part. In an argument drawn from associated things, the conclusion does not *necessarily* follow from the premise because two associated things are only generally, not inseparably, connected. But an antecedent is the antecedent of a previously established conditional, and so, contrary to the case of associated things, the conclusion *must* follow from its premises. Second, attention has to be paid to the temporal relation between two associated things when an argument from associated things is made. In the case of antecedents, however, even though temporal relations may be important in constructing the conditional involved in the argument, once that conditional is established and the antecedent is postulated, the conclusion must follow; and one need not (at that point) have any concern for temporal relations between antecedent and consequent. It seems at first, then, as if arguments from associated things and those from antecedents or consequents differ only because in the latter case there is a conditional understood or taken as a premise and in the former case there is not. But I think the point is that in the case of associated things there cannot be the appropriate sort of conditional because things regularly associated are sometimes not associated. One could not legitimately take as premise a conditional such as If someone loves another, he has previously met that person, as Boethius himself points out (1198B1ff.). But the things referred to in the antecedent and consequent of a conditional that can be legitimately taken as premise are inseparably connected in some way; for example, "If she has borne a child, she has lain with a man."

58. 1200D8 (71.34); "issue." Themistius's intermediate Topics are *conjugates, cases,* and *division* (see 1192B8ff.). Later in this book (1203A6ff.), Boethius discusses in what way Themistius's intermediate Topic *division* is subsumed under the Ciceronian intrinsic Topics. Cicero's Topic *conjugates* comprises both the remaining Themistian intermediate Topics, *conjugates* and *cases.*

59. 1201A6 (72.5); "*quantity.*" By "comparison of quantity" Boethius seems to mean nothing more than comparison of the greater and comparison of the lesser.

60. 1202A5 (72.28); "parts." Boethius says "it is inevitable," I think, at least in part because each of the two divisions is supposed to be an exhaustive division of triangles, so that in one way or another the parts of one division must match or overlap the parts of the other.

61. 1202B9 (73.3); "mind." It is clear that Boethius means to give a diagram here and in the two other places indicated below, but whether the diagrams preserved in the *Patrologia* text are in any way ascribable to Boethius is not clear. The diagram given here contains some infelicities, if not inaccuracies, in the listing of Themistius's Topics.

62. 1203A6 (73.10); "description." Boethius here begins his explanation of what in Themistius's division matches each piece of Cicero's division. In this paragraph, he is concerned to show the Themistian Topics that correspond to Cicero's Topic *from the whole.* So, though Themistius's Topic *from substance* includes *definition, description,* and *explanation of the name,* Boethius here gives only the first two because only the first two correspond to Cicero's Topic *from the whole.* For the initial discussion of these Topics in their own divisions, see 1187A1ff. and 1196C2ff.

63. 1203A8 (73.16); "division."[1] Just as in the immediately preceding case the Ciceronian Topic corresponded to only part of the Themistian Topic listed, so here, too, Cicero's *from enumeration of parts* corresponds not to the whole Topic *from division* but only to one part of it, namely, partition—and then not to all of what Boethius describes as partition but only to the kind in which all the things divided can exist simultaneously. Partition includes the division of genus into species and whole into parts; and these match enumeration of parts. For the initial discussion of the Themistian and Ciceronian Topics, see 1192C13ff. (especially 1192C2-D6 and 1193C12–1194A2) and 1196D2–1197A11.

64. 1203A11 (73.17); "before." Boethius's point here seems to be that if we want to draw a conclusion using Cicero's Topic *from enumeration of parts,* we will have to use the parts of the subject or predicate in the question at issue; and so we will have to divide the subject or predicate into its parts (either integral or specific parts). Consequently, Cicero's Topic *enumeration of parts* is a sort of division, or works by division, and *division* is Themistius's Topic.

65. 1203B1 (73.20); "way." What Boethius says here is highly confusing. When he begins this part of the paragraph, it looks as if he is going to contrast the placing of the two corresponding Topics: the Themistian Topic is placed among intermediate Topics; the Ciceronian Topic, among intrinsic Topics. But, contrary to what we might expect, Boethius tells us

that the Ciceronian Topic *enumeration of parts* is placed in the treatment of genus. That remark seems simply not true. *Enumeration of parts* is one of the four main Topics that comprise the Ciceronian intrinsic Topics. The Topic *from genus,* on the other hand, is one of several Topics that fall within the scope of another of those four main topics, namely, the Topic *from related things.* Furthermore, the Ciceronian Topic *from genus* corresponds not to the Themistian Topic *from division* (as *enumeration of parts* does) but rather to the Themistian Topic *from the whole,* as Boethius himself says just below. The example from Cicero that follows here only increases the confusion because it is a discussion of the Topic *from genus* and not of the Topic from *enumeration of parts,* though some enumeration of parts does occur in the particular argument used.

66. 1203B6 (73.26); "genus." The reader will avoid confusion by taking 'genus' here as if it were nothing more than 'sort.'

67. 1203B7 (73.26); "solid." For this quotation, see Cicero, *Topica* ix.40.

68. 1203B9 (73.28); *"name."* For the initial discussions of these two Topics, see 1187D9–1188A5 and 1197A11–B4.

69. 1203B10 (73.29); "both." What Boethius says here is not quite accurate. The Ciceronian Topic *from conjugates* corresponds to two of Themistius's Topics, rather than to just one, as the text suggests. The Themistian Topic *from conjugates* and the Themistian Topic *from cases* are both comprised by the corresponding Ciceronian Topic. Cf. 1192B10–C5 and 1197B4–10.

70. 1203B11 (73.31); *"whole."* For the initial discussions of these Topics, see 1188B7–C2 and 1197B10–C3.

71. 1203B12 (73.33); *"species."* For the initial discussions, see 1188C9–D11 and 1197C3–12.

72. 1204A1 (73.40); "divisive." For help in understanding Boethius's point here, cf. 1178B5–C4. The initial discussions of these Topics are in 1188B7–C2, 1188C9–D11, and 1197D5–10.

73. 1204A3 (75.3); "extrinsically." The initial discussions are in 1191B11–1192A2 and 1197D10–1198A10.

74. 1204A5 (75.6); "substance." The Themistian Topic here, too, is broader than the Ciceronian; associated accidents either cannot or generally do not leave their subjects, but associated things are only those things that generally do not leave their subjects. For the initial discussion of these Topics, see 1190B3–11 and 1198A11–B14.

75. 1204A9 (75.9); "thing." Which things are consequent to which things is discussed at length in 1179A3–B2. Description and explanation of the name are not discussed in that passage, but since Boethius classes them as sorts of definition, perhaps what he says of definition in 1179 should be understood as applying also to description and explanation of the name.

76. 1204A10 (75.12); "cause." Boethius discusses these relationships in 1179B2–6, but there he says only that sometimes an effect follows from its cause and sometimes a cause follows from its effect. Here he seems to be elaborating part of his point there: an effect follows from its efficient or from its material cause.

77. 1204A12 (75.14); "subject." Cf. 1179B12–14.

78. 1204A13 (75.15); "another." Cf. 1179B8–12.

79. 1204A14 (75.16); "many." In his earlier list of things that follow (1179A3ff.), Boethius includes several things that might have been mentioned here: whole and parts, for example, or privation and possession. Why they are omitted here is not clear.

80. 1204B4 (75.22); "opposites." As Boethius says above (1204A1–2), the Themistian Topic *from opposites* is the same as the Ciceronian Topic *from contraries*. But in his discussion of Cicero's Topics, Boethius takes pains to show (1200B8–14) that the Ciceronian Topic *from contraries* and the Ciceronian Topic *from incompatibles* are not the same. So it seems that Cicero's Topic *from incompatibles* cannot be included in Themistius's Topic *from opposites*. For the initial treatment of these Topics, see 1191B11–1192A2 and 1198D14–1199A6.

81. 1204B5 (75.23); "causes." For Boethius's point here, compare the initial discussions of these Topics: 1189C7–D7 (especially D4–7) and 1199A7–15.

82. 1204B7 (75.25); "end." What Boethius says here is odd. By 'the end of something,' Boethius means that for which, for whose sake, the thing in question comes to be or exercises its function (cf. 1188B1–2 and 1189C3–7); but it is not immediately clear that every effect of a cause is that for which or for whose sake the cause comes to be or exercises its function. For the initial discussion of these Topics, see 1189D7–13 and 1199A15–B5.

83. 1204B9 (75.28); *"lesser."* For the initial discussion, see 1190D7–1191A11 and 1199B5–C6.

84. 1204B9 (75.29); *"equals."* Reading *parium* for *partium*. The Paris 1537 edition reads *parium* (p. 57).

85. 1204B12 (75.31); "equality." Cf. 1190C12–D7 and 1199C6–12.

86. 1204B14 (75.34); *"judgment."* Cf. 1190C3–12 and 1199C12–D13.

87. 1205A15 (77.10); *"equals."* Reading *parium* for *partium*.

88. 1206A3 (77.20); *"transumption."* There are others of Themistius's division that have no counterpart in Cicero's division; the Topic *from form* (formal cause) is an example. But the unmatched Themistian Topics which Boethius does not mention are subdivisions of some larger Topic, for example, *from form* is a subdivision of the Topic *from causes*. Though some of these subdivisions may not be matched, all of the main Topics, with the exceptions Boethius notes here, are matched to Cicero's Topics.

89. 1206A7 (77.24); *"effects."* Both Boethius's points in this paragraph are difficult to understand. Perhaps when he talks about use as a producer of something, he means that use produces an activity; but such a view seems to require some sophisticated distinctions between the use and the activity the use produces. Or perhaps he has in mind that any use is undertaken for some purpose and so may be thought to produce whatever is purposed; so, for example, riding (a use) is undertaken for pleasure or for health and is productive of pleasure or health. Boethius's second point, that a use is itself produced, is even harder to deal with. In what sense,

for example, could riding (Boethius's example of a use) be thought to be produced? Is Boethius perhaps thinking of riding as ambiguous between a use, on the one hand, and an activity produced by the use, on the other? In this way, riding might possibly be thought of either as the use of a horse or as an activity produced by the use of a horse. For the initial discussions of these Topics, see 1190A3–B3 and 1199A7–B5.

90. 1206A11 (77.28); *"effects."* Boethius's point here is more easily understood if one has firmly in mind what he says about the Themistian Topic *from effects.* In the context of that discussion, effect is more like generation than like the effect of a cause, and perhaps Boethius is thinking of effect here as production. 'Production' can be taken in two ways. It can mean either the process of producing something or the finished product of that process; 'Your production is impressive' could be said about an efficient assembly line or an excellent camera. Understood in the first sense of 'production', the Themistian Topic resembles the Ciceronian Topic *from efficient causes;* in the second sense, it is like the Ciceronian Topic *from effects* (that is, the effects of efficient causes). For the initial discussion of these Topics, see 1190A3–B3 and 1199A7–B5.

91. 1206A15 (77.33); *"body."* Cf. 1190A3–B3 and 1199A7–15.

92. 1206B3 (77.35–36); *"similarity."* But Boethius himself seems to argue against such a view in 1191B5–8. Perhaps he means that in many cases where two things have the same quality (and so are similar), each of those two things has the same relationship to each of two other things (which also share a quality). For example, in Cicero's Topic *from similars,* each of the two similar things also has the same relationship to each of two other similar things; rulers of ships and rulers of states each have the same relationship to what they rule, ships and states. Furthermore, this one example can be used both as an example of similarity and as an example of proportion, depending on what is picked out as the same. If we pick out the attribute of being a ruler, it seems to be an example of similarity because the same quality is shared by two things. But if we pick out the relationship of ruling, then it is an example of proportion because the same relationship is manifested in two cases. For the initial discussion of these Topics, see 1191A15–B11 and 1197C12–D5.

93. 1206B6 (77.40); *"equals."* Cf. 1192A2–B6 and 1199B5–C12.

Book III
Ciceronian and Corresponding Themistian Topics

Ciceronian		Themistian	
1196C2-D2	Whole	1187A1-D9	Substance
1196D2-A11	Enumeration of parts	1192C13-1194A14	Division
1197A11-B4	Designation	1187D9-1188A5	Explanation of the name
1197B4-10	Conjugates	1192B10-C5	Conjugates
1197B10-C3	Genus	1188B7-C2	Whole (genus)
1197C3-12	Kind	1188C9-D11	Parts (species)

Ciceronian and Corresponding Themistian Topics (*Continued*)

Ciceronian		Themistian	
1197C12-D5	Similarity	1190C12-D7	Similar
1197D5-10	Differentia	1188B7-C2; C9-D11	Whole or part
1197D10-1198A10	Contrary	1191B11-1192A2	Opposites
1198A11-B14	Associated things	1190B3-11	Associated accidents
1198B15-D14	Antecedents and consequents		"mingled with many"
1198D14-1199A6	Incompatibles	1191B11-1192A2	Opposites
1199A7-15	Effective things	1189C7-D7	Causes
1199A15-B5	Effects	1189D7-13	End
1199B5-C6	Comparison of greater and lesser	1190D7-1191A11	Greater and lesser
1199C6-12	Comparison of equals	1190C12-D7	Similars
1199C12-D13	Judgment	1190C3-12	Judgment
1199A7-B5	Effective things or effects	1190A3-B3	Uses, Effects, Destructions
1197C12-D5	Similars	1191A15-B11	Proportion
1199B5-C12	Comparison of greater, lesser, or equals	1192A2-B6	Transumption

Maximal Propositions (explicitly given) and Differentiae

	Differentia	Maximal Proposition
1196D1	Definition	Whatever the definition is absent from, the thing defined is also absent from.
1197A2; A10	Integral parts	Whatever things the parts are absent from, the whole is also absent from.
1197B3	Designation	A thing is clarified by the explanation of its name.
1197B9	Conjugates	The nature of conjugates is the same.
1197C2	Genus	Things whose genera are different are themselves also different.
1197C11	Kind	The attributes of genera are observed in their kinds.
1197D4	Similars	Regarding similars, the judgment is one and the same.
1197D10	Differentia	Regarding differing things, the judgment is not one and the same.
1198A7	Contraries	Contraries cannot agree with each other when they are adverse, privative, or negative; and when they are relative, they cannot occur without each other.
1198B14	Associated things	Things that are associated with other things are judged on the basis of those things.

Maximal Propositions (explicitly given) and Differentiae (*Continued*)

	Differentia	Maximal Proposition
1198D12	Antecedents and consequents	Once the antecedent has been asserted, the consequent follows; once the consequent is taken away, the antecedent is taken away.
1199A6	Incompatibles	Incompatibles cannot occur together.
1199A14	Efficient causes	Where the cause is, the effect cannot be absent.
1199B3	Effects	Where the effect is, the cause cannot be absent.
1199B12	Comparison of the greater	What holds good in the greater things holds good in the lesser.
1199C6	Comparison of the lesser	What holds good in the lesser holds good in the greater.
1199C11	Comparison of equals	Regarding equals, the judgment is one and the same.

Distribution of Differentiae by Predicable in Question

	Genus	Accident	Definition	Property
1196C12	Definition (whole)			
1196D8	Enumeration of parts (integral)			
1197A5		Enumeration of parts (species)		
1197A13	Designation			
1197B7		Conjugates		
1197B13			Genus	
1197C6	Kind			
1197C14		Similars		
1197D6			Differentia	
1198A2		Contraries		
1198B8		Associated things		
1198D5		Antecedents		
1199A4		Incompatibles		
1199A10; B1		Effective things or effects		
1199B8		Comparison of greater		
1199B15		Comparison of lesser		
1199C9		Comparison of equals		
1199D5		Judgment (?)		

NOTES TO BOOK IV

1. 1205C6 (79.7); "Topics." The reader will find the discussion in this Book easier to follow if he refers to the tables and diagrams appended to this section of the notes.

2. 1205C7 (79.9); "disciplines." Cf. the note on *facultas*, Book I, note 5.

3. 1205C7 (79.9); "*facultatum*." Aristotle's *Rhetoric* is the ultimate source, at least indirectly, of Boethius's discussion of rhetoric; but the im-

mediate source, the book Boethius seems to have had at his elbow while writing on the rhetorical Topics, is Cicero's *De inventione* (*De inv.*). The discussion of rhetoric that occupies the first half or so of this Book closely resembles the order and content of *De inv.*; furthermore, in 1210C1 Boethius says he has taken the preceding material from Cicero and adds a direct quotation from *De inv.* I will cite parallel passages from *De inv.* only when they are important for explaining the text here. We do not know for certain whether Boethius used Aristotle's *Rhetoric* in writing Book IV; but that book is extremely important in Western rhetorical tradition, and I will cite passages from it when they clarify the text here. In general, my concern with this fourth Book is philosophical and not rhetorical; matters of purely rhetorical interest are not part of my study. Hence, these notes will not attempt to trace the rhetorical tradition between Cicero and Boethius, the relation of rhetorical theory to Roman jurisprudence, or other such issues. The sources for traditional Roman rhetoric (which is the basis of much of Book IV) are given in detail in, for example, the footnotes of the *Rhetorica ad Herennium*, ed. Harry Caplan, Loeb Classical Library (Cambridge, Mass., 1954), and the footnotes in the Loeb edition of *De inv.*

4. 1205C15 (79.17); "hypotheses." For discussion of the terms 'thesis' and 'hypothesis,' see Book I, note 43.

5. 1205D4 (79.19); "means." That is, who did the action or crime, what he did, where he did it, when he did it, why he did it, how he did it, and by what means he did it.

6. 1206C3 (79.27); "it." The point is that rhetoric deals with questions about particular things done by particular people at particular times, while dialectic deals with abstract or general questions not tied to individuals. If dialectic brings individuals into its discussion, it does so to help establish its abstract, general point. Similarly, rhetoric may use abstract and general statements, but will do so in order to make its case about some particular person or action. See also 1215D1–1216C11.

7. 1206C7 (80.2); "enthymemes." Aristotle says that the business of rhetoric is to persuade (*Rhet.* I.i.14; 1355b15–16), and it uses enthymemes rather than syllogisms because frequently a premise is obvious, and the aim of persuasion is not served by saying what is obvious to everybody (*Rhet.* I.ii.13; 1357a13–18).

8. 1206C12 (80.8); "questioning." For a discussion of conjectures about the judges in dialectical disputation, see the chapter on Aristotle.

9. 1206D6 (80.18); "questions." The rhetorical questions Boethius is talking about here seem to be just those that *are* issues. Cf. 1209A6–8 and 1207A10–13.

10. 1206D7 (80.19); "*constitutionibus.*" In 1209A6–8, Boethius says that the technical terms '*quaestio*' and '*constitutio*' are synonymous; both refer to the issue that occasions a debate or a legal case. When John Erhlichman was first brought to trial, the *constitutio* was whether or not he authorized the Ellsberg burglary. When Nixon was taken to court for the initial set of Watergate-related tapes, the *constitutio* was whether or not he had a right to withhold evidence on the grounds of executive privilege.

11. 1207A5 (80.23); "examined." What Boethius says here is not just a roundabout way of claiming that the nature of rhetoric is hard to under-

stand; I think he means just what he says. The following discussion indicates that the different things that compose rhetoric are related to one
another in very complicated ways. For example, as Boethius goes on to
say, rhetoric may be divided both into species and into integral parts.
Considered as a genus, rhetoric is wholly in each one of its three species.
In addition, these species act as forms for the (subject) matter of rhetoric,
so that rhetoric's subject matter is divided into three kinds according to
the three species of rhetoric. There are five integral parts of rhetoric, and
all five are in each one of the species of rhetoric. Rhetoric also has an instrument, and it is divided into six parts. Each of the six parts of the instrument contains all five integral parts of rhetoric, but all six parts of the
instrument are contained in each of the three species of rhetoric. And
there are other relationships as well, though these I have just given are
perhaps the most important; certainly they suffice to justify Boethius's
claim about the internal complications of rhetoric.

12. 1207A9 (80.28); "all." Boethius's claim is disturbing because much
of what follows—the basic points about the genus and species of rhetoric
and so on—is part of the rhetorical tradition common by Cicero's time.
But what he claims is so difficult to understand is not the nature of rhetoric but rather "the internal complication of the rhetorical art." So perhaps
Boethius's claim to originality should be restricted to the work he does
relating the various divisions of rhetoric to one another; and such a restricted claim may well survive scholarly scrutiny.

13. 1207B2 (80.36); "deliberative." A judicial speech is one made in a
law court during a trial—for instance, Socrates's speech at his trial in
Plato's *Apology*. An epideictic speech is one that praises or censures
someone or something; Pericles's funeral oration is a famous example. A
speech that argues for or against some course of action is a deliberative
speech. Demosthenes's Olynthiac orations, urging Athens to take certain
actions against Philip, are examples. The division of rhetoric into these
three kinds is an old one; see, for example, Aristotle's *Rhet.* I.iii.2–3
(1358b2ff.).

14. 1207B3 (80.37); "is". There may be more in Boethius's easy comment here than there seems to be. From what follows in this Book, it is
clear that one of Boethius's immediate sources is Cicero's *De inv.;* and the
list of things Boethius proposes to discuss (1207A10–13) very closely resembles the list Cicero gives in a similar context at the beginning of *De
inv.* Cicero, however, gives a genus for rhetoric different from the one
Boethius gives; according to him, "the oratorical discipline is to be put in
the genus of political science" (I.v.6). What Boethius says here is a nice
correction of Cicero and perhaps also a veiled rebuke to him, which many
of his educated readers probably would have been able to appreciate. If
'oratorical discipline' is a synonym for 'rhetoric' and Cicero is looking for
the genus of oratorical discipline, then clearly, as Boethius says, the genus
is not *political science* but rather *discipline*, just as the genus of rational
animal is *animal*.

15. 1207B5 (80.39); "them." That is, the whole genus *rhetoric* is found in
each of its species.

16. 1207B5 (81.1); "cases." In *De inv.* I.vi. 8, Cicero quotes the defini-

tion of case (*causa*) given by Hermagoras of Temnos, a rhetorician of the second century B.C.; and though Cicero attacks Hermagoras on some points, he does not dispute the Hermagorean definition of case. Whether that definition is one Boethius deliberately adopted, it seems to fit Boethius's use of the term in this Book. According to Hermagoras as Cicero quotes him, a case is basically a verbal dispute having to do with specific individuals ("*res quae habet in se controversiam in dicendo positam cum personarum certarum interpositione*"). In the terms of Book IV, we might say that it is a verbal dispute involving a hypothesis (rather than a thesis).

17. 1207B7 (81.2); "cases."[2] Boethius's choice of words here is misleading. He gives the impression that there is a hierarchy of genera of this sort: first, we have *discipline,* which is the genus of rhetoric; then *rhetoric,* which is itself a genus for judicial, epideictic, and deliberative kinds of rhetoric; and then these three, which are species of rhetoric, are themselves genera of cases. But this is an incorrect picture of the hierarchy; judicial, epideictic, and deliberative are not species of rhetoric and genera of cases in one hierarchical line of descent. Judicial, epideictic, and deliberative (the three species of rhetoric) are supposed to be three genera, under each of which we find the species *case.* Now, it never happens that there are several genera for one species unless the genera involved are hierarchically arranged under one another; but the three species of rhetoric are not hierarchically ordered among themselves. So it cannot be that the three species of rhetoric are genera under each of which is found the one species *case.* What is going on here, I think, is that judicial, epideictic, and deliberative occur in two different schemes of division and are species (and subaltern genera) of two different genera—of *rhetoric,* in one division, and of *case,* in the other. Used in the first scheme of division, they give three species of rhetoric. Used in the second to divide cases, they yield three species (or subaltern genera) of verbal disputes for speeches: judicial verbal disputes, epideictic verbal disputes, and deliberative verbal disputes.

18. 1207B8 (81.2–3); "individual." The distinction "special-individual" seems to be a distinction between what is abstract or universal and what has to do with some particular, individual speech or action. Just below Boethius gives as an example of a special case that having to do with war or peace and as an example of a corresponding individual case that having to do with the war or peace of Pyrrhus.

19. 1207C4 (81.15); "question." Perhaps Boethius says what he says here because he thinks that in theory one may make a speech on any subject whatever but that in practice speeches are generally made on matters of public interest that have come into controversy. Cicero (*De inv.* I.v.7) says that the ancient rhetorician Gorgias (the sophist Gorgias) thought an orator was someone who could speak well on any subject, but Aristotle restricted rhetoric to judicial, epideictic, and deliberative speeches (speeches on subjects of public interest or public controversy, and hence political speeches). Cicero sides with Aristotle.

20. 1207C7 (81.19); "later." The explanation seems to follow almost immediately, in 1207D1–14.

21. 1207C9 (81.22); "rhetoric." Boethius here is playing with the Aristotelian analysis of things into matter and form. The "matter" of rhetoric is the political question, and the "form" of rhetoric is the three species into which rhetoric is divided. One does not find the matter by itself; rather, all political questions are "shaped" by one or another of rhetoric's species and exist in the "form" of a judicial, epideictic, or deliberative political question. The matter together with the various forms imposed on it, that is, the political question shaped by the three species of rhetoric, constitute rhetoric as the matter and form of a table constitute a table.

22. 1207D4 (81.32); "parts."¹ And species are a kind of part.

23. 1207D7 (81.35); "*negotiorum.*" Boethius defines *negotium* in this context as a "person's deed or speech for which he is brought to trial" (1212A12).

24. 1208A3 (82.6); "delivery." In *De inv.*, Cicero discusses all these five parts of rhetoric (I.vii.9). Discovery, he says, is the thinking out of true or plausible things that make one's case readily believable. Arrangement is putting the things thought out in appropriate order. Expression is fitting appropriate words to the things thought out. Memorization is a firm grasp on the words and things involved. And delivery is control of the voice and body appropriate to those words and things.

25. 1208A11 (82.15); "rhetoric." In other words, discovery, arrangement, and the rest are all found in each one of the three species of rhetoric.

26. 1208A12 (82.16); "actions." By "political actions" Boethius seems to mean not much more than political questions, since the political question is informed by the species of rhetoric (cf. 1207C2–D1).

27. 1208A12 (82.16); "discussed." Action (*negotium*) is defined and discussed in 1212A12ff.

28. 1208B5 (82.24); "not." Boethius's point here is that, though discourse is the instrument of rhetoric, it is not used by rhetoric alone; as is made clear by what follows, he has in mind, among other things, that dialectic, too, uses discourse. What he means by "political genus" is not clear; in 1208B8–10 he uses "political cases" as roughly equivalent to "political genus."

29. 1208C2 (82.35); "opponent." For Boethius's earlier discussion of the points in this paragraph, see 1205C12–1206D5.

30. 1208C5 (82.38); "peroration." For detailed discussion of these parts of a speech, see Cicero's *De inv.* I.xiv.19 and ff.

31. 1208C8 (82.40); "species." The point seems to be that these six parts of discourse are in rhetoric, and rhetoric is in its species, and so these parts are also in rhetoric's species. But this inference seems fallacious, deriving from an equivocation on 'is (are) in.' Discourse is the instrument for rhetoric and so also the instrument for rhetoric's species; but it is not in either rhetoric or the species of rhetoric as rhetoric itself is in its species. Rhetoric inheres in its species as genus and is part of the substance of the species; but if something's instrument can be said to inhere in it at all, it clearly does not inhere in it in the same way its genus does.

32. 1208C9 (83.2); "species." The point of this sentence is not at all

clear; there are at least two possible explanations, and perhaps both are correct. First, Boethius's concern here may be to emphasize that discourse and its parts are the *instrument* of rhetoric and so are *used* by the species of rhetoric at least to the same extent as they inhere in those species. In other words, since Boethius has made the point that the parts of the instrument inhere in the species of rhetoric, he may be concerned here not to leave their status as instrument obscured. Second, Boethius seems previously to have made a distinction between the three species of rhetoric and the corresponding three genera of cases (cf. note 17 above). The three genera of cases might be thought to function by means of the corresponding species, since the cases (verbal disputes) are carried on by means of judicial, epideictic, or deliberative rhetoric (the three species of rhetoric). On this interpretation, Boethius's point is that the parts of the instrument are not only in the species of rhetoric but also in the three genera of cases that work by means of rhetoric's species. If both interpretations are correct, then Boethius's point is that the six parts of discourse are in rhetoric's species and are also the instrument used by the three genera of cases.

33. 1208C15 (83.9); "Since." The paragraph that begins here seems to belong before and not after the immediately preceding paragraph. In this paragraph, Boethius discusses the relationship of the parts of rhetoric's instrument to the parts of rhetoric itself.

34. 1208D1 (83.10); "disciplines." Boethius's point here looks as if it might involve the fallacy of division; it is not true in general that the parts of a whole share the genus of the whole. But if *facultas* here is translated 'capability' or 'competence,' then in this particular case the conclusion is true, even if the inference is suspect.

35. 1209A6 (83.35); "cases."[2] See note 17.

36. 1209A8 (83.38); "*quaestiones.*" In other words, Boethius takes '*status,*' '*constitutio,*' and '*quaestio*' as synonyms. I have taken the first two as synonyms and translated them by the one word 'issue'; but I have tended to translate '*quaestio*' simply as 'question' because it is an equivocal term and does not always clearly refer to an issue.

37. 1209A10 (83.40); "describe." Reading *ordiamur* for *ordinamur*. The Paris 1537 edition (p. 66) and the Orleans MS. (p. 83) read *ordiamur*.

38. 1209A10 (84.1); "beginning." Much of the discussion that follows is similar to material in *De inv.*; especially I.xii.16ff., I.xi.14ff., and I. viii.9ff.

39. 1209C9 (84.31–32); "administered." The different elements in the list of what is in doubt should be seen in this way. The first involves a doubt about the occurrence of some action, whether a certain action was committed or whether it was the defendant who committed that action. The second is a question about the nature of the action in question; the definition of the action is being requested. The third is a question concerning what qualities the action has, and Boethius takes it in a more circumscribed way than Cicero does (cf. *De inv.* I.viii.10); according to Boethius (1209D1–2), this question seeks the genus of the action committed. The first three of these questions are explicitly discussed in what follows; the fourth is not.

40. 1209C11 (84.35); "issue." The issue has this name because it is

based on a question not about the interpretation of something or about the force of a law but simply about what really happened. So it must be settled not by philosophical discussion or legal debate but by circumstantial evidence about what happened, that is, by "conjectures" about facts. Cf. *De inv.* I.viii.10.

41. 1209C15 (84.36); "definitional." Boethius thinks of definition as showing the whole essence or substance of what it defines (cf. 1187A1–3). And since asking what a thing is (*quid sit*), as distinct from asking what qualities it has, is understood as a question about substance, the appropriate answer to the question is a definition.

42. 1209D3 (85.2); "qualitative." What Boethius says here is troublesome because, as he knows, the question regularly said to call for genus as part of the answer is *not* a question about what sort of qualities something has (*quale sit*) but rather a question about what a thing is (*quid sit*).

43. 1209D4 (85.3); "employed." Quality and quantity are dealt with explicitly in what follows immediately. Comparison is discussed in 1210B10–12. Cf. also *De inv.* I.xi.15.

44. 1209D13 (85.12); "*negotialis.*" Boethius goes on to discuss and divide the juridical issue, but he drops the subject of the legal issue with this mention of it. According to Cicero, the legal issue has to do with what the legal judgment of something should be, taking equity and public custom into account (*De inv.* I.xi.14–15; cf. *De inv.* II.xxi.62ff.). Boethius's fourth division of the rhetorical question (1209C8–9) is perhaps related to the legal issue.

45. 1210A3 (85.16–17); "assumptive." The fourfold division that follows is a division of the assumptive issue; the absolute issue is not discussed any further here. An absolute issue seems to be one in which there is agreement that a certain deed was done and that it has a certain nature but one party argues that the deed was wrong and the other that it was right; the job of the judge(s) is to determine whether or not the action was a wrong one. Cf. *De inv.* II.xxiii.69–71 and *Rhet. ad Her.* I.xiv.24.

46. 1210A12 (85.25); "issue." Cf. 1212D3–10 and 1212B9–C8.

47. 1210B10 (85.39); "did." That is, the crime is transferred in the sense that the defendant's strategy is to put his accuser on the defensive; he turns the tables on his accuser by alleging that what he, the defendant, did was only just punishment for the crime his accuser committed.

48. 1210B12 (86.2); "advantageous." At first glance, this issue seems to rest on the idea that the end justifies the means. But, in fact, what is being compared with the act committed is not the end for which that act was done, but rather the act the defendant would have had to do or acquiesce in had he not done what he did. The strategy involved in this issue seems to be arguing that the defendant had a choice of two evils and chose the lesser of them; hence, he did what he did as a result of choosing the better or more advantageous. Cf. *De inv.* II.xxiv.72ff.

49. 1210C2 (86.8); "else." Boethius discusses the purpose of the work in 1205C1–12.

50. 1210C9 (86.13); "cases." The quotation from Cicero is taken from *De inv.* I.x.13. According to Cicero, Hermagoras held that among the dif-

ferent sorts of the generic issue were the deliberative generic issue and the epideictic generic issue; that is, he took deliberative and epideictic as species of *generic issue*. Cicero's first point against Hermagoras is that deliberative and epideictic are among the (highest) genera of all cases and so they cannot be species of some one kind of case. The passage quoted by Boethius contains his second point against Hermagoras: if epideictic and deliberative cannot be species of some one kind of case, still less can they be species of a part of a case, but every issue is a part of a case; and so epideictic and deliberative cannot be species of an issue, as Hermagoras held that they were. Boethius cites this passage not because he has any interest in the particular controversy between Cicero and Hermagoras but because he wants to discuss the view that issues are parts of a case.

51. 1210C14 (86.18); "case." Boethius's point here seems to be this. One case may contain a number of issues. (That he means only 'may contain' and not 'contains' emerges in the following paragraphs.) Now one genus, too, may contain several species; but any one particular member of such a genus can belong to only one species of that genus, so that in a member of a genus the species of that genus "cannot mingle with each other." But since there may be many issues, in a case issues (unlike species) can "mingle with each other" in a particular case. And so issues cannot be species of case.

52. 1210D3 (86.20); "it." The substance of a species is its proximate genus plus constitutive differentia, and one species is separated from another within the same genus because the differentiae of the two species are contraries or contradictories. Since contraries or contradictories do not "work together" but are opposed to and "destructive" of one another, no species aids the substance of the species opposed to it.

53. 1210D10 (86.28); "*status*." That is, an issue is not a part of a particular, actual case.

54. 1210D12 (86.30); "one." Boethius has something of this sort in mind. In any given actual case there may be more than one issue; but if so, one issue will be the primary or principal one and whatever others there are will be accidental (see the example he gives at the end of this paragraph). But if a case were a genus of which its issues are species, it could not be that one issue is principal and the others have some lowered status, because species of a genus are all on a par. So the difference in rank among issues of a case is evidence that the issues are not species of case.

55. 1210D14 (86.31); "disputes." [2] This point seems to be one of Boethius's reasons for saying that an issue is not an integral part of a case. An action gives rise to as many issues as disputes, but every dispute may have a corresponding case. So every issue can have its own case, and one issue is enough to produce a case. But Boethius claims that a whole cannot be composed of only one part (as he says just above), and so for an actual case arising from a particular action, an issue cannot be a part.

56. 1211A6 (86.38); "definitional." 'Definitional' and 'conjectural' are terms that Boethius has used before only of issues and not of cases; but

presumably a case takes its name from its (principal) issue (cf. 1211A12–15).

57. 1211A9 (87.3); "case." And a whole cannot be composed of only one part. Since the whole case is composed of or constituted by its issue, the issue cannot be a part of that case.

58. 1211A11 (87.5); "issues." Reading *constitutiones* for *constitutionis*. The Paris 1537 edition (p. 69) and the Orleans MS. (p. 85) read *constitutiones*.

59. 1211A12 (87.6); "way." Boethius means to show that Cicero is right and that issues are parts of cases, even in the face of the arguments he has marshaled against that conclusion, by distinguishing two sorts of cases or perhaps two senses of 'case,' a broader and a narrower sense. One can take the description 'the case arising from the action of copulation in a brothel' in two ways. On the one hand, it is a particular case, an actual dispute that might or did arise. For example, if the young man denies that he performed the action, there is a point of dispute (an issue) about the action, from which the case arises. In this sense of 'case' the case cannot contain both a conjectural and a definitional issue; the young man cannot both deny that he had copulation in a brothel and admit that he did but deny its adulterousness. It is also possible, however, that 'the case arising from copulation in a brothel' be taken to refer indefinitely to any one of the cases possible given such an action (or the alleging of it). Taken in this way, the case in question is something like the genus of possible cases corresponding to a particular action. The case understood in this way contains many issues; both the conjectural and definitional issues, for example, are included in the case arising from copulation in a brothel. So there are two ways of understanding this case. In the first way, one issue constitutes the whole case. In the second way, there are several issues for a case, and the issues are species of their case, because the different issues correspond to the different kinds of cases contained within the case that is their genus. In this way, the case arising from copulation in a brothel can be thought of as a genus that is divided by different issues into its species, *the conjectural case arising from copulation in a brothel, the definitional case arising from copulation in a brothel,* and so on.

60. 1211B2 (87.11); "transference." Boethius does not discuss the issue of transference; Cicero places it on a par with the conjectural issue, the definitional issue, and the rest. An issue of transference, according to Cicero, is one in which there is dispute whether the right person has brought the suit, whether the suit is brought before the right court, under the right statute, and so on (*De inv.* I.viii.10). It is called an issue of transference because what is in question is whether some part of the suit needs to be transferred to a different court or different statute and so on.

61. 1211B9 (87.18); "discipline." In this paragraph Boethius is giving a summary of preceding material; cf. 1207A15–1209A4.

62. 1211C9 (87.34–35); "[species]." What Boethius says here is troublesome. First, it is hard to see what four issues he has in mind. The most likely are the four issues corresponding to the four things he says may be

in doubt in any rhetorical question: whether it is, what it is, what qualities it has, and whether judgment can be lawfully and morally administered (1209C7–9). There is no other obvious grouping that consists in four
issues, but Boethius mentions by name at least six issues: conjectural,
definitional, and generic; the subdivisions of generic, legal and juridical;
and the subdivisions of juridical, absolute and assumptive. If Boethius
here is talking about the four sorts of issues mentioned in 1209C7–9,
though, he is not taking all issues into account, because he is neglecting
one of the two main subdivisions of issues, namely, the group of issues
having to do with a document.

63. 1211D1 (88.3); "species." It is difficult at first glance to understand
how Boethius's example of an utterance is analogous to rhetoric and the
political question; but I think the example gives the reader a feeling for
what Boethius has in mind, however appropriate it may be in its particulars. As Boethius has explained the divisions of rhetoric's matter (which is
the political question), they seem not altogether to make sense. Judicial,
epideictic, and deliberative are the genera or subaltern species of cases,
but so are issues. So it seems as if the genus *case* is divided by two different sets of species that are not related to each other as genus and
species. But Boethius here shows that he is thinking of issues almost as if
they were integral parts rather than species of cases; the example of an utterance provides a picture for what he has in mind. An utterance is a
complex thing that can be divided internally into different parts. The
whole utterance, complete with its internal divisions, however, may have
a sort of external division; for example, it may be divided according to its
being heard by one individual or another. Some such distinction between
an external and an internal division is what Boethius wants to use to
explain how *case* can appear to be divided by different and unrelated sets
of species.

64. 1211D2 (88.3); "matter." For the earlier discussion of what Boethius
has in mind here, see 1207C4ff.

65. 1211D6 (88.7); "issues." Boethius is concerned to establish and explain that discovery, arrangement, and the other parts of rhetoric are in
each of the kinds of issue. The conclusion he wants is plausible enough,
but his reasoning is troublesome. It requires the species of rhetoric and so
also the genus *rhetoric* to be in the issues. The species of rhetoric are also
the genera of *case,* and so it might seem that issues are made up of the
genera of *case* (plus certain differentiae); but such an interpretation is
ruled out by the preceding argument about the parts of cases
(1211C9–D1). Because Boethius's words at the start of this paragraph recall
his earlier discussion of rhetoric's species as forms imposed on rhetoric's
matter, perhaps what he has in mind is the following. The species of rhetoric are in the matter as forms; so all the cases and issues that are part of
rhetoric's matter are informed by rhetoric's species. Since the species are
forms of issues, they are in issues, and so the genus constituting the
species is also in the issues. Consequently, the parts of that genus,
namely, the parts of rhetoric, will also be in the issues.

66. 1211D9 (88.11); "rest." Boethius's conclusion seems right, but here, too, the way in which he arrives at it is troublesome. He seems to move illegitimately from saying that rhetoric's matter brings with it rhetoric's instrument to saying that the parts of the instrument are in rhetoric's matter.

67. 1211D12 (88.11); "persuading." Boethius's frequently used notion that one element of rhetoric brings with it another is hard to interpret. Perhaps what he means is simply that the two are connected and in such a way that the second is logically or conceptually dependent on the first. Such an interpretation makes some sense here, since the instrument's work is just the instrument in action.

68. 1212A7 (88.23); "separately." It is not clear what passage, if any, Boethius is referring to here.

69. 1212A10 (88.28); "action." The person and the action are for rhetoric what the subject and predicate of the question under discussion are for dialectic: they are the givens around which or from which one's case has to be built. The conclusion one wants to draw will involve at least one of them, and so the case one makes has to use things related in one way or another to one of them. See also the following note.

70. 1212C8 (89.15); "person." Boethius's point in this paragraph is analogous to one he makes about the subject and predicate in the question under discussion in dialectic; cf. *ICT* 288.4–9 (*PL* 1059C6–12).

71. 1212C14 (89.22); "case." For a detailed discussion of these circumstances, see *De inv.* I.xxiv.34ff. By "manner" Cicero means the state of mind in which an action is done or the manner of doing an action from which a certain state of mind can be inferred. The two basic subdivisions of manner are intention and lack of intention.

72. 1212D3 (89.26); "action." Cf. *De inv.* I.xxiv.34 and 37–38.

73. 1212D10 (89.34); "trial." See *De inv.* I.xxiv.34ff. Nature has to do with one's sex, people, country, family, and age, according to Cicero. Mode of life includes one's education and upbringing, friends, occupation, and home life. Feeling seems to be the general emotional state of the defendant around the time of the alleged crime.

74. 1212D14 (89.38–39); "itself." For this and the following points attributed to Cicero here, see *De inv.* I.xxvi.37.

75. 1213A9 (90.9); "person." That is, the deeds mentioned in the list of eleven things related to the person; see 1212D3–10.

76. 1213A15 (90.15); "action." See *De inv.* I.xxvi.38ff.

77. 1213B1 (90.16); "actions." The first part, of course, is the immediately preceding "what" and "why." Those two are part of the action itself; these four are the circumstances in which the action was performed. In all, the attributes of the action are divided into four parts: those contained in the action itself ("what" and "why"), those in the performing of the action (the last four circumstances), those that are associated with the action (1214A2ff.), and those that are consequences of the action (1214C8ff.).

78. 1213B8 (90.23); "Topics." The Topics, then, are the seven circum-

stances and their subdivisions. For the way in which these circumstances can be used for arguments both by the prosecution and by the defense, see *De inv.* II.v.16ff.

79. 1213C7 (90.39); "means." The first "while it occurs" includes just those occurrences that constitute the crime itself. There is a second "while it occurs" in the attributes connected with the performing of the action because these attributes contain what is contemporaneous with the action (as well as what is prior and posterior to the action). The different circumstances connected with the performing of the action have various temporal relations to the action; method, for instance, might be thought to include what comes before and continues after the action (cf. *De inv.* I.xxiv.34ff).

80. 1213C10 (91.4); "whatever." Boethius's point is that "while it occurs" is an action, namely, the heart of the action that is being prosecuted; the things connected with the performing of the action, however, have to do not with actions but with things that in some way adhere to actions. We might think the point an odd one for Boethius to be making since he has been at some pains earlier (1212B9–C8) to show that the very action that is being prosecuted cannot be a Topic, that is, cannot be what the argument is built around; what he says here about the "while it occurs" seems directly to contradict that earlier point. But the action being prosecuted involves not only striking with a sword (Boethius's example for "while it occurs") but also seizing a sword in a state of excitement and so on (see 1213A2–6); so the action in "while it occurs" is a *part* of the action being prosecuted. And Boethius regards a part of the action as an attribute of the action and not as the action itself.

81. 1213C12 (91.4); "said." There seems to be no better candidate for Boethius's reference here than what he says in the immediately preceding 1213C10.

82. 1213C15 (91.6); "performed." That is, they retain their status as adherents to the action even though in some accounts of what happened they may be presented as among the actions of the defendant.

83. 1214A2 (91.19); "about." In other words, the two groups of circumstances Boethius has discussed so far are analogous to the intrinsic Topics in dialectic.

84. 1214A3 (91.21); "performed." These are the third and fourth groups of circumstances; cf. note 77.

85. 1214A12 (91.31); "action." These are the circumstances Boethius has just finished discussing: who, what, why, when, where, how, and by what means.

86. 1214A15 (91.35); "to." Boethius's point is that circumstances of different actions can be related and compared to one another (cf. *De inv.* II.xii.41–42). If the circumstances of one action are related to those of another action in such a way that the second is contained in the first, the first is a genus of the second.

87. 1214B4 (91.38); "equal." Things associated with the action, then, are genus, species, contrary, result, greater, lesser, and equal. For more detailed discussion of these, see *De inv.* I.xxviii.41ff. and II.xii.41–42.

88. 1214B7 (92.1); "different." Reading *disparatum* for *disperatum*. The Paris 1537 edition (p. 75) and the Orleans ms. (p. 87) read *disparatum*.

89. 1214C7 (92.17); "action." ² Boethius's point is that a Topic that is a thing associated with the action has to do not with contrariety (for example), as the corresponding dialectical Topic does, but rather with the particular thing that is a contrary. The point is explained in greater detail in 1216B1ff.

90. 1214C12 (92.22); "comparison." Boethius here is distinguishing the fourth group of attributes of the action from the first two groups, on the one hand, and from the third group, on the other hand. The first group ("what" and "why") and the second group ("when," "where," "how," and "by what means") are inseparably connected with the action (1214B11–13). The third group (things associated with the action) is acquired by a comparison of actions or their circumstances (1214A12–C3). The explanation of this part of the text, suggested by the *PL* editors here, seems altogether misguided: "It is not in the things themselves because what is in the things themselves is in the substance of the things."

91. 1214C13 (92.23); "performed." For Cicero's discussion of this Topic, see *De inv.* I.xxviii.43; for some suggestion about how the Topics might serve in arguments, see *De inv.* II.xii.42.

92. 1214C14 (92.23–24); "extrinsic." In the passage that follows, Boethius's characterizations of each part of this Topic are taken either verbatim or very nearly verbatim from *De inv.* I.xxviii.43.

93. 1214D11 (92.38); "time." In the preceding paragraph, Boethius explains consequence as something that goes before or comes after the action. So perhaps 'follow' (*consequi*) here should be expanded in the same way; such an expansion seems to be required by the sense of the passage, though it is a strain on the word '*consequi*.' If 'follow' and 'precede' are taken as referring to logical as well as temporal following and preceding, then it does seem possible, with some work and goodwill, to see all the circumstances mentioned in this passage as preceding or following from the action. Especially in legal contexts, one can consider what name applies to a certain action after the action is done. The performers of the action are before the action; approvers, both before and after it. If the type of an action is being discussed, then it may be thought of as giving rise to a certain custom or law; if the particular action itself is considered, then it falls under the aegis of some previously existing custom or law. What men tend to do and how certain actions tend to occur are in some sense prior to the action, as is the tendency of men to defend or not to defend such actions.

94. 1215A4 (93.3); "above." Cf. 1213A6ff. and 1213C6ff.

95. 1215A6 (93.4); "previously." See 1213C8ff.

96. 1215A7 (93.7–8); "performed." If Boethius means that he formerly divided things associated with the action into two groups, what he says seems simply wrong; in no place in the preceding passages does he present things that are related (or compared) and things that follow as two subdivisions of things associated with the action. The preceding passages in which he discussed these two divisions are 1214A11–B10 and C8–D11.

97. 1215A14 (93.14); "Themistius." See 1186D6ff.

98. 1215B5 (93.21); "intermediate." The person and the action are for rhetoric what the predicate and the subject are for dialectic. Hence, for rhetoric, the three divisions intrinsic, extrinsic, and intermediate have to do with the relation of the Topic to the person or action. Cf. notes 69 and 70 above.

99. 1215B7 (93.23); "action." [2] Boethius here seems to be presenting the circumstances involved in the performing of the action (the second group of attributes of the action) as intrinsic Topics. But he says nothing about the circumstances contained in the action (the first group of attributes of the action) or about the attributes of the person; and surely these are closer to the action than the second group of attributes of the action.

100. 1215B9 (93.25); "Topics." Things associated with the action are species, genus, contrary, result, greater, lesser, and equal. In Themistius's division, *species, genus,* and result (*effects*) are intrinsic; and *contrary, greater, lesser,* and equal (*similar*) are extrinsic. None of these Topics is among the intermediate Themistian Topics. Perhaps Boethius says that things associated with the action are intermediate Topics, even though their Themistian analogues are intrinsic or extrinsic because in order to use the associated things some other action that is external to the one at issue has to be brought into the discussion (see 1214A11ff.). So, for instance, in order to use the rhetorical Topic *genus,* the arguer has to mention not only the action at issue and one of its circumstances, but also some other action and one of the circumstances that is the genus of the first action's circumtance. And so in rhetoric, these Topics have to do both with the action at issue and with something external to that action. But in dialectic, in order to use the Topic *genus* nothing has to be brought into discussion but the genus of the subject or predicate of the question.

101. 1215C3 (93.34); "way." For Cicero's division, see 1195D5ff.

102. 1215C6 (93.38); "related things." Both the first two groups of the attributes of the action and the third group (things associated with the action) are intrinsic Topics since *related things* is among the intrinsic Topics in the Ciceronian division (cf.1195D10–14). The seven Topics that are things associated with the action all have their corresponding dialectical Topics among Cicero's *related things;* cf. 1196B5–12.

103. 1215D4 (94.12–13); "circumstances." For Boethius's earlier discussion of this point, see 1205C12–1206C3 and 1206C12–D1.

104. 1215D6 (94.15); "other." In other words, dialectic deals with what is universal (theses) and rhetoric with what is particular (hypotheses).

105. 1216A10 (94.24); "circumstances." So the arguments, like the cases and their Topics, will be about individual or particular things.

106. 1216A13 (94.27); "posterior." The priority and posteriority in question here must be logical or conceptual priority and posteriority. Aristotle says that the more general is prior in nature; the more particular, posterior (cf. *An. Pos.* 71b34–72a5). Presumably, since the subject matter of dialectic is prior to that of rhetoric, the dialectician (considered as dialectician) is in some sense prior to the rhetorician.

107. 1216A15 (94.29); "circumstances." Perhaps Boethius has in mind

something such as a complicated induction, in which one of the particulars of the induction is first disputed, then proved, and then used to help establish the universal conclusion of the induction.

Outline of Book IV

I. Differences between rhetoric and dialectic 1205C–1206D
II. Nature of rhetoric 1207A–1209A
III. Issues 1209A–1210C
    A. Over a document 1209A–C
    B. Not over a document but over the thing itself 1209C–1210C
        1. Whether it occurred 1209C
        2. What kind of thing it is 1209C
        3. What qualities it has 1209C–1210C
        4. Whether judgment can be lawfully or morally administered 1209C
IV. How issues are parts of a case 1210C–1211B
V. Summary of preceding 1211B–1212A
VI. Division of rhetorical Topics 1212A–1215A
    A. Into attributes of persons or actions 1212A–C
    B. Division of circumstances 1212C–1214A
    C. Division of things associated with action 1214A
        1. Comparison (relationship) of action 1214A–C
        2. Consequents of (things that follow) the action 1214C–1215A
    D. Summary of division of rhetorical Topics 1215A
VII. Comparison of rhetorical and dialectical Topics 1215A–C
VIII. Difference between dialectic and rhetoric 1215D–1216C
IX. A difference between Cicero's *Topica* and Aristotle's *Topics* (about dialectical disputation) 1216D

The Nature of Rhetoric

Genus: discipline
Species (= genera of cases): judicial, epideictic, deliberative
Matter: political question
Parts: discovery, arrangement, expression, memorization, delivery
Instrument: discourse
Parts of the instrument: prooemium, narration, partition, confirmation, refutation, peroration
Work: To teach and to move
Function of speaker: To speak appropriately for persuasion
End: To have spoken well or to have persuaded

PART TWO

*Dialectic in Ancient
and Medieval Logic*

Dialectic and Aristotle's *Topics*

To do justice to Aristotle's *Topics* in one chapter is difficult. The book has generated a great deal of literature recently, and the subject itself is complex. Aristotle's concept of a Topic is not easy to comprehend and is the subject of considerable controversy. Since Aristotle uses Topics in the *Rhetoric* also, a thorough account of an Aristotelian Topic would require discussing the *Rhetoric* as well as the *Topics*. But then it becomes necessary not only to interpret the *Rhetoric* and examine the relevant technical terms, such as 'enthymeme,' but also to investigate the similarities and differences between the Topics in the two treatises so that one does not confuse rhetorical and dialectical notions. There is also the troublesome question of the *Topics'* date of composition and its relationship to the *Analytics* and the theory of the syllogism contained therein. Scholars not uncommonly treat the *Topics* as a superseded attempt to discover what Aristotle formulated successfully in the *Analytics*. [1] Such a view, I think, is based on a misunderstanding of the *Topics;* and to the extent to which this view has influenced conclusions about the work's date of composition, it would be worthwhile reexamining those conclusions. [2] Clearly, the scope and intricacy of all these issues could easily supply the material for a whole book. For my purposes here, however, it is sufficient to present only as much of Aristotle's theory of Topics as will aid comprehension of Boethius's *De topicis differentiis* and put the Boethian treatise in its historical perspective. So in what follows, I will confine myself as much as possible to Aristotle's exposition of Topics in the *Topics*, omitting questions about the work's relation

1 See, for example, David Ross, *Aristotle*, 5th ed. (London, 1966), p. 59.

2. See, for example, Richard L. Van der Weel, "The *Posterior Analytics* and the *Topics*," *Laval Théologique et Philosophique*, 25 (1969), 130–141.

to syllogistic logic and touching on the *Rhetoric* only where necessary.

The purpose of the Topics, as Aristotle says at the beginning of his treatise on them,[3] is to provide a τέχνη of dialectical disputation, but at first glance the major part of the *Topics* seems to contain not a τέχνη but a repetitious and disordered listing of Topics. Showing the existence and nature of the art in the *Topics* is my concern in this chapter.[4] The bulk of Aristotle's treatise is concerned with Topics. Six of the eight Books of the *Topics*, Books II–VII, consist almost solely of Topics; and these, as I will argue, are the means for discovering particular arguments. But the arguments to be found are dialectical. They are meant for use in dialectical disputation, and the purpose of the *Topics* is to make a man good at such disputation. So before considering Aristotle's art of discovering arguments, I want to give some idea of the context in which those arguments were meant to be used.

A dialectical disputation arises from a problem (πρόβλημα), which is a question of this form: "Is the world eternal or not?" or, "Is pleasure to be chosen or not?"[5] Not every question of this form is a problem, but only those that are controversial, because problems are issues for disputation, and no disputant would be willing to argue for what is altogether unbelievable or against what seems to be established truth. So to be a dialectical problem, a question of this form must be one stemming from disagreement among the many, among the wise, or between the many and the wise.[6]

In a dialectical disputation, one participant is a questioner and the other an answerer; each participant upholds one side of the problem as true. The answerer, for example, may hold that the world is not eternal and the questioner that it is eternal. What the questioner upholds as true is called a dilectical proposition (πρότασις); and since a dialectical proposition is the questioner's thesis, it is generally in the form of a question, such as, "Pedestrian biped animal is the definition of man, isn't it?"[7] For each

---

3. *Top.* 100a18–24; cf. also *Soph. El.* 183b23–184a8.
4. Similarities and differences and historical connections between Aristotle's and Boethius's methods are considered in the Introduction and the chapter "Between Aristotle and Boethius."
5. *Top.* 101b28–33, 104b7–8.   6. Cf. *Top.* 104a4–8 and 104b1–5.
7. "ἆρά γε τὸ ζῷον πεζὸν δίπουν ὁρισμός ἐστιν ἀνθρώπου" *Top.* 101b30–31.

dialectical problem, then, there is a dialectical (interrogative) proposition that expects either a yes or a no answer.[8]

The questioner tries to establish his own thesis and to refute the answerer's thesis by asking the answerer questions designed to compel his agreement to the questioner's thesis. The answerer tries to prevent the questioner from achieving his aim. But though the questioner and the answerer have opposite aims, they have a common task,[9] because neither the questioner nor the answerer alone has the power to make the disputation a good one. If the questioner does his job well but the answerer answers perversely or contentiously (for example), or if the answerer does his job well but the questioner asks questions in a way that lacks cogency or efficacy (for example), the disputation will not be a good one.

The questioner works in this way. Since he wants to make the answerer accept his thesis, he needs to find an argument with that thesis as its conclusion. This argument, which is found by means of a Topic, forms the basic structure of the questioner's side of the disputation; Aristotle calls the premises of this argument the necessary (that is, required) premises.[10] Once the answerer has granted the necessary premises, he is obliged to grant the questioner's thesis as well. But the answerer may not be willing to grant all the necessary premises, and so the questioner must find a subsidiary argument for each of the necessary premises which the answerer might be unwilling to accept. Each of these subsidiary arguments, then, will yield one of the necessary premises as its conclusion. The necessary premises and the premises in the subsidiary arguments and anything else that may be part of the questioner's contribution to the disputation must be in the form of questions to which the answerer can respond properly with "yes" or "no." When all the appropriate questions have been chosen, they must be arranged. Part of the questioner's art is to conceal from the answerer which are the necessary premises crucial for producing the conclusion, because in this way the answerer is more likely to answer as he thinks and less likely to balk perversely or ingeniously at the important questions. Aristotle has a number of rules of thumb to help the questioner conceal the structure of his argument. He says, for example, that the premises should not be asked for in their natural order but out of sequence

8. *Top.* 101b28–36.   9. *Top.* 161a19–21.   10. Cf. *Top.* 155b3–28.

and separated from the other premises they naturally go with.[11] He advises the questioner to ask for a needed premise in some form other than that wanted in the argument; for instance, if the questioner wants a premise about contraries, he should ask for one about opposites.[12] Other, more general suggestions are designed to help the questioner achieve his aim. Aristotle says, for example, that the questioner should never try to establish his thesis by a *reductio* if he is arguing with someone not well trained in reasoning. Such people are only confused by a *reductio* and frequently will not grant a conclusion arrived at in such a way.[13]

The answerer's aim is to block the aim of the questioner; to avoid having to agree to the questioner's thesis or having to say what is not readily believable (ἀδοξότατα) in order to avoid agreeing with that thesis.[14] He prepares for his part in the dispute by arguing the questioner's case against himself to learn how to parry the questions he is likely to be asked.[15] Hence, he goes through much the same procedure as does the questioner; and the Topics, designed to aid the questioner directly, are useful for the answerer, too. In addition, Aristotle offers several rules of thumb specifically for the answerer. The answerer, for example, should see whether his thesis is generally accepted as true. If it is, he should try to grant only those premises that are themselves generally accepted or seem to be so. If, on the other hand, his thesis goes against public opinion, then again he should try to grant only premises of the same sort. There are two advantages for the answerer in following this rule. First, he will seem consistent. Secondly, because the questioner's thesis is the opposite of his, if the answerer's thesis is generally accepted as true, the questioner's thesis must go against public opinion, and vice versa. Hence, since the questioner's thesis will have to be established by premises that are like it (generally accepted or rejected), if the answerer grants only premises of the same sort as his own thesis, he is likely to block the establishment of the questioner's thesis.[16]

The questioner is limited to yes-or-no questions, but the answerer is not restricted to saying only "yes" or "no." If he thinks a question is vague or unclear, he can ask for a clarification.[17] If he recognizes that a question contains an ambiguous word, he may

---

11. Cf. *Top.* 155b20–156a26.   12. *Top.* 156a27–156b3.
13. *Top.* 157b34–158a2.   14. Cf., for example, *Top.* 159a18–22.
15. *Top.* 160b14–16.   16. Cf. *Top.* 159a38–159b27.   17. *Top.* 160a18–23.

ask the questioner in what sense of the word the question is meant; or, if he sees that the word is ambiguous sometime after he has answered the question, he may object that he assented to that question only in one particular sense of the word.[18] In some cases, the answerer is *obliged* to say more than "yes" or "no." If, for example, he has granted all the particulars of an induction and then refuses to grant the universal, he must give a reason for refusing to do so; he must give an instance in which the universal does not hold or in some other way argue against the universal.[19] The answerer can also bring objections against the questioner's line of argument—for instance, he can argue that the questioner's argument is based on some fallacy—and in this way he can work actively at demolishing the questioner's argument.[20]

The disputation can be ended in several ways. The questioner may have all his premises granted, and so succeed in establishing his conclusion. The answerer may destroy the questioner's argument by showing that it rests on a fallacy or by bringing other objections against it which the questioner cannot refute. Or the questioner may not succeed in establishing his thesis within a certain period of time. Aristotle says[21] that one kind of objection (ἔν-στασις)[22] has to do with time. This kind of objection is not an objection directly about time; the answerer does not object that the time for the disputation has expired. Instead he presents an obstacle or impediment to the questioner's bringing the argument to a successful close by raising objections that take longer to deal with than the time available for the disputation. Aristotle clearly thinks of these disputations as having a certain time limit, but whether they are limited by an official rule, by custom, or by the stamina and patience of the participants is not clear.[23]

18. *Top.* 160a23–33.   19. Cf. *Top.* 160b1–13 and 157a34–157b2.
20. Cf. *Top.* 160b23–161a15.   21. *Top.* 161a9–12.
22. It might be better to translate 'ἔνστασις' here not as 'objection' but rather as 'obstacle' or 'impediment.'
23. Paul Moraux in his "La Joute dialectique d'après le huitième livre des *To-piques*," (in *Aristotle on Dialectic, Proceedings of the Third Symposium Aristotelicum*, ed. G. E. L. Owen [Oxford, 1968]), p. 285 says, "Enfin, il est probable que les deux interlocuteurs n'avaient pas le droit de prolonger indéfiniment leurs débats, mais que les organisateurs pouvaient les interrompre, et peut-être même qu'ils avaient fixé d'avance une durée que la joute ne pouvait dépasser." For this opinion he cites only 158a25–30 and 161a9–12. But neither passage is evidence for Moraux's strong claim. The point of 161a9–12 is (as I have already pointed out) simply that some people bring up objections to a questioner that take more time to argue than is

Aristotle also gives the impression that the participants in a disputation are judged,[24] but it is unclear whether the judging is done by official judges, teachers, friends, or just casual bystanders.[25] A good questioner, Aristole says, is one who succeeds in getting the answerer to grant the questioner's thesis or forces the answerer to say what is not readily believable in order to avoid granting that thesis;[26] and a good answerer is one who prevents the questioner from succeeding in his goals. If the answerer has to say what sounds strange, it should seem to be not his fault but rather a consequence of the thesis he is upholding.[27] It seems clear

---

available for that particular discussion; it provides no evidence whatever for the view that time limits were set for the disputants by anyone. The point of 158a25–30 is that someone who keeps on asking one question for a long time is a bad questioner, and the passage seems altogether irrelevant to Moraux's claim. Gilbert Ryle shares Moraux's views on this subject. In *Plato's Progress* (Cambridge, 1966), p. 196, he says, "The answerer is victorious if he has made no such admissions [that is, admissions inconsistent with his thesis] by the moment when time is up." In this passage he cites no evidence for his notion of a set time limit, but earlier (p. 105) he says, "The 'time's up' seems to be referred to in the *Topics* 161a10 and 183a25." The passage in 161a9–12, as I have just remarked, provides no evidence for a time limit's being *imposed* on the disputants. And 183a23–26 (actually in *Soph. El.*) seems to be making much the same point as 161a9–12: a solution sometimes takes more time than the period available for arguing it out. The claim Moraux and Ryle make about time limits, then, is simply unwarranted by the textual evidence they adduce.

24. Cf., for example, *Top.* 161b16–18, 158a8–11, 162a8–9, 162b16–18.

25. Moraux, "La Joute dialectique," 277, says, ". . . il ne fait aucun doute que maîtres et disciples assistaient à ces tournois avec autant d'intérêt que notre jeunesse à des matches de boxe ou de football"; and, on p. 285, "Qui portera pareil jugement, sinon le maître et les disciples déjà formés qui auront assisté au tournoi?" For the second passage, he cites no textual evidence at all; for the first, he refers to *Topics* 160b21–22 and *Topics* VIII.11. The passage at 160b21–22 is "Men hate him who says such things [as that pleasure is the good], thinking not that he maintains them for the sake of the argument but that he says what he believes." *Topics* VIII.11 is a discussion of what makes arguments and arguers good or bad. Neither reference supports Moraux's claim about the nature of the judges of the disputation. Ryle's view is that disputations were officially decided by an audience (*Plato's Progress*, pp. 105 and 198). As evidence from Aristotle's writings, he cites (p. 198) *Topics* 1169b31 and 1174a37. The references are clearly mistaken; the highest Bekker number in the *Topics* is 164. It is possible that Ryle means to refer to *Soph. El.* 169b31 and 174a37. The first passage says, "The same things which make it seem to those listening as if the conclusion has been proved from the question asked make it appear so to the answerer as well"; and the second is "Sometimes people think that they have granted [a universal proposition] and appear to those listening to have done so, because they remember the induction." Neither of these passages is anything like sufficient evidence to show that the disputations of Aristotle's τέχνη were decided in some official way by their audiences.

26. Cf. *Top.* 159a18–20.   27. Cf. *Top.* 159a20–22.

that at least some disputants maintained theses other than those they held personally, arguing sometimes both sides of a problem and sometimes the theses of famous thinkers.[28] So Aristotle distinguishes between faults that belong to a thesis and faults that the defender of a thesis is responsible for. A questioner does his job badly if he argues fallaciously without realizing it or if he argues contentiously in any way.[29] The answerer is blameworthy if he refuses to grant what follows from something he has previously granted, if he is inconsistent in what he grants as true, if he refuses to grant what is quite apparently true, or if he argues contentiously.[30] The questioner and the answerer can also be judged on the relative difficulty of their tasks: it is easier to block than to construct the proofs for some things.[31] The argument itself is also judged. Some problems are much harder to argue than others;[32] and, in general, an argument is faulted for lacking cogency or elegance.[33]

Clearly, in order to be good at the sort of disputation that has been described here, both the questioner and the answerer must be capable of thinking up good arguments quickly. The sophists wanted to make their students adept at argument; and what they did, according to Aristotle, was to have their students simply memorize common arguments or sets of questions and answers. Aristotle, however, wants to teach not arguments but a method for arguing,[34] and the Topics are the heart of that method. It is by means of a Topic that a particular argument may be found in any given case.

One of the main difficulties in understanding Aristotle's *Topics* is that Aristotle devotes almost no attention to what a Topic is; he seems to assume that the meaning of 'Topic' as a technical term is familiar. He discusses Topics also in the *Rhetoric,* and perhaps rhetorical Topics were already commonly used by contemporary rhetoricians. Furthermore, Aristotle explains the usefulness of dialectical Topics by comparing them to mnemonic Topics, and it is possible that 'Topic' as a technical term originated and by Aristotle's time was well established in Greek arts of memory, where it

28. *Top.* 163a29–163b3 and 159b27–35.
29. *Top.* 162b16–20, 161a33–34, 161b1–5.
30. *Top.* 160b10–13, 161a17–19, 161b11–17.   31. *Top.* 158a31–158b4.
32. *Top.* 158b5ff. and 161b34–162a2.
33. *Top.* 161b19–33, 162a24–34, 162b2ff.   34. *Soph. El.* 183b36–184a8.

meant one of the places in an edifice by means of which things memorized could be recalled.[35]

In any case, even though Aristotle does not explicitly explain the nature of a Topic, Books II–VII of the *Topics* are almost exclusively lists of Topics, and we can get an idea of what Aristotle thinks a Topic is by looking at the sorts of Topics he gives in those Books. Here are the first Topics from the first Book of the *Topics* in which specific Topics are given.

(1) One Topic is to consider if [your opponent] has given as an accident what belongs in some other way. . . . For the predicate of a genus is never said paronymously of the species [of that genus], but all genera are predicated unequivocally of their species, for species take both the name and the formula of their genera. [109a34–b7]

(2) Another [Topic] is to consider those cases in which [a predicate] has been said to belong to all or to none and to examine them by species and not in their infinite numbers, for then the examination will be better and in fewer stages. [109b13–15]

(3) Another [Topic] is to make formulae of the accident and of that to which it belongs, either of both separately or of one of the two, and then examine if anything untrue has been taken as true in the definitions. . . . For so it will be clear whether what is said is true or false. [109b30–110a1]

(4) Furthermore, [one ought to] make the problem into a dialectical proposition for oneself and raise an objection against it, for the objection will be an argument against the thesis. This Topic is almost the same as examining cases in which something is said to belong either to all or to none, but it differs in method. [110a10–13]

(5) Furthermore, [one ought to] define what kinds of things one ought to call as the many call them and what kinds of things ought not to be so called, for this is useful both for establishing and for tearing down [a thesis]. [110a14–16]

In contemporary discussions of the *Topics* it is not uncommon to find Topic (1) and those like it taken as standard or representative Topics. Though analyses of Topics vary, they tend to begin by assuming such a presentation of a Topic. Walter de Pater, who has done the most useful, insightful, and thorough study of Aristotle's *Topics* I know of, puts it this way: "L'expression disant qu'il faut regarder quelque part . . . revient toujours dans la première par-

---

35. *Top.* 163b28–32; for a discussion of the mnemonic Topics, see Introduction, above.

tie du lieu. Cette formule est une règle . . . qui indique à celui qui fait usage du lieu l'objet vers lequel il doit diriger son attention. La deuxième partie du lieu, précédée par le mot γάρ, dit ce qui *est;* elle est donc une loi. Plus précisément, elle est une loi logique ou (dans *Top.* iii. 1–4) une loi axiologique."[36] A very clear case exemplifying De Pater's view is this Topic: "If the species is a relative, [one must] examine whether the genus is also a relative; for if the species is a relative, the genus is also."[37] In this example, Aristotle is doing two things. First, he is giving a strategy or line of argument or tack to take in dealing with one's opponent in a dispute. The answerer, say, maintains that some particular species is a relative. The questioner, then, ought to consider whether the genus of that species is a relative; if it is not, then neither is the species a relative. Second, in the Topic Aristotle is giving a principle or a law that explains or justifies the strategy: whenever a species is a relative, its genus is also a relative.

It is not clear in this case whether Aristotle thinks that both the strategy and the principle are the Topic or only one or the other, and there is further reason for uncertainty. Aristotle gives many Topics that are only lines of argument and many others that are only principles. For example, in 120b36-37 Aristotle says, "[You must see] if the genus and the species are not in the same [category], but one is a substance and the other a quality, or one a relative and the other a quality." Here, unlike the example in the preceding paragraph, the statement of the strategy is not followed immediately by a γάρ clause containing a principle; sometimes, as in the example given here, a corresponding principle occurs later in the discussion, but the strategy alone is called the Topic.[38] In other places, the situation is reversed, and the Topics are principles alone. In 117b10–11, for example, Aristotle gives this Topic: "Another Topic: what is nearer to the good is better and more worthy of choice and also what is more like the good." In such cases, the strategy tends not to be given at all.

Of the two ancient commentators on the *Topics* whose work is extant, Theophrastus thinks that a Topic consists only in a princi-

36. De Pater, "La Fonction du lieu et de l'instrument dans les *Topiques,*" in *Aristotle on Dialectic,* ed. Owen, p. 165.
37. *Top.* 124b15–16.
38. Cf., for example, Topic (1) above; for the principle corresponding to the example given here, cf. 121a5–7.

ple and not in the corresponding strategy as well; and Alexander of Aphrodisias thinks that both the strategy and the principle are equally Topics, though he thinks the strategy is called 'Topic' derivatively from its frequent association with the principle.[39] De Pater's account, then, agrees with that of the Greek commentators; his interpretation is allied with Theophrastus's views, and such an account is not uncommon among modern scholars.[40] But I think a case can be made on the other side. I think that Aristotle considers a Topic primarily as a strategy for arguing, though it is a strategy that will work, and work in many cases because it is founded on some basic principle.

If we look at the first five Topics from Book II given above, we can see that the Topic consisting in "règle" and "loi logique" is *not* standard. Topic (2) begins with a rule or strategy, but what follows in the γάρ clause is "then the examination will be better and in fewer stages," which is hardly a logical law. Similarly, Topic (3) begins with a strategy, but the only significant γάρ clause attaching to the strategy can scarcely be considered a logical law: "For so it will be clear whether what is said is true or false." Topics (4) and (5) also are only strategies and have no adjoined logical law. The γάρ clause in (4) is simply "the objection will be an argument against the thesis," and in (5) it is "this is useful both for establishing and tearing down [a thesis]." Of these five Topics, then, only one has the form of strategy and logical law. Even in that one, Topic (1), the logical law or principle is considerably separated in the text from the strategy, and only the strategy is called the Topic. All five Topics, though, include a strategy.

De Pater deals with observations of this sort by saying, "il s'agisse de lieux en un sens plus faible."[41] He divides Topics into

39. Alexander of Aphrodisias, *In Aristotelis Topicorum,* in *Commentaria in Aristotelem Graeca (CAG),* ed. Maximilian Wallies (Berlin, 1891), sup. vol. II, pt. ii, p. 5.21ff. and p. 126.12ff. For further discussion of the commentators, see the chapter "Between Aristotle and Boethius."

40. Cf. De Pater, "La Fonction du lieu," p. 174. For scholars who agree with De Pater, see, for example, Eugène Thionville, *De la Théorie des lieux communs dans les Topiques d'Aristote* (Paris, 1855; reprinted Osnabrück, 1965), pp. 30ff.; and Friedrich Solmsen, *Die Entwicklung der aristotelischen Logik und Rhetorik* (Berlin, 1929), pp. 163–166. Solmsen's account has a somewhat different emphasis in his article "The Aristotelian Tradition in Ancient Rhetoric," in *Rhetorika,* ed. Rudolf Stark (Hildesheim, 1968). Cf. also William Grimaldi, *Studies in the Philosophy of Aristotle's Rhetoric* (Wiesbaden, 1972), pp. 117–119.

41. "La Fonction du lieu," p. 174.

those that are Topics "au sens strict," which always contain or consist in a principle, and those "au sens faible," which may consist in nothing but a strategy. De Pater readily admits that Aristotle did not explicitly make such a distinction, but he thinks it is necessary to do so if we are to give a coherent interpretation of an Aristotelian Topic. Though I think De Pater is right in thinking that we must take into consideration those Topics explicitly called Topics and consisting in strategies alone, his method of dealing with them seems simply to define them out of account; and I think it is possible to give a consistent description of an Aristotelian Topic without doing so.

First, the form of Topics (1)–(5) above is typical of that in the rest of the treatise. In the presentation of a Topic, even in those cases in which it includes both a strategy and a principle, Aristotle consistently says that the Topic is the strategy; the principle is added in a γάρ clause to explain or support the strategy. Second, all the examples I have found of Topics given as principles alone come from Book III. But in that Book, only one sort of dialectical problem is under consideration, namely, whether one of two things is better or more worthy of choice than the other; and *one* strategy governs the whole Book, which Aristotle gives at the very beginning of the Book: "Our inquiry has to do . . . with things that are closely related and concerning which we dispute . . . because we do not see any superiority of the one over the other. So it is clear . . . that if one or more points of superiority is shown, the mind will agree that *this,* whichever of the two happens to be superior, is more worthy of choice."[42] How does one get one's opponent to agree when the question is which of two things is better or more worthy of choice? Aristotle gives one sensible strategy at the outset: find some point of superiority of the one over the other. Having provided this general strategy, Aristotle throughout the rest of the Book contents himself with describing various principles about what makes one thing superior to another. Third, it is important to notice the general emphasis of the *Topics.* The eighth Book, which deals with the disputation itself and with methods for getting the better of one's opponent, is in keeping with what goes before. The preceding discussions of individual Topics are couched in terms of disputation rather than

42. *Top.* 116a4–12.

abstract logic or metaphysics; the discussion of a Topic is not an elaboration of a principle, explaining the logical relations involved in the principle, but has to do rather with what one's opponent has done and what can be said against him in consequence. The following discussion of a Topic is typical:

Again, if an accident which has a contrary is asserted, you must look to see whether what admits of the accident admits also of its contrary, for the same thing admits of contraries. For example, if your opponent has said that hatred follows anger, then hatred would be in the spirited faculty; for anger is in that faculty. You must, therefore, look to see whether its contrary, namely, friendship, is also in the spirited faculty; for if it is not there but in the appetitive faculty, then hatred cannot follow anger. Similarly, too, if he has declared that the appetitive faculty is ignorant; for if it were ignorant, it would also be capable of knowledge, and it is not a generally accepted opinion that the appetitive faculty is capable of knowledge.[43]

So I think that in the *Topics* a Topic is at least primarily a strategy for argument, a strategy not infrequently justified or explained by a principle.

In the *Rhetoric*, Aristotle makes two significant additions to the discussion of Topics as it occurs in the *Topics*.

First, he divides Topics into those that are common and those that are proper. Common Topics are those that will work equally well for a disputation or speech about any subject; proper Topics are those that function only in a disputation or speech about some particular subject, so that there are Topics proper to ethics, Topics proper to physics, and so on.[44] Though the distinction is not mentioned explicitly in the *Topics*, in the *Rhetoric*[45] Aristotle says that this distinction is common to both the *Topics* and the *Rhetoric*. Possibly, for Aristotle, a Topic that is a principle alone is a proper Topic and a Topic including or consisting in a strategy is a common Topic. De Pater argues that the Topics in Book III of the *Topics* are all proper rather than common Topics because, he says, they are the same as the Topics given in *Rhetoric* I.vii as proper Topics.[46] De Pater does not cite any passages from the *Rhetoric* in which the principles in *Rhetoric* I.vii are explicitly called Topics, and I have not been able to find any such passage. Instead, De

---

43. *Top.* 113a33–b6.   44. Cf. *Rhet.* I.ii.21–22 (1358a10–35).
45. *Rhet.* I.ii.22 (1358a29–30).   46. "La Fonction du lieu," p. 180.

Pater quotes Aristotle's identification of at least certain sorts of principles with εἴδη, and he argues that for Aristotle εἴδη and proper Topics are the same. Hence, if the principles in *Rhetoric* I.vii are εἴδη (as they seem to be), they are Topics. But, as De Pater admits, the evidence for whether or not εἴδη are proper Topics appears contradictory; and in one place Aristotle seems to distinguish principles, especially the group including those in *Rhetoric* I.vii, from Topics. In II.xxii.16 (1396b28–33), just as he is about to present the major discussion of Topics in the *Rhetoric*, Aristotle says that because he has earlier given propositions relating to the good and bad, noble and shameful, just and unjust, and so on; he has, in effect, already provided Topics on these subjects.[47] Aristotle seems to be saying that earlier in the book he has given propositions or premises (προτάσεις), not Topics; but that, in virtue of having provided such propositions, he has established for his reader the appropriate Topics for the subjects in question. The propositions he is referring to are those given in I.vi.1ff. (1362a15ff.), and very many of them are what I have been calling principles. If Topics *are* principles, at least sometimes, then there seems to be no point to Aristotle's remark; he could have said merely that the Topics for the subjects in question had been given previously.

Second, Aristotle defines a Topic in the *Rhetoric*. A Topic, he says, is an element encompassing many enthymemes: "I mean the same thing by 'element' and 'Topic,' for an element or a Topic is that within whose province many enthymemes fall."[48] But this second addition to the theory of Topics is not of much more help than the first for determining whether a Topic is primarily a strategy or a principle or for understanding the art in the *Topics*. It is hard to know precisely what Aristotle means by 'element' (στοιχεῖον),[49] especially as applied to dialectic and rhetoric; and enthy-

---

47. "σχεδὸν μὲν οὖν ἡμῖν περὶ ἕκαστον τῶν εἰδῶν τῶν χρησίμων καὶ ἀναγκαίων ἔχονται οἱ τόποι· ἐξειλεγμέναι γὰρ αἱ προτάσεις περὶ ἕκαστόν εἰσιν, ὥστε ἐξ ὧν δεῖ φέρειν τὰ ἐνθυμήματα τόπων περὶ ἀγαθοῦ ἢ κακοῦ . . . ὡσαύτως, εἰλημμένοι ἡμῖν ὑπάρχουσι πρότερον οἱ τόποι."

48. "τὸ γὰρ αὐτὸ λέγω στοιχεῖον καὶ τόπον· ἔστιν γὰρ στοιχεῖον καὶ τόπος εἰς ὃ πολλὰ ἐνθυμήματα ἐμπίπτει." *Rhet*, II.xxvi.1 (1403a17–18).

49. For a preliminary study of the term, see Walter A. De Pater, *Les Topiques d'Aristote et la dialectique platonicienne: La méthodologie de la définition* (Fribourg, 1965), pp. 110–115.

memes might equally well be thought to fall within the province of a principle or a strategy.

As for what Aristotle explicitly calls Topics in the *Rhetoric*, they are of this sort: "One Topic for demonstrative enthymemes is from opposites; for it is necessary to see if an opposite belongs to an opposite. . . . For example, temperance is good, for incontinence is harmful."[50] Or, again, "Another Topic is from a judgment concerning the same or a similar or an opposite case";[51] or, "Another [Topic is this]: since in most things it happens that some good and bad accompanies the same thing, one can persuade or dissuade, accuse or defend, and praise or blame on the basis of what results from [the thing being discussed]."[52] These Topics are all strategies rather than principles, though as in the second example, the strategy is not completely spelled out; almost all the Topics Aristotle gives for enthymemes are clearly of the same sort.[53]

So I think that the evidence in the *Rhetoric*, too, tends to indicate that a Topic is primarily a strategy rather than a principle and confirms the similar impression gained from the *Topics*.[54] Part

50. *Rhet.* II.xxiii.1 (1397a7–10). By 'demonstrative enthymeme' Aristotle seems to mean a constructive rather than a destructive enthymeme; in *Rhet.* II.xxii. 14–15 (1396b23–27), he says, "Demonstrative enthymemes differ from refutative enthymemes as syllogism and refutation differ in dialectic; the demonstrative enthymeme draws conclusions from premises agreed to [by the opponent], but the refutative enthymeme draws conclusions which have been in dispute."

51. *Rhet.* II.xxiii.12 (1398b21). 52. *Rhet.* II.xxiii.14 (1399a11–14).

53. Cf. *Rhet.* II.xxii.13–II.xxiii.30 (1399a7–1400b33).

54. But cf. De Pater, "La Fonction du lieu," and *Les Topiques d'Aristote*, pp. 140ff. According to De Pater ("La Fonction du lieu," p. 173), a Topic is "une formule de recherche," either "des propositions" (principles) or "des types (classes) de propositions (*loci a persona* ou 'lieux des contraires')." He thinks that in the *Topics* a Topic is "une formule de recherche en tant qu'il est une règle," whereas in the *Rhetoric* it is "une formule de recherche en tant qu'il est une loi . . . ou du moins en tant qu'il n'est pas formulé comme une règle" (ibid.). Surprisingly, in "La Fonction" De Pater considers only the passage in Book I of the *Rhetoric*, where it is not at all clear that Aristotle is presenting Topics, and he leaves altogether out of account the passages in Book II in which Aristotle talks directly about Topics. Consequently, De Pater cites the lack of strategies in the *Rhetoric*'s presentation of Topics as evidence for his view that a Topic is a law or principle. Even in the *Topics*, he concludes, "le lieu . . . est une formule de recherche non pas en tant qu'il est formulé comme une règle, mais déjà en tant qu'il est une loi. En d'autres termes: la règle explicite la loi; celle-ci suffirait" (ibid.). But thinking of the Topics in the *Rhetoric* as *laws*, if it is not to seem simply flying in the face of the evidence, requires justification and explanation which De Pater does not supply. For a recent discussion of De Pater's work, see H. Roelants, "De methodologie van de *Topika*," *Tijdschrift voor Filosofie*, 28 (1966), 495–517, and the excellent study by Jürgen Sprute, "Topos und Enthymem in der aristotelischen Rhetorik," *Hermes*, 103 (1975), 68–90.

of the importance of this conclusion is that it ties the concerns of the *Topics* more closely to the context of disputation, making it less a peculiar treatise on logic than a handbook on how to succeed at playing Socrates; and this view of the *Topics* will make a difference in the way we understand the art it wants to teach. Clearly, however, a strategy and its corresponding principle are very closely related: once one has chosen a particular principle, one is committed to certain strategies, and a particular strategy may require certain principles.

How an individual Topic functions in finding arguments is not hard to determine.[55] A Topic is, as Theophrastus says, definite in outline but indefinite in regard to particulars;[56] that is, a Topic is a general statement (or strategy) that can cover many specific cases. Take, for example, one of the Topics mentioned earlier: "[You must see] if the genus and the species are not in the same [category], but one is a substance and the other a quality, or one a relative and the other a quality. . . . To speak generally, the genus must be under the same category as the species."[57] This Topic can be used to refute a number of arguments, namely, all those in which the opponent maintains that one thing is the genus of something else and the two things in question fall into different categories. Aristotle gives an example in the same passage. Suppose the arguer's opponent maintains that knowledge is a species of what is good; the arguer chooses the strategy of seeing whether the putative genus and species fall into the same category, and he sees that they do not. Then he makes his argument as follows. He gets the opponent to admit first that goodness is a quality and then that knowledge is a relative; he then brings the argument to a conclusion by implicitly or explicitly using the principle that a species and its genus must be in the same category. Depending on the relative obscurity of the principle and the obtuseness of the opponent, the principle may or may not be an explicit part of the argumentation; and, of course, not every strategy requires a particular principle.

A Topic, then, is something like a basic recipe or blueprint, ac-

55. For a detailed but, I think, mistaken account of the way in which a Topic functions, see De Pater, *Les Topiques d'Aristote*, pp. 93–100, 129–139, 147–150.

56. "τῇ περιγραφῇ μὲν ὡρισμένος . . . τοῖς δὲ καθ' ἕκαστα ἀόριστος"; in Alexander of Aphrodisias, *In Top.*, CAG; II, pt. ii, pp. 5.2ff.

57. *Top.* 120b36–121a7.

cording to which one can produce many things the same in structure but differing in detail and in material. Only a few, or perhaps even only one, of these blueprints for argument will serve to produce an argument for a given dialectical problem. For example, the Topic having to do with genus and species being in the same category will not produce a refutation if the genus and species in question are in the same category or if the question is not about genus and species. Faced with a particular problem for which he wants to find an argument, the arguer must apparently go through the various Topics in his mind to find one that will work for his problem; and, since Aristotle gives several hundred Topics in the *Topics*, the procedure for finding arguments seems unwieldy. One is tempted to think that, though Aristotle has not given his students simply a variety of finished products in lieu of an art, like the Sophists he disapproves of,[58] still, what he has done amounts only to giving his students a boxful of blueprints for producing such finished products. Such an impression, I think, is erroneous.

It is clear that the Topics are generally ordered according to the predicables. Topics useful for problems where the predicate is an accident are discussed in Books II–III; Topics involving genus and property are found in Books IV and V respectively; and Books VI–VII contain Topics involving definition. If Aristotle's *Topics* seems like a boxful of blueprints, it is, at any rate, equipped with indexing tabs. Once the arguer has determined which predicable is being used in his problem, he has specified the section of the *Topics* in which Topics appropriate to his problem are found. Still, the unwieldiness of this method is only a little reduced.

But what has been frequently overlooked is that the Topics on a particular predicable are ordered, too. In Book IV containing Topics about genus, for example, principles associated with Topics from the first part of the Book are of this sort:[59]

(1) The genus is predicated of everything under the same species. [120b 19–20]
(2) The genus must be under the same category as the species. [121a5–7]
(3) The species admits the definition of the genus, but the genus does not admit the definition of the species. [121a13–14]

58. *Soph. El.* 183b36–184a8.
59. I pick principles rather than strategies or strategies combined with principles to compare here because the principles alone are shorter and more quickly and easily brought together to provide an overview.

(4) Whatever the species is predicated of, the genus must also be predicated of. [121a25–26]

(5) What partakes of the genus must also partake of one of the species [of that genus]. [121a34–35]

Those in the middle of the Book are different:

(1) The genus and the species are synonymous.[60] [123a28–29]

(2) Every genus is predicated of its species in its proper [that is, unmetaphorical] sense. [123a34–35]

(3) The contrary species must be in the contrary genus, if there is a contrary to the genus. [123b6–7]

(4) If the genus is contrary to something, so is the species. [123b31–32]

The Topics in the last part of the Book frequently do not have accompanying principles; what principles there are tend to be of this sort:

(1) There are some things which cannot be placed in one genus [only]. [126b8]

(2) There are several things which accompany everything; for example, being and oneness are among those that accompany everything [and what accompanies everything cannot be a genus]. [127a27–28]

(3) [When both the genus and species have contraries, and one contrary is better than another in each case], it is generally held that the genus of the better species is also the better genus. [127b12–13]

This ordering of the Topics within a Book can be interpreted or characterized in different ways. Eugène Thionville, who apparently originally discovered this ordering, characterized it as "d'abord les lieux qui proviennent de la nature du prédicable en question; ensuite ceux des choses inhérentes au sujet ou à l'attribut traité (son antécédent, son conséquent, ses inflexions et coordonnés), et finalement ceux du rapprochement avec d'autres sujets ou attributs (les contraires, les comparaisons)."[61] De Pater criticizes Thionville's ordering as inaccurate, and suggests the following order: "d'abord les lieux qui se tirent de la nature du prédicable, et ensuite les lieux les plus utiles [for example, Topics from opposites or from the more and the less]."[62]

But perhaps we should look at these different groups of Topics

---

60. That is, they share a name that has the same definition in each case; see *Cat.* 1a6ff.

61. As De Pater puts it in *Les Topiques d'Aristote*, p. 206; cf. Thionville, *De la Théorie des lieux communs*, p. 63.

62. De Pater, *Les Topiques d'Aristote*, p. 206.

as at least some of the Greek commentators and Latin rhetoricians who discussed Topics did. In light of the Ciceronian and Themistian treatments of the Topics, we might look at the ordering of Topics within a Book as intrinsic, intermediate, and extrinsic.[63] First are the Topics that depend in some way on the nature of the predicable in question; for example, a genus must be in the same category as its species, or, the genus must be predicated of all the things its species is predicated of. These are intrinsic Topics. Then there are Topics that in part have to do with the nature of the predicable but in part also with something outside the predicable. A Topic such as the one that genus and species share a name (are synonymous) seems to be intermediate. Last, there are those Topics that are not about the basic nature of the predicable but instead give peculiarities of the particular predicable or corollary rules about its use.

Whatever the precise characterization of the order of Topics within a Book, there clearly is some order and it includes a movement from Topics closely related to the nature of the predicable to those related only tangentially.

Seeing this order gives us, I think, an important key to the τέχνη in the *Topics*. Previous interpretations of the Topics have included a complicated process for employing Topics. De Pater gives the following analysis of an argument using a Topic:[64]

Phase indépendante de la preuve	Preuve
[Enquête] (premier instrument)	[Garanties] Une même chose est susceptible des contraires (lieu commun)
(données)	[Raison] La partie appétitive de l'âme n'est pas susceptible de science; 'science' est le contraire d' 'ignorance'.	[Conclusion] L'ignorance ne réside pas dans la partie appétitive de l'âme.

63. See the chapter on Boethius below. The use Boethius makes of these terms is slightly different from the use I make of them here. For Boethius, a Topic is intrinsic if, for example, it has to do not with the nature of the *predicable* in question (for example, genus) but rather with the nature of the *specific instance* of the predicable (for example, animal).

64. "La Fonction du lieu," p. 187.

It is important to notice two things about this interpretation of the τέχνη in the *Topics*. First, the primary function of a Topic in this scheme is not in *finding* arguments but in *validating* them. De Pater assigns some heuristic function to a Topic, but it is the minor one of aiding the instrument to find the *"données."* The chief role of a Topic is probative. A Topic is employed in De Pater's scheme not to discover the *"raison"* for the conclusion or the conclusion itself but to "guarantee" the *inference* from the *"raison"* to the conclusion. But the ancient tradition growing out of Aristotle's *Rhetoric* and *Topics* clearly assigns the Topics to *inventio*, to the job of finding rather than judging or validating arguments.[65] And it makes sense that the function of a Topic should be discovery. The Topics are the heart of a method intended to make a man a ready arguer, good at both the questioner's and the answerer's roles in a dialectical disputation. It is not so clear how being able to validate the passage from premises to conclusion will make a man good at dialectical questioning and answering, but it is perfectly plain that the ability to find arguments will do so.

Second, though De Pater's scheme of reasoning is complicated and neat, the dialectical art that corresponds to it is the opposite. Since on De Pater's view Topics are general principles whose function is to validate arguments and the *Topics* amounts simply to a boxful of such principles, the τέχνη which the *Topics* claims to present is basically just the unwieldy method I described earlier. A person who wants to argue for a certain dialectical thesis will go through the three hundred or four hundred Topics in Aristotle's list until he finds one that suits his conclusion and then will build his argument around that Topic. The division of the list according to the predicables and the ordering within each of the four groups reduces the unwieldiness of this method only a little. Furthermore, a good deal of a dialectical disputation involves extemporaneous arguing, since one cannot know ahead of time what line his opponent will argue; and the cumbersomeness of this method makes it is hard to see how it can help with extemporaneous arguments at all.

But once we have seen Aristotle's emphasis on the predicables, I think we can sketch another interpretation of his τέχνη. According to Aristotle, every dialectical problem, question, and conclusion is

65. Cf. Solmsen, "Aristotelian Tradition," pp. 331–337.

predicative or reducible to one that is predicative, and arguing for a dialectical conclusion will consist in showing that the predicate is or is not a predicate of the subject at issue.[66] Every predicate is subsumed under one or another of the predicables, and the list of Topics is grouped according to the four predicables. Within the group for each predicable, the Topics are ordered by the degree to which they have to do with the nature of the predicable of that group. So what we seem to have in the *Topics* is a kind of complicated lore of predicables. The ordered lists of Topics can be thought of as manifesting or teaching the essence and accidents of each of the predicables. A genus, for example, has a certain nature. It is predicated of *every* member of the species falling under it. It is always part of the essence of whatever it is predicated of. And so on. In addition, it has certain accidents and peculiarities. It shares a name (is synonymous) with its species. It cannot accompany everything. If two species are contraries and one is better than another, the genus of the better species is the better genus. And so on. Book IV of the *Topics,* from which these observations about genus are drawn, will make a careful reader so familiar with the character of genus that he will readily recognize when a given predicate in a thesis is a genus and when it is not.

It would be foolish to make use of the *Topics* by trying to memorize all the Topics in the treatise and then searching one's memory for the appropriate Topic to use on any given occasion; one would then be treating the *Topics* as if it were an indexed but unwieldy boxful of blueprints for arguments. But one can use the *Topics* to become thoroughly familiar with the nature of the predicables and the way they work. With such a thorough grasp on the predicables, one can dispense with blueprints. Because one understands the nature of the predicables, strategies and principles having to do with them will suggest themselves naturally. Since all dialectical problems involve predicables, a man familiar with the nature and behavior of the predicables will be able to find arguments quickly, and so he will be able to argue well extemporaneously, as he needs to do in a dialectical disputation. If Aristotle's Topics are learned and understood, then, they do constitute a τέχνη for dialectical disputation.

66. *Top.* 101b15–36, 103b1–19.

Dialectic and Boethius's
De topicis differentiis

De topicis differentiis [1] (De top. diff.) is an advanced treatise on
Topics that builds on Boethius's In Ciceronis Topica (ICT).[2] De top.
diff. is Boethius's attempt to present a definitive work on Topics
and to produce a cogent method for discovering arguments. He
explains two main divisions of dialectical Topics, Cicero's and
Themistius's, and reconciles one with the other; he also expounds
rhetorical Topics and shows their differences from and similarities
to dialectical Topics.[3] The first Book of De top. diff. is a general introduction, containing definitions and discussions of key terms.
The next two Books contain his treatment of dialectical Topics.
Book II describes Themistius's division of the Topics and gives examples for each of his twenty-eight Topics. In Book III, Boethius
expounds Cicero's division, much as he did Themistius's in the
preceding Book; he completes the Book by comparing and recon-
ciling the two divisions. The fourth Book is completely devoted to
rhetorical Topics, explaining what they are and comparing them
with dialectical Topics. It includes a theoretical discussion of the
nature of rhetoric, which Boethius claims is original work and not
to be found in his sources.

In this chapter, I will not consider rhetorical Topics.[4] They are
very different from the dialectical Topics of Cicero or Themistius—

1. Ed. J. P. Migne, Patrologia Latina, LXIV, 1173–1216.
2. PL, LXIV, 1039–1174; Ciceronis Opera, ed. J. C. Orelli and G. Baiterus (Zurich,
1833), V, pt. I. References to this treatise will be given for both the Orelli and the
PL editions.
3. For background information on De top. diff. and for Boethius's views of dialectic, see the Introduction.
4. For some discussion of the rhetorical Topics, see my notes to Book IV of De
top. diff.

or of Aristotle—and require a completely separate treatment. The dialectical Topics are so complicated and difficult, and so little has been written by modern scholars on Boethius's understanding of dialectic, that it is enough for this work to provide a preliminary analysis of Boethius's dialectical Topics.

Unlike Aristotle, Boethius recognizes two different types of Topics. First, he says, a Topic is a maximal proposition (*maxima propositio*), or principle; but there is a second kind of Topic, which he calls the differentia of a maximal proposition, or just Differentia.[5] Both 'maximal proposition' and 'Differentia' are technical terms that will be explained in detail in this chapter. The Differentiae are the real instruments of Boethius's art of finding arguments; but maximal propositions are also important; and Boethius begins his theoretical discussion of the Topics[6] by explaining what a maximal proposition is and showing how it functions.

Boethius thinks maximal propositions are what Aristotle calls Topics.[7] When Aristotle gives a Topic, he generally presents both a strategy for argumentation and a principle. Some interpreters of Aristotle's Topics, such as Theophrastus, consider only the principles to be Topics; others, such as Alexander of Aphrodisias, think Aristotle means both the strategy and the principle to be Topics; and it is not impossible that Aristotle understood the strategies alone to be the real Topics.[8] In suggesting that maximal propositions are Aristotle's Topics, Boethius is in effect allying himself with Theophrastus's interpretation. And, I think, Boethius begins his treatment of dialectical Topics by discussing maximal propositions, even though his main interest is in the Differentiae, at least in part because he wants to begin with what he understands as the traditional, Aristotelian method before he gives the newer method that relies on the Differentiae.

Boethius takes pains to make clear what a maximal proposition is. In *De top. diff.* 1185A8–B5, he says:

There are some propositions which not only are known per se but also have nothing more fundamental by which they are demonstrated, and these are called maximal and principal [propositions]. And there are others for which the first and maximal propositions provide belief. So of

5. I am capitalizing 'differentia' when it is used to refer to a Boethian Topic to avoid confusion with differentia as one of the predicables.
6. *De top. diff.* 1185A3ff.   7. *ICT* 282.44–283.2 (*PL* 1054B2–6).
8. See my discussion in the preceding chapter on Aristotle.

all things which are brought into question, the very first to be agreed to must be those which can provide belief for other things in such a way that nothing more known than they can be found. For an argument is what produces belief regarding something which is in doubt, and it ought to be more known and more readily believable than what is proved. Hence, those maximal [propositions] known per se so that they need no proof from without must impart belief to all arguments.[9]

So maximal propositions are truths known per se, or self-evident truths. They are not proved by any other propositions, and knowledge of them is not derived knowledge, drawn from other known propositions; they are, as Boethius would say, more known than any other propositions.

Maximal propositions have two major functions in argumentation. To see what those functions are, it will be helpful to examine and dismiss a plausible misconception of their function.

So far, Boethius seems to mean that the role of maximal propositions in argumentation is to ensure the truth of a conclusion by ensuring the truth of its premises either directly or indirectly; and here Boethius seems to be relying on Aristotle's theory of demonstration. Aristotle holds that most knowledge comes from previously acquired knowledge. The premises of an argument intended to produce knowledge must be better known than the conclusion, or they could not constitute evidence for what is in doubt, and the premises of one such argument may be the conclusions of other arguments. But unless there is an infinite regress, there must be some starting point for the hierarchy of things known, and there cannot be an infinite regress if there is to be knowledge. In other words, there must be propositions known not by being proved from other, better-known propositions, but by being known per se. Such propositions are the source for all demonstration because all other known propositions are derived directly from propositions known per se or from other propositions that are so derived.[10] Each science has its own set of truths known

9. "Nam cum sint aliae propositiones quae cum per se notae sint, tum nihil ulterius habeant quo demonstrentur, atque hae maximae et principales vocentur, sintque aliae quarum fidem primae ac maximae suppleant propositiones, necesse est ut omnium quae dubitantur, illae antiquissimam teneant probationem, quae ita aliis facere fidem possunt, ut ipsis nihil notius queat inveniri. Nam si argumentum est quod rei dubiae facit fidem, idque notius ac probabilius esse oportet quam illud est quod probatur, necesse est ut argumentis omnibus illa maxima fidem tribuant, quae ita per se nota sunt, ut aliena probatione non egeant."

10. Cf. *An. Pos.* 71a1–72b25.

per se that are fundamental to it and are not demonstrable by any propositions within the science in question or (except in the cases of subaltern sciences) by any propositions from other sciences.[11] By deriving conclusions from these truths known per se, the science arrives at the body of knowledge proper to it.

Boethius's maximal propositions seem to be just such self-evident truths. All true propositions, Boethius seems to be saying, are either self-evident or not self-evident; those that are not self-evident are shown to be true by being traced back to self-evident propositions. Hence, self-evident propositions provide the basis of belief for all argument. The conclusion of an argument is derived either from a maximal proposition or from propositions that are themselves derived, directly or indirectly, from maximal propositions. So Boethius seems to mean to teach the finding of arguments by teaching what look like Aristotle's axioms or first principles of the sciences; given the first principles of each science, from which the rest of the science is derived, one should be able to find arguments regarding whatever is in question.

But if the account of Topics that I have been sketching were correct, then the art of Topics would begin to collapse into demonstration; the art of finding arguments would be the art of producing a proof of some proposition from the first principles of the science appropriate to that proposition. As Boethius[12] and Aristotle[13] both clearly indicate, however, the art of Topics belongs to dialectic; and dialectic and demonstration are very different, as Boethius himself is keenly aware. In the introductory Book of *De top. diff.*, he spends some time elaborating on the difference,[14] sketching, for example, the different aims of the "demonstrator" (philosopher) and the dialectician, and explaining the different sorts of argument appropriate to each of the two. He points out that the art of Topics is useful primarily to the dialectician but that the demonstrator will find it helpful as well, and he supports his point by explaining what sorts of argument the Topics provide. In light of his elaborate distinction between dialectic and demonstration and his detailed explanation showing that the Topics belong primarily to dialectic, it is not sensible to suppose that Boethius means maximal propositions to function in argumenta-

11. Cf. *An. Pos.* 75b37–76a30.   12. Cf. *De top. diff.* 1182B5–15.
13. *Top.* 100a18-25.   14. 1181C10-1182C12.

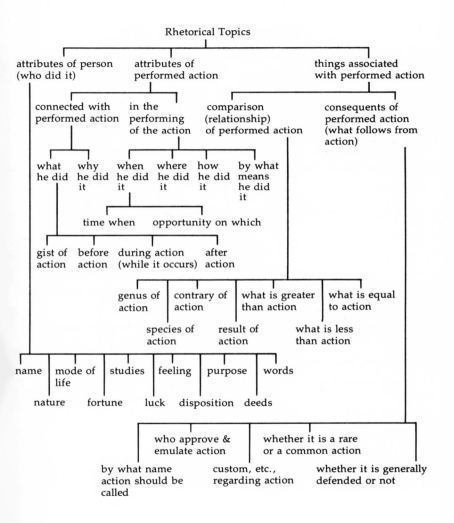

INSERTION FOLLOWING PAGE 155

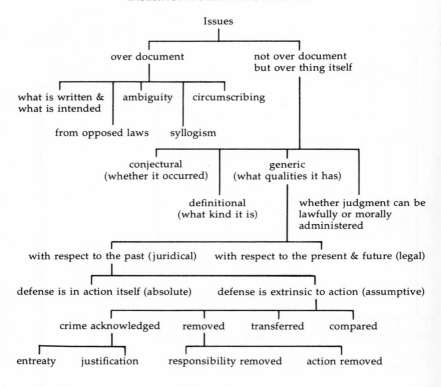

tion as Aristotelian first principles; and, consequently, the account of Topics as axioms of the sciences is not viable.

How, then, do the Topics function in argumentation? After his theoretical discussion of maximal propositions (quoted in part above), Boethius gives an example to make his point clear: "Suppose the task is to demonstrate that an envious man is not wise. An envious man is one who disparages the good of others. But a wise man does not disparage the good of others. Therefore, an envious man is not wise. . . . belief for this syllogism is provided by that proposition by which we know that things whose definitions are different are themselves also different."[15]

Here it is possible to make another very misleading mistake. Boethius gives the premises of the argument in the example as indefinite propositions. Indefinite propositions may be read either as universal or as particular; so the first premise of the argument may be taken to mean either 'Every envious man disparages the good of others' or 'Some envious man disparages the good of others.' We know, however, that the argument has to do with the definitions of the things being discussed, and definitions are never particular. So it is tempting to suppose that Boethius means his indefinite premises to be read as universals and that the argument is a syllogism with one negative and one affirmative universal premise; that is, it is tempting to read the argument in the example as if it were this:

(1) No wise man disparages the good of others.
(2) Every envious man disparages the good of others.
(3) Therefore, no envious man is wise.

This argument, as Boethius unquestionably knows, is a valid, second-figure Aristotelian syllogism (Cesare); so the maximal proposition is not needed for the validity of the argument. In this case, furthermore, the maximal proposition—"Things whose defi-

---

15. 1185C10-D3. "*Sit propositum demonstrare quoniam invidus sapiens non est. Invidus est qui alienis affligitur bonis; sapiens autem bonis non affligitur alienis; invidus igitur sapiens non est. . . . Est enim huic syllogismo fides ex ea propositione per quam cognoscimus, quorum diversa est diffinitio, ipsa quoque diversa esse.*" Contemporary usage tends to take 'definition' to mean the defining proposition; ancient and medieval usage, on the other hand, often takes 'definition' to mean the predicate of a defining proposition. To avoid complicating the terminology, I am using 'definition' in a systematically ambiguous way. For Boethius's use of '*syllogismus*,' see note 5 to Book. II above and note 43 below.

nitions are different are themselves also different"—clearly is not a principle on which either the first or the second premise is based; it does not ensure the truth of either (1) or (2). On this interpretation, then, the maximal proposition seems to have no role to play in the argumentation; it is not required as a rule of inference, and it is no evidence for the truth of either premise.

Such a result should show that it is a mistake to neglect the indefinite quantity of the premises in the argument as Boethius gives it. The argument as it occurs in the text is not a syllogism in Cesare and does need its maximal proposition in order to be valid. If we keep Boethius's premises indefinite, the argument he gives amounts to this:

(4) *One who disparages the good of others* is a definition of envious man.

(5) A wise man does not disparage the good of others.

(6) Every definition is predicated (primarily) of its species and (secondarily) of every individual under that species.

(6¹) Therefore, *one who disparages the good of others* is not a definition of wise man.

(6²) Everything that is defined has one and only one definition.[16]

(7) Therefore, the definition of envious man is different from the definition of wise man.

(8) Things whose definitions are different are themselves also different.

(9) Therefore, an envious man is not wise.

(8) is, of course, the maximal proposition; and in this analysis of the argument, in which Boethius's premises are kept indefinite, it is necessary for the validity of the argument.[17]

---

16. Premises (6) and (6²) are taken from standard ancient views of definition. See the two chapters on differentia below.

17. This argument is much more complex than it appears to be, and whether it is really valid is unclear. It is enough for my purposes in this chapter to show how the maximal proposition functions on Boethius's view if the quantity of the premises is not altered, but I want to sketch here a few of the difficulties with this argument. First, from (4) to (7), the argument seems to be about species, and (7) might be read as 'The definition of the species *envious man* is different from the definition of the species *wise man*.' But the conclusion clearly is meant to be about individuals: for every man, if he is envious, he is not wise. The maximal proposition presumably is meant to span the gap between the conclusion about species and the conclusion

Boethius gives examples of arguments for all the Topics, and the premises of these arguments are almost always indefinite.[18] In some of the arguments, it is very clear that the maximal proposition is required for validity. For example, in 1189C15–D3 Boethius says, "Again, if someone argues that the Moors do not have weapons, he will say they do not use weapons because they lack iron. The maximal proposition: where the matter is lacking, what is made from the matter is also lacking."[19] Here the only premise is 'The Moors lack iron.' To make a valid argument for the conclusion Boethius wants, we need to recognize the relationship between iron and weapons and to include the maximal proposition in the argumentation.

---

about individuals. But to do so, the maximal proposition would have to be taken as 'Things belonging to species whose definitions are different are themselves different,' and such a statement is not true; *animal* and *man*, for example, have different definitions, but the same thing can belong to both species. If the maximal proposition is taken as 'Individual things whose definitions are different are themselves different' or as 'Species whose definitions are different are themselves different,' then on ancient and medieval views of definition the maximal proposition is true; but on such a reading of (8), the inference from (7) to (9) is no longer valid. The context of the argument suggests that Boethius might be thinking of the maximal proposition as 'Things belonging to species whose definitions are *incompatible* are themselves different (or incompatible).' But the argument seems to establish at most that the definitions in question are different, not that they are incompatible. Second, in analyzing the argument one must be careful to take into account that *envious man* and *wise man* are not true species but only species *per accidens*; the definition of a true species is predicated *as a definition* of its members, but the definition of a species *per accidens* is predicated of its members as an accident. *One who disparages the good of others* is not the definition of any individual man who happens to be envious but only one of his accidents. I am indebted to Nicholas Sturgeon for pointing out many of the difficulties in this argument.

18. The fact that Boethius gives almost all his examples for Topics with indefinite rather than universal or particular propositions, a practice imitated by later medieval writers on Topics, is highly suggestive, but frustrating. Indefinite propositions seem to be carefully relegated to dialectic and universal and particular propositions to syllogistic demonstration. But the reason for such a separation is altogether obscure. Did Boethius think of dialectic and demonstration as different kinds of reasoning that had as their natural subject matter these two different kinds of propositions? Or is it simply that dialectic grew out of spoken disputations, in which indefinite propositions are more common than universal or particular propositions? Does Aristotle perhaps hold some theory requiring such a separation and is Boethius simply following well-established tradition? Though Boethius and later medievals maintain the separation rather consistently, none of them, as far as I know, makes much of it or gives an explanation for it.

19. "*Rursus si quis Mauros arma non habere contendat, dicet idcirco eos armis minime uti, quod his ferrum desit. Maxima propositio, ubi materia deest, et quod ex materia efficitur, desit.*"

Both the examples I have just given are predicative arguments;[20] but Boethius gives conditional arguments as well, and there the role of the maximal proposition is somewhat different. For instance, in 1188D11–1189A4, Boethius says: "Similarly, [arguments are made] from those parts which are called parts of a complete thing. Suppose there is a question whether the art of medicine is advantageous. . . . We will say: if it is advantageous to drive out disease and minister to health and heal wounds, then the art of medicine is advantageous; but to drive out disease, minister to health, and heal wounds is advantageous; therefore, the art of medicine is advantageous."[21] The maximal proposition for this argument is given earlier, in connection with the preceding argument: "What inheres in the individual parts must inhere in the whole" (1188D7–8).[22] The argument Boethius gives here is a straightforward example of *modus ponens*, and the maximal proposition is not needed to make the argument valid. But it is required to verify the first premise of the argument; it validates the passage from antecedent to consequent in the argument's conditional premise. The conditional premise can be thought of as the conclusion of an argument very like that we saw in the two predicative arguments we had before. It is derived from an argument in which, as before, we need to recognize a relationship and apply the maximal proposition:

(10) Driving out disease, ministering to health, and healing wounds are the parts of the art of medicine.

(11) What inheres in the individual parts inheres in the whole.

(12) Therefore, if advantage inheres in driving out disease, ministering to health, and healing wounds, it also inheres in the art of medicine.

20. 'Categorical' and 'predicative' are, respectively, Greek-based and Latin-based terms for the same thing. Similarly, 'hypothetical' and 'conditional' are Greek- and Latin-based equivalents. Boethius uses now one, now another, member of each pair, without any change in meaning (see 1183C5-7); and my discussion of his work follows suit.

21. *Item ab his partibus quae integri partes esse dicuntur; sit quaestio an sit utilis medicina. . . . dicemus: si depelli morbos salutemque servari mederique vulneribus utile est, utilis medicina est; at depelli morbos, servari salutem, mederique vulneribus utile est, utilis igitur medicina est."*

22. For a discussion of this maximal proposition, which seems to be a formula for committing the fallacy of composition, see my notes to the appropriate passage of the text.

So maximal propositions function in argumentation as guarantors of validity or of soundness. In Boethius's predicative arguments based on indefinite propositions, they are general premises essential to the validity of the argument; in hypothetical arguments, they validate the passage from antecedent to consequent in the conditional—that is, they verify the conditional premise. Boethius's summary of his discussion of maximal propositions confirms the view of them acquired by looking at his examples. He says that a maximal proposition "gives force to arguments and to propositions"[23] (1185D10–11); "by means of them the consequent arises and the conclusion becomes ratified"[24] (1185D14–1186A1); and they "contain within themselves . . . the deriving of the conclusion itself"[25] (1186A3–4).

So far I have presented one function of maximal propositions—supporting arguments—but they have another as well. What Boethius wants to teach in *De top. diff.* is, after all, not a method for supporitng certain dialectical arguments containing indefinite or conditional premises, but rather a method for finding arguments. How do maximal propositions aid in finding arguments?

If we look at the three examples of maximal propositions we have had so far—

(8) Things whose definitions are different are themselves also different.

(11) What inheres in the individual parts inheres in the whole.

(13) Where the matter is lacking, what is made from the matter is also lacking.—

it is clear that all three can be expressed as conditionals:

(8') If the definitions of things are different, the things themselves are different.

(11') If something inheres in the individual parts, it inheres also in the whole.

(13') If the matter is lacking, what is made from the matter is also lacking.

The conclusions of the two predicative arguments are

23. *"vim tamen argumentis et propositionibus subministrat."*
24. *"per eas fit consequens et rata conclusio."*
25. *"intra se . . . . ipsius conclusionis consequentiam tenent."*

(9) An envious man is not wise (is not a wise man).

(14) The Moors lack weapons.

The conclusion of the hypothetical argument is

(15) The art of medicine is expedient.

The conclusion of the argument justifying the conditional premise used in that hypothetical argument is

(12) If advantage inheres in driving out disease, ministering to health, and healing wounds, it also inheres in the art of medicine.

Thus, (9), (14), and (15) are instantiations of the consequents in (8'), (13'), and (11') respectively; that is, if the maximal propositions are thought of as conditionals, the conclusions of both the predicative and hypothetical arguments supported by those maximal propositions are particular cases of the consequents in their maximal propositions. The conditional premise (12) is different. It is an instantiation of the whole conditional (11') which is its maximal proposition; it is a particular case not of the consequent of its maximal proposition but of the entire maximal proposition.

But to think of Boethius's predicative maximal propositions as conditionals may be a mistake. Boethius is sensitive to the difference between predicatives and conditionals, and he elaborates the distinction in Book I of *De top. diff.*[26] Most of the maximal propositions he presents are given as predicatives rather than as conditionals; and if he chooses one form over the other, he may do so deliberately, though no appropriate and significant reason for doing so is apparent from the text. Perhaps, then, in the interest of accuracy the maximal propositions should be kept as predicatives and not read as conditionals.

If the maximal propositions presented as predicatives[27] are considered as such, the conclusions of the arguments in Boethius's three examples might be thought of more roughly as instances of

---

26. See 1175A12ff.; see also 1177B7–1180A11.

27. Boethius occasionally gives a maximal proposition as hypothetical. It is easy to distinguish between those given as predicative and those given as hypothetical, though the distinction is sometimes easier to see in Latin than in English. For example, it seems that (13) "Where the matter is lacking, what is made from the matter is also lacking" could be read as either predicative or hypothetical, but the Latin construction strongly suggests a predicative reading.

their maximal propositions or as cases falling under the generalization that is the maximal proposition. For instance, we might think of (9) 'An envious man is not wise' as presenting a particular case covered by its maximal proposition. Its maximal proposition is (8) "Things whose definitions are different are themselves also different," and (9) seems to come to this: 'An envious man and a wise man (that is, things whose definitions are different) are (themselves also) different.' (14) might be read in this way: 'Moors (that is, people who lack the matter iron) lack weapons (that is, what is made from iron).' And so on.

Maximal propositions, then, are generalizations that prove some conclusion because the conclusion is an instance either of the whole generalization or of the generalization's consequent in case the maximal proposition is a conditional. A maximal proposition helps in finding arguments because it is the principle that gives the argument its force; it is the generalization on which the rest of the argument depends. Once one has the appropriate maximal proposition for a dialectical question, it is not hard to construct the argument or the general outline of the argument for that question.[28] For example, given the question 'Is an envious man wise?' and the maximal proposition "Things whose definitions are different are themselves also different," an arguer has the heart of his argument; the rest of the argument will consist in giving the definitions of wise man and envious man and showing that the two are different. Even if the arguer cannot immediately construct the argument (because of his ignorance, for example, of the definition of envious man), he knows what is needed to do so, namely, differing definitions.

It may occur to someone to wonder why Boethius fusses with such complications. The argument about the envious man, for example, can easily be turned into an Aristotelian syllogism, as I showed above. Why bother with all the complexities of dialectical argument when straightforward syllogism seems so much simpler? To see the answer to the question, it is important to notice that Boethius defines an argument in psychological rather than logical terms: an argument, he says, is what produces belief regarding what was in doubt (1180C4–5). The word to emphasize here, I

---

28. Boethius leaves the criteria for appropriateness to his reader's intuition. The way one acquires the maximal proposition for a given question will be discussed later.

think, is 'belief': the dialectician's purpose is to produce belief. The aim of the questioner in a dialectical disputation is to get the answerer to agree to the questioner's thesis; both the questioner and the answerer work at producing conviction for their positions.[29]

Because the aim of dialectic is conviction, the techniques of demonstration and syllogistic argument are unsuited to it. Take, for example, the argument about the envious man, which is a syllogism in Cesare. Unless the hearer of the argument knows Aristotelian logic and knows how to recognize examples of valid syllogistic moods, belief in the conclusion of the argument will not be provided for him because he recognizes the *form* of the argument as a valid Aristotelian syllogism. For hearers without that specialized knowledge (and these are most hearers) belief will in fact come because the conclusion has been shown or assumed to be an instance of or a case falling under a tacitly understood and generally accepted truth. Aristotle himself says that in most cases even if the arguer can make his argument by demonstrative science (by scientific, demonstrative syllogisms), he ought to make the argument instead by means of the Topics because most people will not be persuaded by demonstration.[30] The trouble with demonstration as a means of making arguments, in Boethius's sense of "what provides belief regarding what was in doubt," is that very many propositions one would like to prove are a long way from the self-evident truths that are first principles. To prove such propositions by demonstration requires going through all the steps from the first principles. If the one for whom the proof is made knows many of the steps along the way, derived propositions instead of first principles can be used as the starting points for the proof; otherwise the proof will have to start from the first principles and go through all the steps up to the desired conclusion. In such a case, the argument is more or less equivalent to teaching all of the science in question up to the desired conclusion, and the process becomes too long and tedious to be useful in debate. An answerer would not stand still for so long a dialogue, and more than one session might be needed. So in many cases, demonstration will be an almost impossibly cumbersome in-

29. Cf. 1206D3–5.   30. *Rhet.* I.i.12 (1355a24–29).

strument for producing conviction, which is the end of dialectic.[31]

The Topics are thought to work where demonstration does not for two reasons: first, maximal propositions are supposed to be both self-evident truths and most general propositions;[32] and second, all true secondary propositions, those that are not self-evidently true but require proof, are instances of one or another maximal proposition.[33] Exactly why Boethius thinks that all true secondary propositions fall under a self-evidently true generalization is not clear. He tends to think of maximal propositions as predicative, though he occasionally gives one as a hypothetical; and a maximal proposition seems to be greater than the secondary propositions that fall under it because at least one of the terms in the maximal proposition can be said of more things (or has a greater extension) than the corresponding term in any of the secondary propositions. He may think of all true secondary propositions as falling under one or another maximal proposition because the terms of any secondary proposition are generalizable and because it seems that the terms of a true secondary proposition can always be generalized in such a way as to produce a self-evident truth. Take, for example, this secondary proposition from *De top. diff.*: "It remains now to disclose what a Topic is" (1185A3–4). It clearly is a hard case for Boethius's view that any true secondary proposition falls under the self-evident generalization that is its maximal proposition. Can one make or find a maximal proposition for such an example? The subject of the secondary proposition is 'disclosing what a Topic is,' and the predicate is 'remains now to be done'; that is, when the rhetoric is stripped away, the sentence seems to be 'Disclosing what a Topic is remains now to be done.' If we leave the predicate the same and generalize the subject, we might make a maximal proposition of this sort for the sentence:

---

31. Cf. Aristotle, *Rhet.* I.ii.13 (1357a7–12). See also *De top. diff.* 1181A11–C10 where Boethius explains that some arguments are arguments (that is, provide belief for what was in doubt) only for certain people, who already have had proved to them the truth of the premises of the arguments at issue. What he says, of course, holds for all arguments other than those whose premises are known per se or are readily traceable to propositions known per se.

32. Cf. for example, *ICT* 280.12–14 (*PL* 1051C6–10).

33. Cf. *De top. diff.* 1176C6–10 and ff. The division of propositions Boethius gives in this passage may not be meant to be exhaustive, but the language he uses—"*propositionum quoque aliae . . . aliae*"—is of the form he regularly uses for exhaustive divisions; cf., for example, 1175A2–4, A12–13; and 1176B1–2.

'What one proposes to do and has not yet done remains now to be done.'

In any event, if the theory is correct and all true secondary propositions are instances of maximal propositions, maximal propositions clearly are very important for dialectic. Any true secondary proposition that is wanted as the conclusion of an argument falls under some maximal proposition; once the arguer has found the appropriate maximal proposition, he will have his argument or the structure of his argument proving the secondary proposition he wants to defend. Since the maximal proposition is self-evident, the arguer's opponent will have to grant it as true, though it may be so obvious that the arguer can leave it unsaid and count on it as a tacit assumption. And since the secondary proposition is a particular case covered by the generalization the opponent has to grant as true, once the arguer has made clear that the conclusion he wants is covered by the maximal proposition, the opponent will have to grant the conclusion as well. Because the maximal proposition is a self-evident truth, it has to be granted as true; and because it is a most general proposition, it covers the cases of a number of secondary propositions.[34] Hence, since all questions that occasion dialectical disputations and require arguments involve secondary propositions,[35] an argument can be made for any dialectical question by finding the appropriate maximal proposition and showing that the conclusion wanted is covered by that generalization. Finally, arguments may be thought of as arising from maximal propositions[36] for two reasons. First, the maximal proposition is the principle or generalization in the proof and hence its most important part; the maximal proposition is chosen first, and the rest of the argument is shaped and structured accordingly. Second, because a maximal proposition is a generalization covering many cases, it will work for a number of different dialectical questions, and one maximal proposition will give rise to a variety of arguments.

Aristotle's Topics, which are principles similar to Boethius's maximal propositions or strategies for argument or both, are the

34. Cf., for example, *ICT* 280.12–24 (*PL* 1051C7–D8).

35. Perhaps 'almost all' would be closer to the truth. Aristotle, for example, discusses a dialectical refutation of those who call into question or deny the law of noncontradiction; *Met.* 1006a11ff., and see also the Introduction above.

36. Cf. *De top. diff.* 1185A3–7 and C6–8.

instruments of an art. Every dialectical question is predicative; so the proposition wanted as conclusion to a dialectical argument is also predicative, and it contains a predicate that is one or another of the predicables—that is, is related to its subject as a genus, definition, or one of the other predicables. In order to prove the conclusion, the arguer will have to show that the predicate inheres in or is separated from the subject, and having a thorough familiarity with the nature of the predicables will make a man ready and quick at just such argumentation. Aristotle presents his Topics in such a way as to teach a man the nature of the predicables and make him skillful at using them. But it is easy to read Aristotle's Topics as if his presentation amounted to no more than a boxful of recipes for aguments, a very long list of Topics to be memorized, from which an appropriate one could be culled for a particular dialectical question. Boethius seems to think of Aristotle's method as such an unwieldy instrument, involving the memorization of prefabricated Topics; and his own method for using maximal propositions seems to be much the same: rote learning of certain self-evident generalizations useful for dialectical arguments. But Boethius is not really interested in maximal propositions as aids to finding argument. Though maximal propositions are needed for dialectical arguments, the real instruments of Boethius's art for discovering arguments are the Differentiae, to which I will turn next.[37]

Maximal propositions differ in content, and they can be distinguished on the basis of that content. Some maximal propositions are about causes, some about contraries, and so on. If the genus is thought of as *maximal proposition*, then it may be divided into its species according to the differing content of the maximal propositions; there will be a species *maximal proposition from causes* and another *maximal proposition from contraries* and so on. In this way, *from contraries* (or simply *contraries*) is a differentia for maximal propositions. Boethius lists Themistius's and Cicero's differentiae for the genus *maximal proposition*. Depending on how they are counted,[38] there are approximately twenty-eight such differentiae in Themistius's list and nineteen in Cicero's.

37. Cf. Boethius's comparison of Differentiae and maximal propositions, 1186B3-12. The relationship between Differentiae and maximal propositions as they function to find arguments will emerge later.
38. Cf. the chapter "Differentia and the Porphyrian Tree" below.

The Differentiae are divided into three main groups by Themistius, two by Cicero: Differentiae are intrinsic, extrinsic, or (in the Themistian division) intermediate. If the argument and the maximal proposition have to do with the nature of the subject or the predicate in the question [39]—if, for example, the maximal proposition is about definition and the argument is based on the definition of the question's subject or predicate—then the maximal proposition and its Differentia are *intrinsic*. If, on the other hand, the maximal proposition is, for example, about contraries and the argument is based on the contrary of the subject or the predicate in the question, then the maximal proposition and its Differentia are *extrinsic* (in the Themistian division) because they have to do with something (for example, a contrary) which is external to the nature of the subject or predicate. Some maximal propositions and their arguments seem in one way to have to do with the nature of the subject or predicate and in another way not to do so—these Themistius calls *intermediate*. Maximal propositions about conjugates and their Differentiae are an example. [40] Beginning with the large divisions of Differentiae—intrinsic, extrinsic, and intermediate (in the case of Themistius's list)—Boethius divides and subdivides until he arrives at the twenty-eight lowest species of maximal propositions and the corresponding twenty-eight Differentiae; [41] he is at some pains to show that the consequent list of Differentiae is exhaustive. [42]

The fact that Differentiae originate as the differentiae of the genus *maximal proposition* has some bearing on the way they work together with maximal propositions in argumentation, but it is not important for their special function in finding arguments, which is what I will consider next. In the discussion immediately follow-

39. The subject and predicate in a dialectical question are, of course, the same as those in the corresponding conclusion.

40. Conjugates are words drawn in different ways from the same word, as 'just' in the neuter (frequently meaning 'just thing') and 'just' in the masculine (frequently meaning 'just man') are conjugates drawn from 'justice'; see *De top. diff.* 1192B12–14.

41. The maximal propositions Boethius is distinguishing and dividing here are only those Aristotle lists among common Topics; Boethius does not discuss the sorts of maximal propositions Aristotle includes among proper Topics. Cf. the preceding chapter on Aristotle.

42. Cf. *De top. diff.* 1194B3–1195A13. It is troublesome to him to have two sets of species for maximal propositions—the Themistian and the Ciceronian—each of which, he claims, is exhaustive of the genus *maximal proposition;* and he spends some time on the problem. See *De top. diff.* 1195B4–C7 and also 1200C14ff.

ing, it will be helpful simply to take 'Differentia' as a technical term whose meaning and use we want to determine.

The Differentiae are instruments for finding arguments. What exactly are they supposed to find? Boethius says that all argument is basically syllogism.[43] There are two terms in a question and in the conclusion of its corresponding syllogistic argument;[44] such an argument arises when the two terms of a question are joined by and to a third term, which is thus an intermediate or middle between the two other terms.[45] Boethius gives as an example the question whether man is a substance. The two terms in the question, which are also the two terms wanted in the conclusion, are 'man' and 'substance.' In order to join 'man' and 'substance,' Boethius says, we need to find a third term that can connect the two terms in the question. 'Animal' is such an intermediate term; it can be joined to 'man'—'A man is an animal'—and also to 'substance'—'An animal is a substance.' So, by means of the intermediate 'animal,' we have an argument enabling us to join 'man' and 'substance' in the conclusion 'A man is a substance.'[46] Since the two terms of a question are connected by an intermediate and the argument for the conclusion arises from that term, Boethius says "an argument is nothing other than the discovery of an intermediate,"[47] so that finding an argument is tantamount to finding some intermediate between the two terms given. Hence, Differentiae must function to find arguments by aiding in the dis-

---

43. *De top. diff.* 1184D7–14; ICT 279.2–6 (PL 1050B9–13). Boethius's use of 'syllogism' is broader and looser than the use of the word we have in mind when we talk about the demonstrative syllogism of Aristotle's *Prior Analytics;* Boethius defines 'syllogism' as Aristotle does in the *Topics:* "Syllogism is discourse in which, when certain things have been laid down and agreed to, something other than the things agreed to must result by means of the things agreed to." *De top. diff.* 1183A11–15. ("*Syllogismus est oratio in qua quibusdam positis et concessis, aliud quiddam per ea ipsa quae concessa sunt, evenire necesse est, quam sint ipsa quae concessa sunt.*") Cf. also Aristotle's *Topics* 100a25ff., and note 5 to Book II above. See also James Duerlinger, "Συλλογισμός and συλλογίζεσθαι in Aristotle's *Organon,*" *American Journal of Philology,* 90 (1969), 320–328.

44. Boethius here uses 'term' to refer to a phrase or an expression as well as a word. Cf. 1175B7–9, D4–8.

45. ICT 279.6–11 (PL 1050B14–C4).

46. Cf. ICT 279.11–24 (PL 1050C6–D7), where Boethius gives a similar but demonstrative argument. The use of Differentiae in demonstrative arguments is discussed later in this chapter.

47. ICT 279.30–31 (PL 1051A2–3): ". . . *nihil est aliud argumentum quam medietatis inventio*"; cf. also Aristotle, *Pos. An.* 90a35–36: "ὅτι μὲν οὖν πάντα τὰ ζητούμενα μέσου ζήτησίς ἐστι, δῆλον."

covery of such intermediates. But what exactly are these intermediates that Differentiae are supposed to find?

Boethius gives the following twenty-eight Themistian Differentiae:

Intrinsic	Intermediate	Extrinsic
From definition	From cases	From judgment
From description	From conjugates	From similars
From explanation	From division	From the greater
From genus		From the lesser
From whole		From contraries
From species		From relatives
From integral parts		From privation and possession
From efficient cause		From affirmation and negation
From material cause		From proportion
From formal cause		From transumption
From final cause		
From effects		
From destructions		
From uses		
From associated accidents		

He gives an example of the sort of argument each of these Differentiae provides. For instance, the argument concluding "Moors lack weapons," quoted above, is an argument provided by the Differentia *from material cause*. The question at issue is 'Do the Moors have weapons?' and we want to argue that they do not, that they lack weapons. To find an argument, we need to find an intermediate between the two terms in the question, something that can be joined to each of the two terms and connects them in the way wanted. Laid out in its steps, the argument Boethius gives is this:

(16) Moors lack iron.
(17) Iron is the matter (or material cause) of weapons.
(18) Where the matter is lacking, what is made from the matter is also lacking.
(19) Therefore, Moors lack weapons.

The Differentia *from material cause* (or just *material cause*) is not itself the intermediate term that gives rise to the argument; the intermediate in this case is 'iron.' The two terms the propounder of the argument wants to connect are 'Moors' and 'weapons'; 'iron' is the intermediate because it is linked to both terms, to the first term by means of (16), which says that Moors lack iron, and to the second term by means of (17), which says that iron is the matter of weapons. The Differentia *material cause*, on the other hand, is the genus of the intermediate in this argument because iron is a species of material cause. The Differentia does not work by providing a particular intermediate term; instead it suggests the *sort* of term that could serve as intermediate—namely, whatever is the material cause of the appropriate term in the question.

In *ICT*, Boethius gives a detailed example showing how to use the Differentia *definition*.

There is a question whether civil law is a useful body of knowledge. Here 'civil law' is the subject, 'useful body of knowledge' is the predicate. What is asked is whether the predicate can inhere in the subject. Therefore, I will not be able to call civil law itself to the argument, for it is a constituent of the question. So I consider what might be incorporated in it. I see that no definition is disjoined from what it defines, so that the appropriate definition cannot be disjoined from civil law. So I define civil law, and I say, "Civil law is equity established among those who are of the same state for the sake of preserving what is theirs." After this, I consider whether this definition can be joined to the remaining term 'useful body of knowledge,' that is, whether equity established among those who are of the same state for the sake of preserving what is theirs is a useful body of knowledge. I see that the equity mentioned above is a useful body of knowledge. And so I conclude, "Therefore, civil law is a useful body of knowledge."[48]

In this example, the two terms in the question are "civil law" and "useful body of knowledge"; and the intermediate is "equity . . . ," which is joined to each of the two terms in the question and links them together in the way wanted. Again, the Differentia *definition* is not itself the intermediate for the argument; but it is

48. ICT 288.4–17 (PL 1059C6–D8). "*Est enim quaestio, an iuris civilis scientia sit utilis. Hic igitur ius civile supponitur, utilis scientia praedicatur. Quaeritur ergo, an id, quod praedicatur, vere possit adhaerere subiecto. Ipsum igitur ius civile non potero ad argumentum vocare; de eo enim quaestio constituta est. Respicio igitur, quid ei sit insitum. Video, quod omnis definitio ab eo non seiungitur, cuius est definitio, ne a iure civili quidem propriam definitionem posse seiungi. Definio igitur ius civile, ac dico:* Ius civile est aequitas constituta iis, qui eiusdem civitatis sunt, ad res suas obtinendas. *Post haec considero, num sic haec definitio reliquo termino, utili scientiae, possit esse coniuncta, id est, an aequitas constituta iis, qui eiusdem civitatis sunt, ad res suas obtinendas, utilis scientia sit. Video esse utilem scientiam dictae superius aequitatis. Concludo itaque: Igitur iuris civilis scientia utilis est.*"

the genus of the term that is the intermediate because *equity* . . . is the definition of *civil law*.

The hypothetical argument concluding (22) "The art of medicine is advantageous" seems to be only a less clear example of the same sort of thing. The two premises proving (22) are

(20) If driving out disease, ministering to health, and healing wounds is advantageous, the art of medicine is advantageous.

(21) Driving out disease, ministering to health, and healing wounds is advantageous.

The maximal proposition is "What inheres in the individual parts inheres in the whole," and the Differentia is *integral parts*. Here, too, the Differentia is a genus of the intermediate in the argument. Driving out disease and the rest are all integral parts of the whole which is medicine; and they form an intermediate between 'medicine' and 'advantage' by being linked to each of those two terms so that the two terms are appropriately joined. So Differentiae provide intermediates for hypothetical as well as for predicative dialectical arguments.

The argument exemplifying the Differentia *definition*, like the argument exemplifying the Differentia *material cause*, is a dialectical argument relying on a maximal proposition for its validity; but, unlike the argument from material cause, the argument from definition could easily be a demonstrative argument. The argument could be given as the first-figure Aristotelian syllogism Barbara:

(23) All civil law is equity, etc.

(24) All equity, etc., is a useful body of knowledge.

(25) Therefore, all civil law is a useful body of knowledge.

In this argument, the two terms in the conclusion are not linked by some word or phrase that can be designated only roughly as some sort of intermediate between them; they are linked in this argument by the middle term of a three-term, demonstrative Aristotelian syllogism. The Differentia *definition*, then, is also a genus of middle terms for demonstrative syllogisms, so that at least some of the Differentiae are useful for demonstration as well as for dialectic. And seeing that they can also provide middle terms for demonstrative syllogisms illuminates the enigmatic remark Boethius makes at the end of his first lengthy discussion of Differentiae. The Differentiae *definition, genus, differentia,* and *causes* are useful for demonstrative syllogisms, Boethius says (*De top. diff.* 1195A14–B2), but all the other Differentiae are useful primarily for dialectical arguments. His point seems to be that, of the Differentiae, *definition* and the others mentioned can provide not only some sort of intermediate between the two terms of a question but also middle terms for demonstrative syllogisms.

The Differentiae, then, aid in finding arguments because they aid in finding intermediate terms. Sometimes the intermediate provided is simply an expression that can be joined in some way to each of the two terms in the conclusion; sometimes it is a middle term for a demonstrative Aristotelian syllogism. In either case, a Differentia does not specify the particular intermediate term to be used in an argument, but rather it gives the genus of intermediates appropriate to that argument, suggesting the sort of intermediate that could join the two terms of the conclusion. And so Differentiae function in finding arguments much as Boethius says they do: they provide not particular arguments but a reasoned path to finding them.[49]

The list of Differentiae is much shorter than Aristotle's list of hundreds of Topics; Boethius claims it is exhaustive, and he means it to be memorized. The man who has memorized Boethius's Differentiae has ready the twenty-eight genera of all possible intermediates for arguments. When he wants to find an argument for some conclusion, he chooses from his list of twenty-eight one that is appropriate for the conclusion he wants to maintain and uses it to find the particular intermediate term that will give him the argument he needs.

It seems clear that interpreting Differentiae as genera of intermediates between the two terms in the conclusions of arguments will work for most of the Differentiae, including almost all of those Themistius designates as extrinsic. They are related to one of the terms in the conclusion straightforwardly, as its subject or predicate; and they are connected to the other term as similar, contrary, conjugate, or whatever the Differentia at issue happens to be.

The hard case for this interpretation of the Differentiae and their role in finding arguments is the Differentia *from judgment.*[50] This

49. See the Introduction.
50. Themistius's Differentia *from division* seems to be another hard case, but Boethius thinks it can be assimilated to Cicero's Differentia from *enumeration of parts.* See *De top. diff.* 1203A6–12 and note 56 to Book III.

Differentia is the genus of opinions that, for one reason or another, are considered authoritative; it gives rise only to arguments from authority. There is a question, for example, whether the heaven is revolvable; and the argument from judgment amounts to saying that it is revolvable because wise men and the most learned astronomers think so. In this argument, the particular instance of the Differentia—the opinion of learned astronomers that the heaven is revolvable—seems to be related to neither of the terms in the question.[51] It was generally recognized, however, that this Differentia and the kind of argument it could provide are different from the other Differentiae and their arguments. Cicero divides all Differentiae into intrinsic and extrinsic, and the Differentia *from judgment* is the only extrinsic Differentia in his list.[52] Both Cicero and Boethius explain that this Differentia and its arguments are generally considered to fall outside the art of the arguer;[53] according to Cicero, the Greeks called the arguments arising from this Differentia '*ἀτέχνοι*', that is, not part of the art in question.[54] This extrinsic Differentia, then, seems to have troubled the ancient writers on the Topics, too, and for much the same reason that it seemed troublesome to us in light of what appears to be the correct interpretation of Differentiae: the particular instances of this Differentia are not connected to either the subject or the predicate in the question.[55]

51. Norman Kretzmann has suggested to me that the conclusion of an argument from judgment might be not '*x* is *A*' but 'it is true that *x* is *A*.' A proof of the latter is not necessarily a proof of the former. In this case, then, the subject of the argument's conclusion would be the proposition that *x* is *A*, and the predicate would be 'is true.' Then these two would be related by the intermediate at issue, somewhat in this way:
   (1) Most of the learned (etc.) say that *x* is *A*.
   (2) What most of the learned (etc.) say is true.
   (3) Therefore, it is true that *x* is *A*.
Kretzmann's suggestion may be the right interpretation of this Topic, but Boethius gives no indication that he thinks of the conclusions for arguments as being of the form 'it is true that *x* is *A*' rather than '*x* is *A*.'
52. See *Topica* IV.24.
53. See *ICT* 309.19–29 (*PL* 1082A8–B6) and 386.8–46 (*PL* 1166D13–1167D4).
54. *Topica* IV.24.
55. It seems hard to imagine what self-evident truth, what maximal proposition, could be associated with this Differentia. The one Boethius gives in *De top. diff.* is not an analytical truth, but it might be thought to be psychologically (if not logically) self-evident: "What seems true to everyone or the many or the wise should not be gainsaid." ("*quod omnibus vel pluribus vel sapientibus hominibus videtur, ei contradici non oportere,*" 1190C9–11).

That this Differentia troubled those authors as it did is confirmation for the interpretation of the Differentiae laid out above, but it raises the question why this Differentia was included in the list of Differentiae and the method of Topics at all. The reason probably is historical. It appears odd at first that Boethius, who knew Aristotle's *Topics* so well, should omit all discussion of strategies from his own account of the Topics. But some evidence[56] in Alexander's and Theophrastus's treatments of the Topics suggests that the strategies might have been shortened until they amounted to little more than the sort of phrase given as Differentia, for example, *from contraries*. The less intrinsic Boethius's Differentiae are, that is, the less they are tied to the nature of either the subject or the predicate of the question, the more they seem to resemble abbreviated strategies. The most extrinsic of the Differentiae, the one *from judgment*, seems to be no more than an instruction: make the argument from judgment (from authority). So it is not unlikely, I think, that the Differentiae in Boethius's work arose as a list of abbreviated Aristotelian strategies and that the explanation Boethius gives for them—that they are the differentiae of maximal propositions that find arguments by providing an intermediate—was added later, perhaps by Greek commentators, as the potentialities of such shortened strategies began to be seen.

This view, furthermore, helps to explain an odd resemblance between Boethius's account of Topics and Aristotle's. Many of Aristotle's Topics bear some resemblance to Differentiae; for example, Aristotle gives a Topic about the conjugate of an accident[57] or about the contrary of a property,[58] and the Boethian Differentiae include *from conjugates* and *from contraries*. In Aristotle, however, Topics are first divided according to the predicable they involve, and then ordered within each predicable's group. The ordering within each of the four groups of Topics seems much the same, and often the same sort of Topic is found in all four groups. Topics about contraries, for example, occur in the list of Topics for each of the four predicables.[59] If the Differentiae began as abbreviated strategies, they are strategies gathered together across the

---

56. See the chapter "Between Aristotle and Boethius" below.
57. *Top.* 114a26ff.   58. *Top.* 135b7ff.
59. Aristotle does not repeat himself, however, as he is often accused of doing. The Topics about contraries, for example, are not the same but differ by being about the contraries of different predicables.

grain of Aristotle's ordering by predicables. It is as if Boethius's predecessors had taken Aristotle's *Topics* as a boxful of blueprints or recipes for arguments, rather than as an art teaching the nature of predicables, and had been dismayed at the great number of blueprints. To facilitate remembering the Topics, they gathered them together into groups across the grain of the predicables: some Topics are about conjugates, some about contraries, and so on. Not all the Differentiae can be explained in precisely this way. The Differentia *from judgment* seems to correspond not to a strategy within the groups of Topics for the four predicables but rather to a general strategy given in the last Book of the *Topics*.[60] But for the bulk of the Differentiae, this is a plausible explanation of the relation between Aristotelian and Boethian Topics.

Though the real instruments for finding arguments are the Differentiae, maximal propositions cannot be dispensed with because they are required to support a dialectical argument, and Differentiae can aid in the discovery of maximal propositions as well as intermediate terms. Since a differentia takes the place of a genus,[61] Differentiae may be thought of as the various genera of maximal propositions;[62] hence, as a genus can be said to contain the things that fall under it, so each Differentia can be said to contain the maximal propositions of which it is the differentia. Consequently, because they contain maximal propositions and because, as genera, they are far fewer in number, Differentiae can also function as aids in finding maximal propositions. When one wants a maximal proposition to support an argument, instead of sorting through the numerous maximal propositions at random, one can run through the small number of Differentiae to find the genus of maximal propositions suitable for the question at issue.

The particular maximal proposition wanted can be specified further with the help of a predicable. When Boethius gives an example in full for a Differentia, after the statement of a question and its corresponding argument, he gives the predicable involved in the question and then the appropriate maximal proposition. For instance, he gives this example for the Differentia *definition:*

Suppose there is a question whether trees are animals and suppose there is a syllogism of this sort: an animal is an animate substance capable of

60. Cf. *Top.* 156b20–23.   61. Cf. *Top.* 1178C2–4.
62. *ICT* 281.18–29 (*PL* 1052C12–D12).

perceiving; a tree is not an animate substance capable of perceiving; therefore, a tree is not an animal. The question has to do with genus, for the question is whether trees should be put under the genus of animals. The Topic which consists in a universal proposition is this: that to which the definition of the genus does not belong is not a species of the genus defined. The higher Differentia of the Topic, which is nevertheless called a Topic: *from definition.* [63]

The predicable involved in the question is *genus*, because if animal inheres in tree, it does so as the genus of tree. But the purpose of explicitly specifying the predicable in this and other arguments exemplifying Differentiae seems obscure. Boethius's method of the Topics is not the art of the predicables that Aristotle's is, and the predicables seem to play almost no role in the Boethian method of the Topics. If Boethius's Differentiae are related to Aristotle's Topics in the way suggested above, however, then a Differentia differs from an Aristotelian strategy not only by being abbreviated, but also by being stripped of its association with a particular predicable. A Differentia seems to be a strategy that has been condensed by leaving out, among other things, the predicable involved in the question at issue. So one of the ways to reconstitute the strategy (and hence the corresponding principle or maximal proposition) from a particular Differentia is to reintroduce the omitted predicable. In the example above, for instance, if we know that the predicable involved in the question is *genus*, we can reconstitute the maximal proposition by combining the omitted predicable and the Differentia (*definition*). The maximal proposition wanted, then, will have to do with the definition of a genus. What else is lacking can be filled in without too much trouble from the context of the particular argument. By considering the context, we can tell that the maximal proposition involving the definition of a genus that is needed to validate the argument has to be something like 'A thing to which the definition of a genus is unsuited is not a species of that genus.' So the predicable Boethius gives in

---

63. *De top. diff.* 1187A6–B1. "*Age enim quaeratur an arbores animalia sint, fiatque hujusmodi syllogismus: animal est substantia animata sensibilis; arbor vero substantia animata sensibilis non est; arbor igitur animal non est. Haec de genere quaestio est, utrum enim arbores sub animalium genere ponendae sint quaeritur. Locus qui in universali propositione consistit, hic est cui generis diffinitio non convenit; id ejus cuius ea diffinitio est, species non est. Loci superior differentia, qui locus nihilominus nuncupatur a diffinitione.*"

the example for a Differentia can work with the Differentiae to find a maximal proposition for a particular argument.

We can summarize in this way. The heart of a dialectical argument is a term intermediate between the two terms in a question, that is, a term that can be linked to each of the question's two terms in such a way that those two terms can be linked to each other in the argument's conclusion. Differentiae are the genera of such intermediate terms, and hence they provide the kind of intermediate term needed; they constitute "a reasoned path" to finding arguments. For Boethius maximal propositions play no role in finding arguments; but they are required to support dialectical arguments—to validate the whole argument in predicative arguments and to validate the passage from antecedent to consequent in the conditional premise of hypothetical arguments. Because Differentiae are the differentiae of maximal propositions, they can be of use in finding maximal propositions as well as intermediate terms. Because they are abbreviated strategies, they can be used in connection with the particular predicable of a given question to specify further the maximal proposition needed for an argument. Maximal propositions are Topics for argument—places from which arguments can be drawn—because they are the generalizations on which the argument is based and of which the conclusion is a particular case. Differentiae, the main instruments of dialectic, are Topics or places for arguments in two senses. First, they are Topics or places for maximal propositions because they contain maximal propositions as their genera, and hence maximal propositions are found with their help. Second, and more important, as genera of intermediate terms, they contain the intermediate terms from which arguments arise for all dialectical questions, and hence they provide arguments.

Between Aristotle and Boethius

As is clear from the preceding two chapters, the discipline of the Topics and the method for finding arguments underwent important changes between Aristotle's time and Boethius's. Perhaps the most significant and certainly the most easily recognizable change is in the notion of a Topic. We can see the difference clearly even on a superficial level: Aristotle expresses his Topics as propositions, but Boethius's Differentiae, the Topics Boethius is really interested in, are expressed as words or phrases whose expansion into appropriate propositions is neither intended nor readily conceivable. Aristotle gives hundreds of Topics, divided into only four groups, depending on which predicable they are concerned with. Boethius gives just twenty-eight Topics (the Themistian Differentiae), and these are highly ordered among themselves, as I show in the chapter "Differentia and the Porphyrian Tree." Aristotle's method for using Topics is strongly tied to oral disputation; the eighth Book of his treatise is given over entirely to a discussion of disputation, and his presentation of each Topic tends to be couched in terms of disputation, for example, what one says to one's opponent when he maintains such and such a thesis. Boethius's exposition centers on the arguments themselves, divorced from disputation and its participants, and the arguments he presents as examples are brief, orderly, and textbookish. Finally, as I argued above, Aristotle thinks of a Topic as a general strategy for argumentation, which is useful for the discovery and construction of a number of different arguments. Boethius thinks of a Differentia as a genus of intermediate or third terms for syllogisms,[1] which provides an appropriate intermediate or third term for a variety of arguments.

1. I am using 'syllogism' in Boethius's broad sense of the word; see *De top. diff.* 1183A11ff. and my notes on the passage.

The difference between the two can be made clearer, perhaps, by an example. As it happens, Aristotle and Boethius both discuss an argument having to do with the definition of genus. Aristotle presents the example as follows. Suppose participant A in a dialectical disputation maintains that x is the genus of y, and participant B maintains that it is not. How is B to refute A? Well, Aristotle says, B "must see whether what is given as the genus partakes of or can partake of the species" (*Top.* 121a14–16). Corresponding to this strategy, which is the Topic, Aristotle supplies the following principle: "The species receives the definition of the genus, but the genus does not receive the definition of the species" (*Top.* 121a13–14). So the notion of a genus partaking of a species, which is employed in the strategy, should be interpreted as the genus "receiving the definition" of the species; that is, x partakes of y only in case the definition of y is predicated truly of x. Further evidence that this is Aristotle's meaning is in his next words: "[if someone gives a genus for being or oneness] it will happen that the genus partakes of the species, for being and oneness are predicated of all things that are, so that their definition is also predicated" (*Top.* 121a17–19). So in refuting A, B is to begin with a Topic, namely, the strategy of seeing whether A's putative genus x in fact partakes of its species y; that is, whether the definition of the species y is predicated truly of the putative genus x. If B finds that x does partake of y, then he employs his principle that the definition of a species is not predicated truly of the genus of that species; since x is in violation of this principle, B concludes that x is not, in fact, the genus of y after all. For Aristotle, then, a Topic is a strategy based on a principle, and Aristotle's method for the discovery of arguments consists in knowing the nature of a predicable (such as genus) and checking to see whether one's opponent has violated some rule regarding it.

The corresponding passage in *De top. diff.* begins with a question: "suppose there is a question whether trees are animals" (1187A6). And suppose that we want to answer in the negative and to support our answer with an argument. How do we find the argument? Boethius's method is to start with the two terms of the question ('trees' and 'animals'), which will also be the two terms in the conclusion of our argument, and attempt to find an intermediate term that will connect them in a syllogism. His list of twenty-eight Differentiae is supposed to include all the possible varieties of third terms. So we go through the list of these twenty-eight to see which one is appropriate for the argument we need, and we see intuitively that the Differentia *definition* can be used in this case. We produce the definiens (what Boethius refers to as the definition) of one of the two terms, namely, 'animal'; and by attaching the definiens to this term, we make the first premise of our argument: 'An animal is an animate substance capable of perceiving.' Next, we connect the definiens in the appropriate way to the other term to produce a second premise: 'A tree is not an animate substance capable of perceiving.' The maximal proposition for this argument, according to Boethius, is this: 'That to which the definition of the genus does not belong is not a species of the genus defined.' If we recognize the relationships among the three terms and apply the maximal proposition, we can conclude validly that trees are not animals.[2] The intermediate term in this case is *animate substance capable of perceiving*, and it is an instance of definition, on Boethius's view. A Differentia, then, is a genus of intermediate or third terms; and Boethius's method for the discovery of arguments consists in selecting one of the twenty-eight Differentiae, finding an intermediate term on the basis of the Differentia, and building a syllogism around that intermediate term.

Plainly, Boethius and Aristotle handle these two very similar cases in very different ways. A rough summary of the difference is that Boethius's method of discovery is more highly ordered and less informal than Aristotle's and that it relies on a type of Topic that must have been developed after Aristotle. What accounts for this change between Aristotle's and Boethius's methods of discovery? How did the discipline of the Topics evolve between these two philosophers? My purpose in this chapter is to sketch the start of an answer to these questions, within certain limitations.

For Aristotle and the tradition after him, Topics were important not only in dialectic but also in rhetoric and mnemonics. In mnemonics, a Topic is literally a place (generally a place in some large edifice) from which by certain mnemonic techniques one can recall a part of what is to be remembered.[3] In rhetoric, there are Topics similar in content and function to dialectical Topics. Aristotle's *Rhetoric* devotes considerable attention to these rhetorical Topics,[4]

---

2. Cf. also in this connection *ICT* 288.4–17 (PL 1059C6–D8).
3. For more discussion of Topics in mnemonic techniques, see the Introduction.
4. Cf., for example, I.ii.21ff., I.v.1ff., II.xii.13ff.

and they are discussed in detail in the rhetorical treatises of Cicero and Latin rhetoricians after him. After Cicero the study of Topics flourished among Latin rhetoricians, who paid attention to Topics because of their usefulness for law and oratory. Tacitus, Quintilian, Victorinus, Martianus Capella, Fortunatianus, and Cassiodorus all wrote something about Topics.[5] But none of these authors has much theoretical discussion of the nature of Topics or of the manner in which Topics provide arguments, and their treatments of the Topics are not likely to have advanced or altered either the conception of a Topic or the method of discovery. Still, the use of Topics in rhetoric and mnemonics almost certainly influenced the discussion of dialectical Topics, and the change in the method of discovery from Aristotle's time to Boethius's has its sources in rhetoric and mnemonics, no doubt, as well as in dialectic. But to consider the traditions of rhetoric and mnemonics is clearly beyond the scope of this study, and I will confine myself to considering the change in dialectic. Within the field of dialectic, furthermore, I am leaving the Stoics out of account. We have Cicero's word that they ignored methods for the discovery of argument and concentrated exclusively on what we now call logic,[6] and I know of no evidence to contradict Cicero's claim.[7]

Of the early Peripatetics, Theophrastus, Eudemus, and Strato are said to have written on the Topics. Strato is cited by Alexander of Aphrodisias[8] as having altered a particular Aristotelian Topic, and Diogenes Laertius attributes to him a work entitled 'τόπων προοίμια'.[9] Eudemus, according to Alexander, wrote a work called 'περὶ λέξεως', in which he discussed types of dialectical ques-

5. Cf., for example, the following: *Cornelii Taciti Dialogus de oratoribus*, ed. Maximum Lenchantin de Gubernatis, Corpus Scriptorum Latinorum Paravanianum (Turin, 1949), p. 31; Quintilian, *Institutio oratoria*, tr. H. E. Butler (London, 1921), V.x.20ff., V.x.100ff., V.xii.15ff.; *Victorini explanationum in Ciceronis rhetoricam libri II*, in *Rhetores Latini minores*, ed. Charles Halm (Leipzig, 1863), pp. 213ff.; *Martiani Capellae liber de arte rhetorica*, in *Rhet. Lat. min.*, pp. 465ff.; *C. Chirii Fortunatiani artis rhetoricae libri III*, *Rhet. Lat. min.*, pp. 105ff.; Cassiodorus, *Institutiones*, ed. R. A. B. Mynors (Oxford, 1937), pp. 125ff.

6. Cicero, *Topica*, II.6.

7. See Benedetto Riposati, *Studi sui'Topica, di Cicerone*, (Milan, 1947), pp. 5–6. See also Charles Thurot, *Etudes sur Aristote: La Dialectique et la rhetorique*, (Paris, 1860), pp. 187ff.

8. Alexander of Aphrodisias, *In Aristotelis Topicorum libros octo commentaria*, in Maximilian Wallies, ed., *Commentaria in Aristotelem Graeca (CAG)*, (Berlin, 1891) II, pt. ii. 340.3ff.

9. Diogenes Laertius, *Lives*, V.59.

tions.[10] As far as we know, neither Strato's nor Eudemus's work on Topics has been preserved. Diogenes Laertius[11] attributes at least two works on the Topics to Theophrastus: ανηγημένων τόπων and τὰ πρὸ των τόπων. And Alexander mentions Theophrastus's Topics[12] and his ανηγημένων λόγων.[13] Though none of these books on the Topics remains, Alexander's commentary on Aristotle's Topics includes a couple of substantial quotations or paraphrases. These Theophrastian remnants are discussions of the nature of a Topic, just the sort of material important for comprehending the change in the conception of Topics.

The first of these passages occurs at the beginning of Alexander's commentary:

As Theophrastus says, a Topic is a source (αρχή) or element, from which we take sources for individual things, and these sources establish the understanding. A Topic is definite in outline (for either [a Topic] encompasses the common and universal, which govern syllogisms, or [a Topic] is able, on the basis of [what is common and universal], to take and demonstrate things of the same sort), but it is indefinite as far as individual things are concerned, for beginning from these, it is possible to provide a readily believable premise for the matter at hand.[14]

The same Theophrastian definition is cited again in In Top. p. 126.12–16, but there Alexander omits the material in parentheses and also the final "for" clause in the passage quoted above,[15] indicating that perhaps this omitted material is Alexander's own thought added to aid comprehension of Theophrastus's definition. The other Theophrastian definition of major importance for our purposes occurs in In Top. p. 135.2–6: "One must understand that Theophrastus says a Topic and a precept are not the same. A

10. Alexander of Aphrodisias, In Top., p. 69.15ff.   11. Lives, V.42–50.
12. For example, In Top., p. 55.11.
13. In Analytica priora, ed. Maximilian Wallies, CAG, II, pt. i, (Berlin, 1883), 340.14–15.
14. "ἔστι γὰρ ὁ τόπος, ὡς λέγει Θεόφραστος, ἀρχή τις ἢ στοιχεῖον, ἀφ' οὗ λαμβάνομεν τὰς περὶ ἕκαστον ἀρχὰς ἐπιστήσαντες τὴν διάνοιαν, τῇ περιγραφῇ μὲν ὡρισμένος (ἢ γὰρ περιλαμβάνει τὰ κοινὰ καὶ καθόλου, ἅ ἐστι τὰ κύρια τῶν συλλογισμῶν, ἢ δύναταί γε ἐξ αὐτῶν τὰ τοιαῦτα δείκνυσθαί τε καὶ λαμβάνεσθαι), τοῖς δὲ καθ' ἕκαστα ἀόριστος· ἀπὸ τούτων γὰρ ἔστιν ὁρμώμενον εὐπορεῖν προτάσεως ἐνδόξου πρὸς τὸ προκείμενον." In Top., p. 5.21–27.
15. "διὸ καὶ ὁρίζεται ὁ Θεόφραστος τὸν τόπον, ὡς ἤδη ἡμῖν ἐν τοῖς πρώτοις εἴρηται, οὕτως· 'τόπος ἐστὶν ἀρχή τις ἢ στοιχεῖον, ἀφ' οὗ λαμβάνομεν τὰς περὶ ἕκαστον ἀρχάς, τῇ περιγραφῇ μὲν ὡρισμένος, τοῖς δὲ καθ' ἕκαστα ἀόριστος.'"

precept is more common and more universal and more simply expressed, and from it a Topic is found. For a precept is the source of a Topic, as a Topic is the source of a dialectical syllogism." [16] Alexander adds what appears to be his own explanation: "For example, a precept is something expressed in this way: One must make a dialectical syllogism from contraries, from coordinates. But an example of a Topic: If one of a pair of contraries has many meanings, then so does the other; or, If one [A] of a pair of contraries [A, B] belongs to one [X] of a pair of contraries [X, Y], then the other contrary [B] belongs to the other contrary [Y]. And again: Whatever is the case for one coordinate is also the case for the rest of the coordinates. For a Topic is a premise arising from a precept." [17]

These passages suggest that Theophrastus thought of a Topic primarily as a principle. According to Theophrastus, a Topic is a source and an element that is definite in outline but indefinite with regard to particulars. This definition, read in light of Alexander's example of a Topic, suggests a basic generalization that can be used in a variety of syllogisms to derive other, less general propositions. On Theophrastus's view, the many passages in which Aristotle appears to identify a Topic with the precept or strategy of an argument are really just giving the strategy from which a Topic arises. In the chapter on Aristotle above, I have argued that such an interpretation is mistaken,[18] and so I think the account of Topics Theophrastus presents as Aristotelian is not really Aristotle's. The change in the discipline of the Topics from Aristotle's time to Boethius's is marked by a progressive shift away from concern with oral disputation and toward interest in written arguments and prepared speeches; this shift is accompanied by a tendency to make the Topics more and more abstract, formal, and organized. Theophrastus's view of Aristotle's Topics

16. "δεῖ δὲ μὴ ἀγνοεῖν ὅτι Θεόφραστος διαφέρειν λέγει παράγγελμα καὶ τόπον· παράγγελμα μὲν γάρ ἐστι τὸ κοινότερον καὶ καθολικώτερον καὶ ἁπλούστερον λεγόμενον, ἀφ' οὗ ὁ τόπος εὑρίσκεται· ἀρχὴ γὰρ τόπου τὸ παράγγελμα, ὥσπερ ὁ τόπος ἐπιχειρήματος." Alexander says that ἐπιχείρημα is a dialectical syllogism in In Top., p. 126.12.

17. "οἷον παράγγελμα μὲν τὸ οὕτως λεγόμενον, ὅτι δεῖ ἐπιχειρεῖν ἀπὸ τῶν ἐναντίων, ἀπὸ τῶν συστοίχων, τόπος δὲ οἷον 'εἰ τὸ ἐναντίον πολλαχῶς, καὶ τὸ ἐναντίον', ἢ 'εἰ τῷ ἐναντίῳ τὸ ἐναντίον ὑπάρχει, καὶ τὸ ἐναντίον ὑπάρχει τῷ ἐναντίῳ', καὶ πάλιν 'ὡς ἓν τῶν συστοίχων, οὕτως καὶ τὰ λοιπά'· ὁ γὰρ τόπος πρότασις ἤδη τις ἀπὸ τοῦ παραγγέλματος γεγονυῖα." In Top., p. 135.6–11.

18. See the chapter on Aristotle.

as principles rather than strategies (or precepts) seems to me to be the first step in that shift. And it is Theophrastus's understanding of Aristotle's Topics that Boethius adopted for his own use and transmitted to the later Middle Ages. For Boethius, an Aristotelian Topic is a principle (that is, a maximal proposition); strategies are not discussed anywhere in either of Boethius's extant works on Topics.

But the strategies, isolated by Theophrastus and denied the status of Topics, may have been important in bringing about the change in the conception of a Topic. To begin with, as Theophrastus conceives of it, a strategy has a certain resemblance to a Boethian Differentia. A Topic is said to arise from a strategy, just as a maximal proposition is said to come from a Differentia. Several Topics may correspond to one strategy,[19] just as several maximal propositions may correspond to one Differentia. And strategies may serve as a means for ordering Topics, just as Differentiae serve to order maximal propositions. Strategies, furthermore, are easily compressible in a way that maximal propositions are not. Aristotle tends to give strategies in this form: "One Topic is to consider if [your opponent] has given as an accident what belongs in some other way."[20] In the *Rhetoric*, he frequently gives strategies in this way: "One Topic for demonstrative enthymemes is from opposites; for it is necessary to see if an opposite belongs to an opposite. . . . for example, temperance is good, for incontinence is harmful."[21] Alexander's example of a strategy is "One must make a dialectical syllogism from contraries."[22] It does not seem a long step from the shortened strategies in Aristotle's *Rhetoric* and Alexander's example to the corresponding Differentia *from contraries*. The strategies pointed out and isolated by Theophrastus may have been the direct ancestors of Boethius's Differentiae, and the attention Theophrastus called to the strategies may have provided the impetus that resulted in the discovery of the Differentiae.[23]

Though Cicero wrote a treatise entirely devoted to Topics, his

19. Cf. Alexander's explanation of the Theophrastian passage, *In Top.*, p. 135.6ff., quoted just above.
20. *Top.* 109a34.   21. *Rhet.* II.xxiii.1 (1397a7–10).   22. *In Top.*, p. 135.7.
23. See also the introductory survey of this period in Jan Pinborg's *Logik und Semantik im Mittelalter* (Stuttgart-Bad Cannstatt, 1972), pp. 21–24, and his "Topik und Syllogistik im Mittelalter," in *Sapienter Ordinare: Festgabe für Erich Kleineidam*, ed. F. Hoffmann, L. Scheffczyk, and K. Feiereis (Leipzig, 1969), pp. 158–160.

work is practically devoid of theoretical foundation for the study of them. His *Topica,* for example, has virtually no discussion of the nature of a Topic or its function in the discovery of argument; instead, it contains only a list of Topics and examples of arguments in jurisprudence for which those Topics are useful. But Cicero's Topics are not strategies or principles expressed in propositions; rather, they are expressed by the words and phrases Boethius later uses to refer to Differentiae. The discussion of Differentiae in the third Book of *De top. diff.* is simply a discussion of the Topics in Cicero's *Topica.* So, I think, a major part of the change in the conception of a Topic must have taken place between Aristotle and Cicero. Although Cicero's Topics are Differentiae rather than principles or strategies, Cicero himself probably did not have the method Boethius had for using them. Cicero, for example, never refers to his Topics as Differentiae; maximal propositions or principles play no part in his discussion of Topics; and there is no suggestion in his work that he thinks Topics provide intermediate terms for arguments.

As for Greek philosophers between Cicero and Boethius, medieval Arabic bibliographers note that Ishaq (tenth century A.D.) translated Ammonius's commentary on the *Topics* and that Yahya ibn 'Adi (also tenth century) said he had Ammonius's commentary on the first four Books of Aristotle's *Topics.* [24] If such a commentary by Ammonius did exist, and if the Ammonius in question is (as seems not implausible) Ammonius Hermiae, then it is possible that Boethius knew and used that commentary. [25] But as far as we know, none of Ammonius's work on the Topics still remains. Themistius and Alexander of Aphrodisias also wrote on the Topics. Alexander's commentary on Aristotle's *Topics* is extant, but only fragments of Themiustius's remain, preserved in some quotations and paraphrases in Averroes's commentary on the *Topics.* [26] One of

24. See F. E. Peters, *Aristoteles Arabus* (Leiden, 1968), p. 20.

25. For Boethius's acquaintance with Ammonius, see, for example, C. J. De Vogel, "Boethiana I," *Vivarium,* 9 (1971), 49–66. See also the Introduction, above.

26. As far as I know, Averroes's short and middle commentaries on Aristotle's *Topics* survive in the original Arabic and also in Latin. For my purposes here, I have used only the Latin middle commentary: *Primi voluminis pars III Aristotelis stagiritae Topicorum, atque Elenchorum libri, cum Averrois Cordubensis in eos media expositione* (Venice, 1562). Exactly the same text is in the edition reproduced by the Minerva Press, Frankfurt am Main, 1962, but in this edition the paragraph letters are sometimes put in carelessly. After an initial search through the middle commentary, I count nineteen quotations or summaries of Themistius: 28A, 43I, 45C,

these passages contains Themistius's definition of a Topic. In that passage Averroes begins with Theophrastus's definition, apparently citing the same passage Alexander cites,[27] and then contrasts Themistius's view:[28] "Themistius, however, says that a Topic is a general proposition which is truer than other propositions of a syllogism; and he says that sometimes such a proposition itself, sometimes its meaning and force, is placed within a syllogism."[29] The Themistian material Averroes preserves here unfortunately deals only with principles or maximal propositions, even though Themistius gives considerable attention to Differentiae, to judge from what Boethius says. In discussing the passage, Averroes maintains that the difference between Themistius and Theophrastus on the nature of a Topic consists mostly in Themistius's insistence that a principle is sometimes used within a syllogism,[30] and I think Averroes's assessment is correct. Both Theophrastus and Themistius pick out the same sort of thing as a principle; the difference between their two definitions of a Topic seems to be only in emphasis, Theophrastus speaking of a principle as a source and element, Themistius referring to it as a general proposition.

Alexander gives Theophrastus's definition and seems to accept it as it stands, emphasizing in his explanation that it is a premise and an aid to finding premises.[31] He disagrees with Theophrastus's rejection of strategies as Topics, though; on his view, both strategies and principles are Topics, and he remarks that Aristotle calls strategies Topics.[32] In this disagreement between the two commentators, Boethius's understanding of a Topic accords with

---

46C, 49I, 50I, 58A, 62B, 67H, 69C, 70A, 72I, 73M, 77C, 79C, 100H, 101G, 106L, 113M. Fur further discussion of these Themistian passages, see my article "Boethius's Works on the Topics," *Vivarium,* 12 (1974), 77–93.

27. At note 14 above.

28. The renaissance editions have parallel colums of two different Latin translations, one attributed to Mantinus, the other to Abram. For the sake of consistency, I am here following and quoting Mantinus's translation.

29. Averroes, *Primi voluminis,* p. 28D. "*Themistius vero dicit, quod locus est propositio universalis, quae est verior ceteris propositionibus syllogismi, et dicit, quod illa propositio, quae ita se habet, quandoque ponitur ipsamet in syllogismo, quandoque vero eius significatum et vis eius.*" Abram's translation has "*sententia*" instead of "*significatum,*" and my English translation here follows Abram at this point.

30. Averroes also refers to a passage from Alexander in which Alexander expressly argues against such a view (28E).

31. *In Top.,* pp. 126.11–12 and 17–19, 5.21ff., and 135.3ff.

32. *In Top.,* pp. 135.18ff.

Theophrastus's rather than with Alexander's; he thinks of Aristotle's Topics as principles only.

So, on the basis of Themistius's and Alexander's extant discussions of the nature and function of the Topics, it seems fair to say that the important differences between Aristotle and Boethius do not stem from either Themistius or Alexander. Theophrastus appears to have begun the change, and the completion of at least a part of the change can be seen in Cicero's work. But the Boethian method for the discovery of arguments seems to be uniquely preserved in Boethius's treatises on the Topics. There is nothing quite like it in the extant work of any of the intermediaries between Aristotle and Boethius considered in this section. Boethius's work on the Topics seems to be the sole surviving representative of a significant development in the history of dialectic. Plainly, however, a good deal of work remains to be done on the tradition of the Topics between Aristotle and Boethius. No doubt there are logic manuscripts from this period that have not yet come to light, and even the material we know about and have available in modern editions has not been fully explored. For example, no one has thoroughly studied Alexander's commentary on Aristotle's *Topics* or supplemented the scanty *CAG* index of passages showing Theophrastus's or Alexander's theory of Topics. Until further research is undertaken, the conclusions in this chapter will have to remain very tentative.

Peter of Spain on the Topics

To put Boethius's work on the Topics in perspective and to understand later changes and developments in the Topics, it is useful to consider treatments of the Topics not only by Boethius's predecessors but also by later medieval philosophers. In this chapter, I will examine the discussion of Topics in Peter of Spain's *Tractatus*,[1] which became a standard textbook of logic and thus a source for later scholastic treatments of the Topics. Its discussion of the Topics is very similar to discussions found in several of the scholastics contemporary with or earlier than Peter. Besides being a representative and influential treatment of the Topics, Peter's discussion is heavily dependent (directly or, more likely, indirectly)[2] on Boethius's account. The chapter on dialectic in the *Tractatus* is like *De top. diff.* in organization. It begins with a series of definitions and then lists the Topics with a description and example of each. The definitions and the listing are those in *De top. diff.*, and in some places Peter's words are equivalent to a quotation from Boethius.[3] Consequently, comparison of Boethius and Peter is not difficult. Some of the recent literature has suggested that Peter's work on the Topics is simply a slightly varied compilation drawn from Boethius's *De top. diff.* Otto Bird, for example, who has published a number of very useful articles on the medieval Topics, says that Peter's discussion of the Topics "is little more than a summary of the first half of BDT [*De top. diff.*],"[4] and that "Peter of Spain made a précis of it [*De top. diff.*] (primarily of the second

1. Ed. L. M. de Rijk (Assen, 1972).   2. Cf., *Tractatus,* p. xciii, n. 5.
3. Cf., for example, Peter, *Tractatus,* p. 55.17 and Boethius, *De top. diff.,* 1180C4–5, Peter p. 55.23 and Boethius 1183A9–10, and Peter p. 56.16–18 and Boethius 1184B13–C1.
4. "The Tradition of the Logical Topics: Aristotle to Ockham," *Journal of the History of Ideas,* 23 (1962), p. 313.

book) and provided additional Maxims in the fifth tract of his Summulae [*Tractatus*]."[5] But such a view shows a mistaken understanding of both Peter and Boethius. In what follows here, I will examine Peter's discussion of the Topics in considerable detail in order to exhibit with some accuracy a method for using Topics that, despite its apparent similarity to Boethius's method, is in fact very different from it; by doing so, I hope to show what Peter's method comes to and as a result to clarify the nature of the Boethian art of Topics.

Peter's treatise on the Topics is not an isolated work on the subject; there are many such treatises from the early scholastic period onward. To understand Peter's discussion, it is helpful to take into account treatments of the Topics in earlier and contemporary works, such as Garlandus Compotista's *Dialectica;*[6] the anonymous treatises *Introductiones Montane minores, Abbreviatio Montana, Tractatus Anagnini, Introductiones Parisienses, Logica "Ut dicit," Logica "Cum sit nostra," Dialectica Monacensis;*[7] William of Sherwood's *Introductiones in logicam;*[8] and Lambert of Auxerre's *Logica.*[9] Abelard produced a very long and detailed treatment of

5. "The Formalizing of the Topics in Mediaeval Logic," *Notre Dame Journal of Formal Logic,* 1 (1960), 140. Jan Pinborg echoes Bird's view of Peter. Cf. "Topik und Syllogistik im Mittelalter," in *Sapienter Ordinare: Festgabe für Erich Kleineidam,* ed. F. Hoffmann, L. Scheffczyk, and K. Feiereis (Leipzig, 1969), p. 164; and *Logik und Semantik im Mittelalter* (Stuttgart-Bad Cannstatt, 1972), p. 75. De Rijk, ed., *Tractatus,* p. xciii, seems to agree at least in part with Bird's view: "This tract [chap. V of *Tractatus*] is not a compilation from Aristotle's *Topica* but from Boethius' *De topicis differentiis I* and *II,* with some additions from Aristotle's *Topics.*" He argues in note 5 on the same page that Peter's treatment is not taken directly from Boethius; rather, he says, it is "useful to point to the treatment of the *loci* in the Logica *Cum sit nostra,* pp. 438–445 or to that in the somewhat older work, *Dialectica Monacensis,* pp. 528–555." De Rijk's point is very likely right, but what can be inferred from the claim in the text and the note is that Peter's work on Topics amounts to an indirect compilation from Boethius's *De top. diff.*
6. Ed. L. M. de Rijk (Assen, 1959), pp. 86–114.
7. For the major treatment of the Topics in these last treatises, see *Logica Modernorum,* ed. L. M. de Rijk, II (Assen, 1967), pt. 2, 47–67, 85–97, 242–251, 365–371, 401–408, 438–445, 528–555 (cf. also 504–506).
8. *Introductiones Magistri Guilelmi de Shyreswode in logicam,* ed. Martin Grabmann, in *Sitzungsberichte der bayerischen Akademie der Wissenschaften,* Heft 10 (Munich, 1937), pp. 30–104. For corrections of Grabmann's text, see John Malcolm, "On Grabmann's Text of William of Sherwood," *Vivarium,* 9 (1971), 108–118. For an annotated translation, see *William of Sherwood's Introduction to Logic,* tr. Norman Kretzmann (Minneapolis, 1966).
9. Lambert of Auxerre, *Logica (Summa Lamberti),* ed. Franco Alessio (Florence, 1971). There is also an incomplete and very general commentary on *De top. diff.* by Martin of Dacia, *Martini de Dacia Opera,* ed. H. Roos, Corpus philosophorum Dani-

the Topics,[10] and he also wrote a commentary on Boethius's *De top. diff.;*[11] but Abelard's treatment tends to be idiosyncratic or allied to accounts of Topics in later scholastics such as Ockham.[12]

Peter's treatise on the Topics begins with a discussion of the word 'ratio' and its different senses, because in one of its senses *ratio* is the genus of argument in Boethius's definition of argument.[13] According to Peter, *ratio* in that definition is a *middle* (or intermediate) entailing or implying a conclusion.[14] An argument, which is a reason (*ratio*) producing belief regarding something that was in doubt, is a middle proving a conclusion, and a conclusion is a proposition that must be confirmed by an argument.[15] To understand clearly what Peter means by 'argument' here, it would be helpful to know more precisely what he conceives of as a middle, but Peter says only that a middle is what has two extremes (p. 55.22). In the context it is hard not to suppose that by 'middle' Peter means to refer to the middle term of an Aristotelian syllogism,[16] but we will see as we go on whether such an interpretation is justified.

After a brief discussion of the difference between argument and argumentation, in which Peter provides Boethius's definition of argumentation,[17] he considers the four different kinds of argu-

---

corum medii aevi (Hauniae, 1961), pp. 317–327; and an unedited commentary by Radulphus Brito ("Questiones Radulphi Brithonis super libro topicorum Boecij," Ms. Bibliotheque royale, Brussels, Cod. 3540–47, ff. 163v–195v).

10. Peter Abelard, *Dialectica,* ed. L. M. de Rijk (Assen, 1970), pp. 253–466.

11. Peter Abelard, *Scritti di Logica,* ed. Mario dal Pra (Florence, 1969), pp. 205–330.

12. This is not to say that Abelard's treatment had no influence on the tradition of the Topics or that it bears no resemblance to the discussions of the Topics in Peter and Boethius. But Abelard's account seems in some respects more sophisticated and advanced than Peter's, so that it might be more sensible to read Abelard in the light of Peter of Spain, rather than the other way around. See Bird, "Tradition of the Logical Topics," pp. 317 and 320.

13. Cf. *De top. diff.* 1174D1–2.

14. "*Medium inferens conclusionem,*" p. 55.12–14.

15. *Tractatus,* ed. De Rijk, p. 55.13–18. Peter says, "*argumentum est . . . medium probans conclusionem que debet confirmari per argumentum*" (p. 55.17–18). He seems to mean something like the two different definitions I suggest here and not one circular definition, for he goes on to spell out the definition of 'conclusion': "*Est enim conclusio argumento vel argumentis approbata propositio*" (p. 55.19).

16. In the passage on enthymemes immediately following, Peter uses '*medium*' to refer to the middle term of a syllogism.

17. "Argumentation is the explication of the argument in discourse . . . the whole discourse composed of premises and conclusion," pp. 55.23, 56.4–5; cf., for example, *De top. diff.* 1174D8–9 and 1183B4–11 in conjunction with 1184D10–14.

mentation. Syllogisms have been treated at length in an earlier treatise (or chapter) of the book, and the bulk of this section on argumentation is devoted to the enthymeme. Peter explains briefly that an enthymeme is a syllogism with a premise missing and then shows how enthymemes are reduced to syllogisms: "It is important to know that every enthymeme must be reduced to a syllogism. In every enthymeme there are three terms, as in a syllogism; of these terms, two are put in the conclusion and are the extremes, and the other is a middle and is never put in the conclusion. Of the extremes, one is taken twice in the enthymeme and the other once. A universal proposition must be produced from the extreme taken once and the middle in keeping with the requirement of [the syllogistic] mood. In this way, a syllogism will be produced."[18] He gives the example, "Every animal is running; therefore, every man is running." The premise needed to make the enthymeme a syllogism, according to Peter's theory above, is a universal proposition composed of the middle, *animal,* and the extreme taken only once, *man.* The proposition can be negative or affirmative, and the middle can be the subject or the predicate; and so the resulting syllogism will be either first or third figure. But there is no valid third-figure syllogism with a universal affirmative conclusion; and the only first-figure syllogism with a universal affirmative conclusion is Barbara. So the missing premise will have to be a universal affirmative with the middle term as predicate, namely, 'Every man is an animal.' Peter simply gives the missing premise in the passage without stating his reasons for choosing this combination of middle and extreme; but the reasoning I have provided to explain that choice of the missing premise seems to be what Peter has in mind when he says that the missing premise ought to be constructed "in keeping with the requirement of the [syllogistic] mood."

Peter begins his general discussion of Topics with a definition of a Topic and a statement of its function. An argument is confirmed (*confirmatur*) by a Topic, Peter says; and a Topic is the seat (*sedes*) of an argument, or that from which a fitting argument for

18. P. 57.3–10. "*Sciendum autem quod omne entimema debet reduci ad sillogismum. Ergo in quolibet entimemate sunt tres termini sicut in sillogismo. Quorum terminorum duo ponuntur in conclusione et sunt extremitates, et alius est medium et numquam ponitur in conclusione. Illarum autem extremitatum altera est sumpta bis in entimemate, altera semel. Et ex illa extremitate semel sumpta et medio debet fieri propositio universalis secundum exigentiam modi et sic fiet sillogismus.*"

the question at issue is drawn.[19] Since Peter has defined argument earlier as a certain kind of middle, what is drawn from a Topic is a middle of some sort. Hence a Topic functions as part of the proof for a conclusion, and it does so by providing a middle.

Included in this general discussion of Topics is some of the basic theory about Topics found in Boethius. Peter divides a Topic into maximal proposition (which he abbreviates as 'maxima' 'maxim') and Differentia, which he defines much as Boethius does: the Differentia is a differentia (specific difference) of maximal propositions, and a maximal proposition, or maxim, is a proposition for which there is no prior or better-known proposition. The Topics are also divided into the three main groups found in *De top. diff.* Book II (the Themistian division of the Topics), namely, intrinsic, extrinsic, and intermediate, depending on whether the argument is taken from the nature of one of the terms in the argument's question or from what is external to their nature or partly from their nature and partly from without (p. 59).

The first Topic Peter gives in detail is the intrinsic Topic *from definition*. The Topic *from definition*, he says, is the relationship of a definition to what it defines (the *definitum*), and the Topic contains four arguments and four maxims (p. 60.10–12). Peter identifies the four arguments by specifying four sorts of premises for enthymemes: "First, by using the definition as the subject in an affirmative proposition; second, by using it as the predicate in an affirmative proposition; third, by using it as the subject in a negative proposition; and fourth, by using it as the predicate in a negative proposition" (p. 60.13–15). Since many things are definitions, this Topic contains not four arguments but four sorts of argument. The rest of the section on this Topic consists in examples of these four sorts of arguments and appropriate maxims for them; and the examples for this and every other Topic in Peter's treatise on the Topics are all enthymemes.

Peter does not say that his examples are enthymemes; and all the examples he gives for Topics, here and in the rest of Treatise V, differ in an important respect from the examples he gives of an enthymeme: the quantity of the propositions in all the examples for Topics is indefinite or singular rather than universal or particular. Nonetheless, I am regarding these examples as enthymemes

19. p. 58.10–13; cf. *De top. diff.* 1185A4–5 and ff.

for three reasons. First, they fit Peter's definition of enthymeme (closely paraphrased from Boethius, 1184B13–C1) at the beginning of this Treatise: "An enthymeme is an imperfect syllogism, that is, discourse in which the precipitous conclusion is derived without all the propositions having been laid down beforehand."[20] The definition does not exclude arguments composed of an indefinite premise and conclusion. Furthermore, when Peter discusses indefinite propositions in connection with complete syllogisms, he does not exclude them altogether; he says only, "A syllogism cannot be produced from propositions which are all particular or indefinite or singular."[21] An enthymeme can be composed of an indefinite premise and conclusion and still be reduced to a complete syllogism by the addition of one premise, provided that that premise is universal. Second, at the start of this Treatise (p. 56.10ff.) Peter gives an apparently exhaustive list of the varieties of argumentation, that is, the varieties of legitimate combinations of premises and conclusions (see p. 56.4–5); they are syllogism, induction, enthymeme, and example. It is hard to see how Peter's combinations of premise and conclusion could be classified except as enthymemes because they are more like enthymemes than they are like syllogisms, inductions, or examples; and Peter gives no other classifications into which they might fit. Third, as far as I can tell, nothing turns on the indefinite quantity of the propositions in Peter's examples; nothing explicit or implicit in Peter's account makes much of the indefinite quantity of the propositions. In the rest of my analysis of Peter, therefore, I will refer to his examples of arguments as enthymemes.[22]

Indefinite propositions can be interpreted either as universal or as particular propositions; for example, 'a man is an animal' should be taken as a universal, but 'a man is a father' as a particular. William of Sherwood's interpretation of indefinites and singulars often seems determined more by the needs of a certain syllogistic mood than by any theory about the nature of indefinites and singulars; for example, he takes 'an animal is not a quantity' as a

20. "*Entimema est sillogismus imperfectus, idest oratio in qua non omnibus antea positis propositionibus infertur festinata conclusio,*" p. 56.16–18.
21. "*ex puris particularibus vel indefinitis vel singularibus non potest fieri sillogismus,*" p. 45.1–2.
22. See also note 18 in the chapter, "Dialectic and Boethius's *De topicis differentiis.*"

particular[23] and 'Socrates is included under "every man" ' as a universal.[24] In the discussion that follows, I will read Peter's indefinite propositions either as universals or as particulars, depending on what the context calls for.

The four enthymemes given for the Topic *from definition* are these:

(1) A mortal rational animal is running; therefore, a man is running.
(2) Socrates is a mortal rational animal; therefore, Socrates is a man.
(3) A mortal rational animal is not running; therefore, a man is not running.
(4) A stone is not a mortal rational animal; therefore, a stone is not a man. (p. 60)

Their corresponding maxims are:

(1') Whatever is predicated of the definition is also predicated of the thing defined.[25]
(2') Whatever the definition is predicated of, the thing defined is also predicated of.[26]
(3') Whatever is removed from the definition is also removed from the thing defined.[27]
(4') Whatever the definition is removed from, the thing defined is also removed from.[28] [*Ibid.*]

If we look at the arguments given for this first Topic in the light of the introductory material Peter presents at the beginning of this Treatise, particularly the special consideration accorded to enthymemes and the method for reducing enthymemes to syllogisms, then it is tempting to suppose that the Topics are the instruments for reduction to syllogism (or to syllogistic inferences). Such a view of the Topics is not uncommon among contemporary writers,[29] and is also taken by some later medievals.[30] Peter's con-

---

23. "*Animal non est quantitas,*" *Introductiones,* Grabmann, ed., p. 59.21; Kretzmann, tr., p. 76.
24. "*Sortes est sub eo, quod est omnis homo,*" *ibid.,* Grabmann, ed., p. 61.32–33; Kretzmann, tr., p. 80.
25. "*quidquid predicatur de diffinitione, et de diffinito.*"
26. "*de quocumque predicatur diffinitio, et diffinitum.*"
27. "*quidquid removetur a diffinitione, et a diffinito.*"
28. "*a quocumque removetur diffinitio, et diffinitum.*"
29. See, for example, Jan Pinborg, "Topik und Syllogistik," p. 159.
30. See, for example, Bird, "Formalizing of the Topics," p. 146; according to Bird, Burley, for example, thinks that the Topics reduce material inferences to formal inferences, inferences that hold good solely in virtue of their form.

temporary, Lambert of Auxerre, also appears to take Topical arguments in this way; at the end of his treatment of the Topics, he says,

> it can be said that [an argument depending on the Topics] is an enthymematic argumentation . . . and can be reduced to a syllogistic argumentation. . . . [For example,] 'a man is running, therefore a mortal rational animal[31] is running' is an enthymeme [composed of] the major [premise] and conclusion. Let the minor premise be put forward, and there will be a syllogism in the third mood of the first figure [Darii] in this way: 'Every man is running; a mortal rational animal is a man; therefore, a mortal rational animal is running.' It should not cause surprise that what is taken as an indefinite in the enthymeme is taken as a universal in the syllogism, because a syllogism cannot be produced without a universal, although an enthymeme can be produced correctly without a universal.[32]

William of Sherwood, another contemporary of Peter's, also regularly reduces Topical arguments to syllogisms.[33] In what follows, I will show the way Peter's discussions of the first five Topics lend themselves to such a view of Topics and how Topics function according to that view. I will then show that Peter cannot have thought of Topics solely or primarily as instruments for reducing enthymemes to syllogisms and that, for Peter, Topics confirm arguments in a more complicated and perhaps a looser way.

If we consider the enthymemes for the Topic *from definition* according to Peter's method for reducing enthymemes to syllogisms, we see that in each enthymeme the middle term is *mortal rational animal* and the term taken only once is *man*. No valid syllogism contains exactly one or three negative propositions; there are three affirmative or one affirmative and two negative propositions in every valid syllogism. And every valid syllogism contains at least one universal premise. So the missing premise in each of the four

---

31. Reading *'animal'* for *'homo.'* The text as Alessio gives it is clearly mistaken.

32. "*dici posset quod est argumentatio empthimemica . . . et ad sillogisticam argumentationem posset reduci . . . 'homo currit, ergo homo rationale mortale currit' empthimema est ex maiori et conclusione; et ponatur minor: erit sillogismus in tertio prime figure sic: 'omnis homo currit, animal rationale mortale est homo, ergo animal rationale mortale currit'; nec mirandum est si sumatur in sillogismo universalis, que sumetur in empthimemate infinita, quia sine universali non potest fieri sillogismus: empthimema vero bene potest fieri sine universali*" (*Logica,* ed. Alessio, pp. 139–140). I have no explanation for the curious assignment of quantity in the syllogism. Lambert's explanation seems both lame and artificial.

33. I do not mean to imply nor is it at all clear that either William or Lambert thinks that the *primary function* of a Topic has to do with reduction to syllogism.

enthymemes is a universal affirmative proposition whose two terms are *mortal rational animal* and *man*.

The first enthymeme will be reduced to a first-figure syllogism if we take the definition as the predicate in the missing premise and to a third-figure syllogism if we take it as the subject. The premise given in the enthymeme is the major premise since the extreme in it is the predicate rather than the subject of the conclusion and hence this extreme is the major term; so the missing premise is the minor premise of the appropriate syllogism. The syllogism, then, will be a syllogism in IAI in either the first or third figures if we read Peter's indefinites as particulars. But since there are no such valid first-figure syllogisms, the enthymeme must be reduced to the third-figure syllogism Disamis; and the missing premise is 'Every mortal rational animal is a man.'

In the second enthymeme, the missing premise is the major premise; and the appropriate syllogism is AII in the first or second figure, depending on whether the missing premise is 'Every man is a mortal rational animal' or 'Every mortal rational animal is a man.' But there are no valid AII syllogisms in the second figure; so the premise needed is again 'Every mortal rational animal is a man,' and the enthymeme reduces to a first-figure syllogism in Darii.

The third enthymeme reduces to OAO in either the first or third figures. There are no valid first-figure syllogisms in OAO; so the appropriate syllogism here is the third-figure Bocardo, and the missing premise is again 'Every mortal rational animal is a man.'

It seems clear that the propositions for the last enthymeme ought to be taken as universals, and the appropriate syllogism is one in AEE. If we add the same premise here as we did to the other enthymemes, namely, 'Every mortal rational animal is a man,' we have an invalid first-figure syllogism. The other possibility is a second-figure syllogism in AEE; and there is such a valid syllogism: Camestres. So for this enthymeme the missing premise is 'Every man is a mortal rational animal.'

The Topic following the Topic *from definition* is the Topic *from what is defined* (the *definitum*); and it, too, has four sorts of arguments and four corresponding maxims. The four enthymemes and the corresponding maxims are these:

(1) A man is running; therefore, a mortal rational animal is running.
(2) Socrates is a man; therefore, Socrates is a mortal rational animal.

(3) A man is not running; therefore, a mortal rational animal is not running.

(4) A stone is not a man; therefore, a stone is not a mortal rational animal. [p. 61]

(1') Whatever is predicated of the thing defined is also predicated of the definition.[34]

(2') Whatever the thing defined is predicated of, the definition is also predicated of.[35]

(3') Whatever is removed from the thing defined is also removed from the definition.[36]

(4') Whatever the thing defined is removed from, the definition is also removed from.[37] [*Ibid.*]

They reduce to the same syllogisms as those from definition: Disamis, Darii, Bocardo, and Camestres. For the first three enthymemes, the missing premise is 'Every man is a mortal rational animal'; and for the last one, it is 'Every mortal rational animal is a man.'

The Topic *from explanation of the name* is the next one provided with examples. In this case, too, we are given four enthymemes with their maxims.

(1) A lover of wisdom is running; therefore, a philosopher is running.

(2) A philosopher is running; therefore, a lover of wisdom is running.

(3) A lover of wisdom does not envy; therefore, a philosopher does not envy.

(4) A philosopher does not envy; therefore, a lover of wisdom does not envy. [p. 62]

(1') Whatever is predicated of the explanation is also predicated of what is explained.[38]

(2') Whatever the explanation is predicated of, that which is explained is also predicated of.[39]

(3') Whatever is removed from the explanation is also removed from what is explained.[40]

(4') Whatever the explanation is removed from, that which is explained is also removed from. [*Ibid.*][41]

---

34. "quicquid predicatur de diffinito, et de diffinitione."
35. "de quocumque predicatur diffinitum, et diffinitio."
36. "quicquid removetur a diffinito, et a diffinitione."
37. "a quocumque removetur diffinitum, et diffinitio."
38. "quicquid predicatur de interpretatione, et de interpretato."
39. "de quocumque predicatur interpretatio, et interpretatum."
40. "quicquid removetur ab interpretatione, et ab interpretato."

In all four, *lover of wisdom* is the middle term, and *philosopher* is the term taken only once in the enthymeme. For the first two enthymemes, the missing premise is 'Every lover of wisdom is a philosopher'; and the enthyemes reduce to Disamis and Darii, as in the Topic *from definition* and the Topic *from the definitum*. The missing premise in the second two enthymemes is 'Every philosopher is a lover of wisdom'; and the appropriate syllogisms are Celarent and Baroco.

One enthymeme is given for the Topic *from genus* (that is, from the relationship of the genus to the species): "A stone is not an animal; therefore, a stone is not a man" (p. 63.16–18); and two for the Topic *from species* (the relationship of the species to the genus): "A man is running; therefore, an animal is running"; and "Socrates is a man; therefore, Socrates is an animal" (p. 64.1–10). The missing premise for all three is 'Every man is an animal'; and the appropriate syllogisms are Camestres, Disamis, and Darii respectively.

In every one of the enthymemes considered above, the Topic is a relationship between the things referred to by the middle term of the enthymeme and one of the extremes—in every case, the extreme taken only once in the enthymeme. When the middle and the extreme taken only once are used to make a universal premise, according to Peter's method for reducing enthymemes to syllogisms, the resulting premise presents an instance of the relationship that is the Differentia, or some part of that relationship. As we have seen, Peter holds that the function of the Differentiae is to confirm arguments and that they do so by providing a middle or intermediate. We might be inclined to think that the middle provided must be a middle term; but an enthymeme already has a middle term and so cannot be provided with, or confirmed by the addition of, a middle term. What does depend on the Differentiae is not a middle term, it seems, but rather a premise that is based on the relationship that is the Differentia or some part of the relationship. That premise, made as Peter says the missing premise for an enthymeme should be made, turns the enthymeme into a valid syllogism and by doing so confirms the inference made in the enthymeme. It seems, then, that the Differentiae provide miss-

---

41. "*a quocumque removetur interpretatio, et interpretatum.*"

ing premises for enthymemes and that Peter's method of the Topics is a method for reducing enthymemes to syllogisms. And the Differentiae do provide a middle as Peter's account requires, not, however, by providing a "middle" proposition (middle in the sense that it is between the premise and the conclusion of the enthymeme), but instead by providing a bridge between the lone premise and the conclusion of the enthymeme, a link that validates the passage from premise to conclusion.

The hypothesis that Differentiae function in this way to confirm arguments is strengthened if we look at the section on the Topics in Garlandus Compotista's *Dialectica*, which may be as much as two hundred years older than Peter's *Tractatus*. Garlandus's treatise on the Topics is in many ways closer to *De top. diff.* than Peter's is, and it seems to be an intermediary between Boethius's method of the Topics and Peter's.

Garlandus's discussion of the first topic *from definition* [42] is fuller than his discussions of the remaining Topics, and it is instructive. In the example he provides for this Topic, he follows Boethius's pattern for giving examples of Topics. First, he raises a question: whether Socrates is a man. Then he gives an argument supporting one side of the question:

(1) Every mortal rational animal is a man.
(2) Socrates is a mortal rational animal.
(3) Therefore, Socrates is a man.

The Differentia and the maximal proposition for the argument are given immediately after the argument. The rest of the discussion of this Topic, however, resembles Peter's treatment of it. Garlandus explains that arguments are taken from this Topic in six ways; and he gives the following six enthymematic inferences as examples (but without the appropriate maxims Peter always provides for enthymemes): [43]

(1) If a mortal rational animal is white, a man is white.
(2) If a mortal rational animal is not white, a man is not white.
(3) If Socrates is a mortal rational animal, he is a man.

42. *Dialectica*, ed. De Rijk, p. 102.
43. Garlandus gives almost all his examples for Topics as hypothetical propositions, but they may be considered as enthymemes in hypothetical form. Like the premises and conclusions of Peter's enthymemes, the antecedents and consequents of Garlandus's hypotheticals tend to be indefinite propositions.

(4) If Socrates is not a mortal rational animal, he is not a man.
(5) If a mortal rational animal exists, a man exists.
(6) If a mortal rational animal does not exist, a man does not exist.

In the context, it seems as if something of this sort is happening. An argument corresponding to the Topic *from definition* has a definition as its middle term and that definition is the definition of one of the extremes. So one obvious premise in any such argument is the premise expressing the relationship between definition and *definitum:* 'Every mortal rational animal is a man' or 'Every man is a mortal rational animal.' The second premise in the syllogism contains the middle and the other extreme; it can vary considerably, depending on the way it is composed. It can be affirmative or negative; the middle term can be the subject or the predicate; and, according to Garlandus, it can be existential or predicative. In the enthymemes Garlandus gives for this Topic, if the premise 'Every mortal rational animal is a man' is added to enthymemes (1), (2), (3), and (5), hypothetical syllogisms are produced. The syllogistic moods for the first three are the same as those for the first three enthymemes of Peter's Topic *from definition:* Disamis, Bocardo, and Darii. The appropriate syllogism for (5), the first existential enthymeme, is also Darii. The premise needed for enthymemes (4) and (6) is 'Every man is a mortal rational animal'; and they both reduce to Baroco in hypothetical form. Each of the existential enthymemes, (5) and (6), reduces to the same syllogistic mood as one of the nonexistential enthymemes above. Perhaps the existential enthymemes are omitted from later treatments of this Topic (and others), as in *Dialectica Monacensis*[44] or in Peter's *Tractatus,* because 'exists' can be treated as a syllogistic extreme, thereby rendering an existential enthymeme merely a special case of one of the predicative enthymemes.

It seems, then, that Garlandus means all six enthymematic inferences as examples of the six forms of argument possible with the Topic *from definition.* He gives an argument in full at the beginning of his discussion of the Topic for the sake of clarity; but when he gives examples of the six types of argument that go with this Topic, he leaves out the obvious premise, which is taken from the Topic. In the discussions of Topics following the Topic *from defini-*

44. Ed. De Rijk, *Log. Mod.,* II, pt. 2, 530–531.

tion, Garlandus abbreviates further and omits the initial, Boethian consideration of the Topic, including the full presentation of an argument from the Topic. For these Topics, Garlandus gives only the varying premise and the conclusion of arguments appropriate to the Topic being discussed. Maxims for these arguments are sometimes given and sometimes not.

The treatment of the Topics found in Garlandus may be one of the historical links between Boethius's method and Peter's. Boethius uses the Topics to provide intermediates or middle terms in order to make arguments from the two terms in a question. In Garlandus's treatment, the Boethian method is ordered and formalized to some extent. The different sorts of argument corresponding to each Topic are catalogued, and catalogued in an abbreviated way; the premise related to the Differentia is omitted, and the different types of argument are given as enthymematic inferences in hypothetical form with varying premises, depending on the way the middle is related to the second extreme. And in Peter, the interest seems to have turned to the abbreviated syllogisms or enthymemes themselves, which are reduced to complete syllogisms (and hence confirmed) by the addition of the premise related to the Differentia.

In William of Sherwood's treatment of those Topics we have been considering in Peter's account, we find explicit the procedure that seems implicit in Peter. William, too, gives enthymemes as examples for Topics, and he reduces almost all his enthymemes to syllogisms. Two of his enthymemes, those serving as examples for the Topic *from species* [45] are the same as Peter's. William reduces them to syllogisms in the way I suggested Peter's enthymemes ought to be reduced. He leaves the enthymeme's propositions indefinite or singular, and he adds a universal premise taken from the Differentia. As I did with Peter's enthymemes, he takes the indefinite or singular propositions as particulars; and he claims that the enthymemes are reduced to Disamis and Darii respectively, the same two moods that Peter's method for reducing enthymemes yields for these examples. [46]

45. *Introductiones*, Grabmann, ed., p. 60; Kretzmann, tr., p. 77.
46. There are more possibilities for arguments than those generated by considering only syllogistic mood and the quality (affirmative or negative) of the propositions. The quantity (universal or particular) of the propositions can be varied, too, to provide different arguments in different moods of the syllogism. For instance, Peter's enthymemes for the Topic *from definition* reduce to syllogisms in Disamis,

So far we have considered in detail the first five Topics in Peter's treatise on the Topics. The sixth is the Topic *from integral whole,* the relationship of the integral whole to its part. One enthymeme is given for this Topic: "A house exists; therefore, a wall exists" (p. 64.12–17). According to Peter's method for reducing enthymemes to syllogisms, we pick out the middle term—*house*—and the extreme taken only once—*wall;* and we combine these two terms into a universal proposition in keeping with the requirements of the syllogistic mood to get a valid syllogism. The premise given in the enthymeme has the middle as subject, and so the appropriate syllogism cannot be in the second figure. The enthymeme's premise is also the major premise and should be read as particular (an I premise), so the first figure is ruled out since it has no valid moods with major premises in I. That leaves the third figure; the missing premise must be a universal premise with *house* as subject and *wall* as predicate; and the premise will have to be affirmative because the conclusion is affirmative. If we proceed straightforwardly to produce the needed premise as a universal affirmative with the middle as subject, we will reduce the enthymeme to a valid syllogism in Disamis. But the premise added will have to be 'Every house is a wall'; and it is absurd to suppose that the enthymeme would be confirmed by such a premise. Peter's method for reducing enthymemes to syllogisms apparently will not work in this case.

We could try to find the missing premise by working directly from the Differentia since the Differentia is supposed to provide the argument and confirm the enthymeme. The Differentia is *from an integral whole;* that is, the enthymeme depends on a relationship between an integral whole and one of its parts. In this case, the integral whole is a house, and its part is a wall. So we might make this premise from the Differentia: 'A wall is part of a house' or perhaps even the universal, 'Every wall is part of a house.' But we cannot use either of these propositions to reduce the enthymeme to a syllogism because in the context *part of a house* would be a fourth term. Apparently this enthymeme cannot

Darii, Bocardo, and Camestres. If enthymemes were generated by varying quantity as well, there would also be enthymemes that reduced to Darapti, Barbara, Felapton, and Baroco (corresponding to Disamis, Darii, Bocardo, and Camestres). And in a later development of the Topics, Ockham, for example, does take the quantity of an argument's propositions into account. See Otto Bird, "Topic and Consequence in Ockham's Logic," *Notre Dame Journal of Formal Logic,* 2 (1961), 69–70.

be confirmed by adding a premise according to Peter's method or directly from the Differentia. However the Topic is meant to confirm the argument here, it does not do so by reducing it to a syllogism.

For the Topic *from an integral whole*, William of Sherwood gives the same enthymeme as Peter; and he adds: "Arguments from an integral whole reduce to the third mood of the first figure [*Darii*], as follows: 'every part of the house exists (since the house exists), a wall is part of the house; therefore a wall exists.' "[47] As William gives it, the argument is this:

(1) A house exists.
(2) Therefore, every part of the house exists.
(3) A wall is part of the house.
(4) Therefore, a wall exists.

The second, third, and fourth steps constitute the syllogism in Darii, and the enthymeme's premise is not one of the premises in the syllogism. The syllogism's minor premise, step (3) in the argument, is the premise generated from the Differentia in question here, and it describes the relationship between wall and house, the particular whole and part in the enthymeme. The syllogism's major premise, step (2), is the conclusion of an enthymeme very similar to the original enthymeme 'A house exists; therefore, a wall exists.' The maxim William gives for this Differentia is "What goes together with an [integral] whole in respect of proportional and perceptible parts (*secundum partes proportionales et notabiles*) goes together with a part."[48] And the inference from step (1) to step (2) in the argument above seems to depend on this maxim, which attributes certain predicates of an integral whole to any and every part of that whole. The inference from (1) to (2) seems to go like this:

(A) What goes together with an integral whole in respect of proportional and perceptible parts goes together with every part of that whole.
(B) Every house is an integral whole.

47. "*Et reducuntur argumenta iuxta hunc locum in tertium prime sic: quelibet pars domus, quia domus est, est. Paries est pars domus quia domus est* [sic!]. *Ergo paries est.*" *Introductiones*, Grabmann, ed., p. 61.6–9; Kretzmann, tr., p. 79.

48. *Ibid.*, Grabmann, ed., p. 60.32–33; Kretzmann, tr., pp. 78–79.

   (C) Existence goes together with some house in respect of proportional and perceptible parts.
   (D) Therefore, existence goes together with every part of that house.

Steps (C) and (D) are equivalent to steps (1)[49] and (2) in William's argument; (B) is the premise related to the Differentia; and (A) is the Differentia's maxim.

So in the argument William provides to show that the enthymeme for this Differentia can be reduced to Darii, one premise of the syllogism in Darii comes from the Differentia (the relationship involved in the enthymeme). The other premise is derived from the enthymeme's premise (premise C above), a premise related to the Differentia (premise B above), and the maxim for the enthymeme (premise A above). The valid inferring of the conclusion depends on the enthymeme's premise, the Differentia, and the maxim.

The Topic *from an integral whole* is typical of most of the remaining Topics in Peter's treatise. Take, for example, the Topic *from a material cause.* One of the enthymemes for that Topic is 'There is no iron; therefore, there are no iron weapons', or more conveniently, for present purposes, 'Iron is not; therefore, iron weapons are not' (p. 68.4–5). The enthymeme's premise is the major premise and *iron* is the middle term; so the appropriate syllogism for this enthymeme must be a first- or third-figure syllogism in OAO. The only combination that gives a valid syllogism is the third-figure syllogism Bocardo; but that mood requires the blatantly false premise 'Everything that is iron is iron weapons.' The proposition describing the relationship that is the Differentia here would have to be something like 'Iron is the matter (or material cause) of iron weapons'; such a proposition would introduce a fourth term if it were added to the enthymeme in order to produce a syllogism.

William of Sherwood gives a similar enthymeme for this Topic: "the Moors do not have iron; therefore they do not have iron weapons."[50] And he says the enthymeme is to be reduced to Ferio

---

49. Except, of course, for the qualification about proportional and perceptible parts, which seems to be taken as understood in (1).
50. *Introductiones*, Grabmann, ed., p. 63.29–30; Kretzmann, tr., p. 85.

in this way: "no people who do not have iron are people who have iron weapons, the Moors are people who do not have iron; therefore the Moors are not people who have iron weapons."[51] The syllogism's minor premise is the premise in the enthymeme; the major premise, however, seems to depend on or be drawn from the maxim for this Differentia: "Where the matter is lacking, what depends on that matter is lacking (*deficiente materia deficit materiatum*)."[52] That maxim and a proposition drawn from the Differentia stating that iron is the matter of iron weapons (the *materiatum*, what depends on the matter) yield the conclusion that all people who lack iron lack iron weapons and so also that no people who lack iron are people who have iron weapons, which is the major premise of William's syllogism.

In much the same way, the maxims and Differentiae in Peter's treatise can be combined to confirm arguments, even for the arguments of Topics that can be confirmed by reduction to syllogisms. For example, the Topic *from definition* has as its first enthymeme 'A mortal rational animal is running; therefore, a man is running' and the corresponding maxim "Whatever is predicated of the definition is predicated also of the *definitum* (the thing defined)" (p. 60). The enthymeme, as we saw above, can be confirmed by reducing it to the third-figure syllogism Disamis, adding a premise describing the relationship of the Differentia. But it can also be confirmed without reduction to a syllogistic mood, by using the maxim and the Differentia:

(1) Whatever is predicated of the definition is predicated of the *definitum*.
(2) Mortal rational animal is the definition of the *definitum* man.
(3) Running is predicated of a mortal rational animal.
(4) Therefore, running is predicated also of man.

The first premise is the maxim; the second is the premise drawn from the relationship in the Differentia; and (3) and (4) are equivalent to the premise and conclusion of the original enthymeme.

Or, for another example, the Topic *from a quantitative whole* has as its first enthymeme "Every man is running; therefore, Socrates is running"; and the corresponding maxim is "Whatever is predicated of a quantitative whole is also predicated of any part of that

51. *Ibid.*, Grabmann, ed., p. 63.32–34; Kretzmann, tr., p. 85.
52. *Ibid.*, Grabmann, ed., p. 63.30–31.

whole" (pp. 64.24–65.5). If we take this as premise from the Differentia: 'Every-man is the quantitative whole of which Socrates is
a part,' then we can make a valid argument that yields the enthymeme's conclusion as we did above, from the premise drawn from
the Differentia, the maxim, and the premise in the enthymeme.

Furthermore, of the different discussions of the Topics taken
into account here,[53] when enthymemes and their confirming
Topics are given, William's treatise is the only one to add appropriate syllogisms and to show that the enthymemes can be reduced to
syllogisms. All the other discussions of the Topics, including Lambert's, leave syllogisms out of consideration and give only the
enthymemes and their maxims. Peter himself, who spends some
time explaining how to reduce enthymemes to syllogisms, makes
no attempt to do so for his examples and presents enthymemes
and maxims without any mention of corresponding syllogisms.

Peter's main interest, then, is not in confirming enthymemes by
reducing them to syllogisms; and though such confirmation by
reduction works for the arguments exemplifying the first Topics, it
does not work for many of the enthymemes Peter gives. The reason Peter introduces his method for converting enthymemes to
syllogisms and the way he means it to relate to confirmation by
maxims are not clear. That valid enthymemes are only imperfect
syllogisms was, of course, part of received doctrine.[54] And in William's treatise, confirmation by reduction to syllogism seems to be
only a second check on the maxims, providing additional evidence
that the enthymeme confirmed by the Topic is valid.

The method of confirmation that seems to work for all the Topics
and seems to be Peter's main method (at least) is that using both
maxims and Differentiae. The maxims are general principles that
specifically validate enthymematic inferences for a certain relationship. They serve as specific inference warrants for certain
enthymemes, and the Differentiae provide the information needed
to apply them. The notion that the function of Topics is to confirm
arguments in this way seems to have prevailed in later treatments
of the Topics as the Topics became absorbed into the study of consequences.[55]

53. See the beginning of this chapter.
54. Cf., for example, *De top. diff.* 1184B13ff.
55. Cf. Bird, "Formalizing of the Topics"; and "Tradition of the Logical Topics,"
pp. 307–323.

Otto Bird argues that many of the maxims work with the Differentiae to validate enthymemes because the maxims in question are laws of class logic. One of Peter's enthymemes for the Topic from genus is "An animal is not running; therefore, a man is not running," and its maxim is "What is removed from the genus is also removed from the species." [56] Bird thinks that the enthymeme's conclusion is validly inferred from the enthymeme's premise, the maxim for the enthymeme, and this premise drawn from the Differentia: 'Animal is the genus of the species man', and he formalizes the argument in this way. Let α and β be classes, and let M be the class of men and A the class of animals. Then,

(1) $\alpha \subset \beta \rightarrow ((x) \sim (x \epsilon \beta \wedge \phi x) \rightarrow (x \epsilon \alpha \wedge \phi x))$
(2) $M \subset A$
(3) $\therefore (x) \sim (x \epsilon A \wedge Rx) \rightarrow (x) \sim (x \epsilon M \wedge Rx)$

And if the enthymeme's premise is added, the argument yields the conclusion of the enthymeme. [57]

Peter's enthymemes, then, work because there is a certain relationship between what is signified by the middle term and what is signified by one of the extreme terms (namely, the relationship spelled out in the Differentia) and because certain inferences are valid given that relationship (those falling under the maxims for a Differentia). Theoretically, a maxim is a self-evidently true generalization; [58] and so the inference in the enthymeme is shown to be valid once the enthymeme has, with the help of the Differentia, been shown to fall under the generalization that is the maxim. And it should be clear now what the middle is that the Differentia provides to confirm arguments: it is the relationship that holds between the middle term and one of the extremes in the enthymeme, on the basis of which the maxim can be applied. So in the first enthymeme for the Topic *from definition*—"A mortal rational animal is running; therefore, a man is running"—the relationship between the middle *mortal rational animal* and the extreme *man* is spelled out in the Differentia *from definition*. Given this relationship, those inferences that fall under the maxim for this enthymeme are valid. The maxim is "Whatever is predicated of the defi-

56. In fact, neither the enthymeme nor its maxim is given in the text of De Rijk's edition of Peter's *Tractatus*, though both are in the apparatus as variants (p. 63). De Rijk's edition was not available at the time Bird was writing.
57. Bird, "Topic and Consequence in Ockham's Logic," p. 73.
58. See Peter, p. 59.

nition is predicated also of the *definitum*"; applied to the enthymeme, it validates the passage from premise to conclusion, and it can be applied to the enthymeme because the middle and extreme have the relationship of definition to *definitum*, which is the Differentia for this example. So the enthymematic argument is "confirmed," as Peter says it is, by the twofold Topic consisting in the Differentia and maxim for this argument.

The method found in Peter's treatment of the Topics, then, is very different from that in Boethius's *De top. diff.* In Peter's treatise, the Topics are almost completely divorced from the predicables and from the dialectical dispute. There is no discussion of the question going with each Topic or of anything related to disputation; and there is no evidence here of the technique of arguing by question and answer, which Boethius thinks is characteristic of dialectic. For Peter, the Differentia is the *relationship* between the things referred to by a middle term and an extreme in the conclusion of an argument (for example, the relationship of definition to *definitum*).[59] For Boethius, the Differentia is simply the sort of thing that the middle term refers to (for example, a definition); and when he thinks of a relationship involving the middle term (or what it refers to), he thinks of it as the relation between the things referred to by the middle term and one of the terms in the *question*. The function of the Differentiae in the two methods is different, too. For Boethius, a Differentia provides a middle term or an intermediate between the two extremes in order to *produce* an argument. For Peter, a Differentia provides a premise or information needed in order to apply the maxim that *validates* the enthymeme's inference. And finally, Boethius's main purpose in *De top. diff.* is to teach the art of obtaining an argument for and belief in a certain conclusion; Peter's main interest is in explaining and justifying the validity of obvious and readily granted inferences that are enthymemes. Boethius explains at length that the method for the Topics belongs to the art of finding arguments rather than to the art of judging them. For Peter, the reverse is true; the func-

---

59. When Peter is giving Boethius's definitions of key terms in the introductory section of this Treatise, he says that arguments may be taken from things that agree with the terms posited in the question (p. 59.28–31). But when he discusses the relationships that are the Differentiae, the relationships are those holding between a term in an enthymeme's premise and another term in that enthymeme's conclusion; see, for example, p. 61.21–25. See also *Dialectica Monacensis*, p. 528, where the point is discussed in some detail.

tion of the Topics in his treatise is solely to confirm arguments, to manifest and guarantee their validity. In Peter's treatment of the Topics, they are an interesting part of scholastic logic and the burgeoning study of "consequences";[60] but with these developments in the method of the Topics, the Boethian art of discovering arguments has been lost.

60. See, for example, Ernest A. Moody, *Truth and Consequence in Medieval Logic* (New York and Amsterdam, 1953).

Differentia and the Porphyrian Tree

Aristotle divides everything in the world into ten categories: substance, quantity, relation, quality, doing, undergoing, place where, time when, position, and having.[1] Examples of substances are an individual man or an individual horse, and also the species and genera of these individual things, such as the species *man* and *horse* and the genus *animal* (*Cat.* 2a11ff.). Examples of the remaining nine are these:

Category	Example	Reference in CAT.
(2) quantity	numbers, surfaces	4b20ff.
(3) relation	double, larger, slave	6a36ff.
(4) quality	virtue, healthiness, sweetness	8b25ff.
(5) doing	heating, cooling	11b1ff.
(6) undergoing	being heated, being cooled	11b1ff.
(7) place where	in the market place	1b25ff.
(8) time when	yesterday, last year	1b25ff.
(9) position	lying, sitting	1b25ff.
(10) having	having shoes on, having armor on	1b25ff.

None of these categories is reducible to or subsumed under any of the others; none of them taken together fall under any other, more general category, but everything is subsumed under one or another of them. Each of these ten is the head (or, perhaps more accurately, the root) of a Porphyrian tree; each is a genus to many other things but is itself not a species of anything. There are, then, ten different Porphyrian trees, which, if they were worked out

1. *Cat.* 1b25ff.

fully, would contain among themselves all the species of things there are in the world.

A Porphyrian tree is constructed with the help of predicables, and the medievals considered knowledge of the predicables essential to a proper understanding of the categories.[2] Porphyry's famous introduction to the *Categories*, the *Isagoge*, consists altogether in an examination of predicables.

In the *Topics* Aristotle makes use of four predicables: definition, property, genus, and accident. A definition, he says, is an expression (λόγος) signifying the essence of something (101b38), and a definition consists in the genus and differentiae of what is being defined (139a28–29). Property is what belongs to one particular species and to no other and is predicated convertibly of the species, but it does not make clear the essence of the thing. One property of man, for example, is *capable of learning grammar;* if something is a man, it is capable of learning grammar, and if something is capable of learning grammar, it is a man (102a18ff.). Genus is what is predicated of many things differing in kind in respect of what they are (that is, in respect of their essence); the genus of *man,* for example, is *animal* (102a31ff.). An accident is what can belong or not belong to a thing; sitting, for example, or whiteness can belong or not belong to something (120b4ff.). Aristotle summarizes his discussion of the predicables in this way:

"It is necessary that everything which is predicated of something be convertibly predicated of that thing or not. If it is convertibly predicated, it will be a definition or property; for if it signifies the essence, it will be a definition, and if it does not signify the essence, it will be a property. . . . If it is not convertibly predicated of the thing, it either is or is not one of the things said in the definition of that thing. If it is one of the things said in the definition of the thing, it will be a genus or differentia since a definition is composed of genus and differentiae. But if it is not one of the things said in the definition, clearly it is an accident. . . . [103b7–17][3]

2. Whether predicables are linguistic entities or nonlinguistic entities of some sort (such as Platonic Forms) was a moot point throughout the Middle Ages. Boethius, like many other medievals, tends to use words referring to the predicables in an ambiguous way; and rather than introducing novel and cumbersome circumlocutions, I intend to follow his lead.

3. "ἀνάγκη γὰρ πᾶν τὸ περί τινος κατηγορούμενον ἤτοι ἀντικατηγορεῖσθαι τοῦ πράγματος ἢ μή. καὶ εἰ μὲν ἀντικατηγορεῖται, ὅρος ἢ ἴδιον ἂν εἴη· εἰ μὲν γὰρ σημαίνει τὸ τί ἦν εἶναι, ὅρος, εἰ δὲ μὴ σημαίνει, ἴδιον. . . . εἰ δὲ μὴ ἀντικατηγορεῖται τοῦ πράγματος, ἤτοι τῶν ἐν τῷ ὁρισμῷ τοῦ ὑποκειμένου λεγομένων ἐστὶν ἢ οὔ. καὶ εἰ

In the *Isagoge*, Porphyry discusses five predicables, omitting one of Aristotle's (definition) and adding two which Aristotle mentions but does not examine in detail (species and differentia), so that for Porphyry the predicables are genus, species, property, accident, and differentia. Genus and property he defines as Aristotle does.[4] His definition of species is analogous to the definition of genus: A species is that which is predicated of many things differing in number and in respect of what they are (*CAG*, p. 4.11–12). Accident he defines both as Aristotle does and as what is present to and absent from a thing without the destruction of that thing (*CAG*, p. 12.24–25). Differentia is what is predicated of many things differing in species in respect of what kind of thing they are; and all differentiae have to do with the essence or substance of what they are predicated of (*CAG*, p. 9.7ff.).

Differentiae can be thought of in two different ways: either they divide a genus, in which case they are divisive differentiae; or they constitute a species, in which case they are constitutive differentiae. The same differentia is both divisive and constitutive, but it is divisive of one thing and constitutive of another. For example, the differentia *rational* is divisive of the genus *animal* and constitutive of the species *man*. A genus that cannot itself be subsumed as a species under some higher genus is called a highest genus—Aristotle's ten categories are the ten highest genera of everything; and a species that can have no species subsumed under it for which it serves as a genus is called a lowest species. Except for lowest species and highest genera, all genera are subaltern genera—that is, they can all be described also as species; and all species are subaltern species—that is, they can all be described also as genera. A subaltern genus or species has two different sets of differentiae, those that divide it (its divisive differentiae) and those that constitute it (its constitutive differentiae). The subaltern genus *animal*, for example, is divided by the differentiae *rational* and *irrational* and constituted by the differentia *capable of perceiving*. Almost all species fall under more than one genus; the species *man*, for example, falls under the genera *rational animal*, *animal*,

μὲν τῶν ἐν τῷ ὁρισμῷ λεγομένων, γένος ἢ διαφορὰ ἂν εἴη, ἐπειδὴ ὁ ὁρισμὸς ἐκ γένους καὶ διαφορῶν ἐστίν· εἰ δὲ μὴ τῶν ἐν τῷ ὁρισμῷ λεγομένων ἐστί, δῆλον ὅτι συμβεβηκὸς ἂν εἴη. . . ."

4. *Commentaria in Aristotelem Graeca* (*CAG*), ed. Adolf Busse (Berlin, 1887), IV, pt. i, 2.14ff., 12.12 ff.

animate corporeal substance, corporeal substance, and *substance.* But the genus immediately above a given species is the proximate genus of that species. For example, *rational animal* is the proximate genus of *man.* Definitions define species and are composed of the proximate genus and constitutive differentia of the species they define.

A Porphyrian tree begins with a highest genus; in ancient and medieval writers, by far the most common example of such a genus and the tree springing from it is that of the first of Aristotle's ten categories, *substance.* The highest genus *substance* is divided by a pair of opposite characteristics, its divisive differentiae, into two species, each of which is picked out by one of the pair of differentiae. *Substance* is divided by the divisive differentiae *corporeal* and *incorporeal* into two species, which do not have their own names but are referred to by the genus plus the appropriate differentia—in this case *corporeal substance* and *incorporeal substance.* Though these two are species of *substance,* they are also genera for other things; and they can be divided by divisive differentiae just as *substance* was. *Corporeal substance* is divided by the differentiae *animate* and *inanimate* into the two species *animate corporeal substance* and *inanimate corporeal substance. Incorporeal substance* is presumably also divided, but I will follow common medieval practice and work out only one branch of this Porphyrian tree. Like *corporeal substance, animate corporeal substance* and *inanimate corporeal substance* are subaltern genera, being species of the genus above them in the tree and genera for what is below them. *Animate corporeal substance* is divided by differentiae into *sensitive* (that is, capable of perceiving) *animate corporeal substance* and *insensitive animate corporeal substance.* These two subaltern genera have names and not just descriptions; the first is the genus *animal,* and the second, the genus *plant. Animal* is divided into *rational animal* and *irrational animal,* or *rational sensitive animate corporeal substance* and *irrational sensitive animate corporeal substance.* The subaltern genus *rational animal* is in turn divided into *mortal rational animal* (*mortal rational sensitive animate corporeal substance*) and *immortal rational animal;* these two also have their own names, *'man'* and *'god.'*

These last two species are mirror images of *substance: substance* is a genus that is not a species of anything and hence is a highest genus, and these two are species that are not genera for anything and hence are lowest species. There is just one highest genus for a Porphyrian tree, but *man* and *god* are two of many lowest species for this particular tree. By working out the other branches of this tree, one would end with a large number of lowest species, all subsumed under the highest genus, *substance*. The Porphyrian tree for *substance* with one branch worked out looks like this:

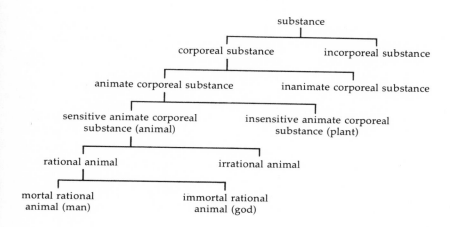

Given this view of a Porphyrian tree and its divisions, there seems to be something odd about the way in which Boethius divides the genus *maximal proposition* in *De top. diff. Maximal proposition* is a subaltern genus; it is a species of *proposition*, and it contains a number of different species—*maximal proposition from efficient cause* and *maximal proposition from contraries* and so on. In the Themistian division of Topics, there are twenty-eight species of maximal propositions and twenty-eight differentiae constituting these species. But it seems as if *maximal proposition* were the proximate genus for all twenty-eight species, as if these species all came directly and without intervening subaltern genera from *maximal proposition*. The twenty-eight species all seem to occur at the same level of their tree, and the differentiae and species are not paired in any way; there is, for example, a differentia *from efficient cause* but no corresponding differentia *not from efficient cause*. The division of *maximal proposition* into species, then, seems to look like this:

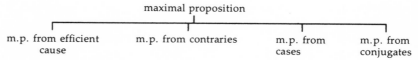

And so on for the remainder of the twenty-eight differentiae of maximal propositions: *definition, description, explanation of the name, complete thing, genus, integral parts, material cause, formal cause, final cause, effects, destructions, uses, associated accidents, judgment, similars, greater, lesser, relatives, privation and possession, affirmation and negation, proportion, transumption,* and *division.*

In his *Liber de divisione,* however, Boethius indicates that he accepts as standard the sort of Porphyrian tree constructed above for *substance.*[5] He says, for example, that a genus is divided only by some pair of opposites (881D4–6; 114.18) and that species are to be separated by means of opposites (882A6–10; 115.20–21). He says, furthermore, that every division of a genus is a division into two (883D12ff.; 118.30ff.). He discusses a case in which it appears that a genus is divided into three parallel species and explains that the three species are really produced from the genus by two sets of division into two. *Three-sided figure* has three species—*three sides equal, two sides equal,* and *no sides equal*—derived from the genus in this way:

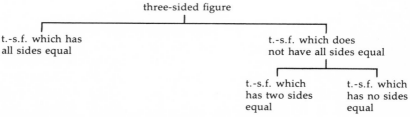

How, then, should his views about the division of a genus be reconciled with his seemingly anomalous division of *maximal proposition?*

If we look closely at the text of *De top. diff.,* I think it is possible to see the outlines of a more conventional division for maximal propositions.

5. *PL,* LXIV, 875D–892A. See also *Trattato sulla divisione,* tr. Lorenzo Pozzi (Padua, 1969); it includes the text of an early edition of the treatise, pp. 107–129. In the following citations of this treatise, I will give first a reference to the *PL* edition and then a reference to the edition in Pozzi's book. The references to Pozzi's book are given by page and section number.

Boethius begins by dividing all differentiae for maximal propositions into three groups: those taken from the terms in the question, those taken from without, and those that are intermediate (1186D6ff.). If we follow Boethius's method for dividing *three-sided figure*, then we could divide *maximal proposition* into subaltern genera in this way:[6] some maximal propositions are drawn from the terms in the question, and others are not; of those that are not, some are connected in some way with the terms in the question or partly inhere in the terms (these are intermediate) and others do not (these are extrinsic).[7]

Then he says (1186D11ff.) that of those drawn from the terms in the question, some are from the substance of the terms and others follow from the substance of the terms. Here we could take as differentiae the pair *from the substance* (of the terms in the question) and *not from the substance*. The second differentia constitutes the subaltern species of maximal propositions that are drawn from the terms in the question but not from the substance of those terms— namely, those that are taken from what follows from the substance.

Those taken from the substance all have to do just with definition, he says; but it turns out that he wants a threefold division here as well: true definition and also description and explanation of the name, which are put in place of a true definition (cf. 1187C6–8). So the subaltern genus *those taken from substance* can be divided in this way: those that are taken from the substance are true definitions, and others are not true definitions. There are two species of the second sort—*those that are from descriptions* and *those that are from explanation of the name*—although what pair of differentiae divide these two from their proximate genus is not suggested in the text.

By these conventional, Porphyrian divisions, we have arrived at what are for Boethius's purposes three lowest species of maximal propositions and three of the differentiae that are Topics: *definition, description,* and *explanation of the name.*

6. The reader may find it easier to follow the discussion of this division if he consults the diagram presented at the end of the chapter.

7. Boethius is, in fact, giving these groups for the differentiae of maximal propositions; but since the differentiae constitute species of maximal propositions, he is also giving groups of maximal propositions. It will be less cumbersome and confusing to talk as if the divisions he makes are of maximal propositions rather than of their differentiae.

All the rest of the intrinsic Differentiae—*genus, complete thing, species, integral parts, the four causes, effects, destructions, uses,* and *associated accidents*—fall under the group of those that follow from the substance. Boethius says nothing explicitly to indicate how the appropriate divisions are to be made, but he does treat these Differentiae in groups. The first four are discussed together, then the four causes, then effects and destructions and uses, and then associated accidents. Perhaps, if he had laid out the divisions explictly for these Topics, he would have done so in this way. Of those that follow from the substance of the terms in the question, some have to do with the thing itself (from whose substance they follow), and others do not. Of those that do, some are from the whole of the thing, and others are not. The second sort—those that follow from the substance of the thing and have to do with the thing itself but not with the whole of the thing—are those that are from the parts of the thing. Those from the whole are divided into two species—*those from genus* and *those from complete thing,* and, similarly, those from parts are divided into species and parts— *those from parts that are species* and *those from parts that are integral parts,* though the differentiae for the last two divisions are simply a matter for speculation. With these divisions, we have again derived lowest species of maximal propositions and differentiae that are Topics: *genus, complete thing, species,* and *integral parts.*

There remains yet a subaltern species of those that follow from the substance—namely, *those that do not have to do with the thing itself* (from whose substance they follow); and we need to get lowest species whose differentiae are the four causes, effects and destructions and uses, and associated accidents. When Boethius is comparing Themistian and Ciceronian Topics, he treats effects, destructions, and uses as if they were sorts of cause or effect (1206A1ff.; see also 1194C4ff.). So perhaps the subaltern genus here should be divided into those that are true causes and those that are not. Those that are true causes will be the four causes (efficient, material, formal, and final). Those that are not true causes can be divided into those that are similar to a cause (or effect) and those that are in no way causes. The latter are those that follow from the substance but do not have to do with the thing itself and are neither true causes nor causes of any sort; the Topic *from associated accidents* fits this description. The former—those that are assimilable to causes or effects—include effects, destructions, and

uses; by 'effects' in this connection Boethius seems to mean generation, the opposite of destruction. The generation of a thing is in
some sense prior to the thing generated, the destruction of a thing
is in some sense posterior to that thing, and the use of a thing is
(at least in most cases) simultaneous with that thing, so that it is
easy to devise the following division of those that are assimilable
to causes or effects (though how Boethius would have made the
division is not clear):

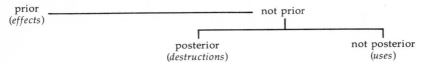

Since the constitutive differentiae of a genus are included, implicitly or explicitly, among the differentiae of its species, those from
uses will be characterized as not prior and not posterior (to the
things of which they are the uses) and hence as simultaneous.

Boethius gives no indication of how the last of the intrinsic
Topics are to be divided into their lowest species; nor does anything in the nature of the Topics readily suggest the divisions he
is likely to have had in mind. So I will not here suggest divisions
for these two groups.

The extrinsic Topics are *judgment,* the four opposites, *greater,
lesser, similars, proportion,* and *transumption.* The first of these
Boethius treats as different from the others in that it is completely
unconnected with the terms in the question. So we might make an
initial division of extrinsic Topics in this way: some are completely unconnected with the terms in the question (and the Topic
judgment constitutes this species); and others, though they are extrinsic, are still in some way connected with the terms in the question. Boethius's discussion of the remaining Topics (1190C12ff.)
and his comparison of the Ciceronian and Themistian Topics (cf.,
for example, 1206B2ff.) suggest that the division of those connected in some way should be made along these lines. Those that
are connected to the terms in the question must be connected by
something, and that something must be equal or not equal to the
term(s) in the question. Of those connected by something equal,
some will be connected by something equal to and like the term(s)
in the question; others, by something equal and unlike. The latter
(equal and unlike) is the subaltern species to which the four op-

posites belong. The former (equal and like) can be divided into two, depending on whether the likeness is a likeness between two things or not. If it is likeness of two things, we will have the lowest species *those from similars*. The group connected by something equal and like, where the likeness is not between two things, includes the lowest species *those from proportion* (likeness of relationship) and *those from transumption* (broadly analogous cases).

So it is possible on the basis of what is explicit or suggested in the text to construct an almost fully worked-out standard Porphyrian tree for maximal propositions, whose lowest species have as their constitutive differentiae the twenty-eight Themistian Topics (see the following diagram). A similar Porphyrian tree could be worked out in the same way for the Ciceronian Topics.

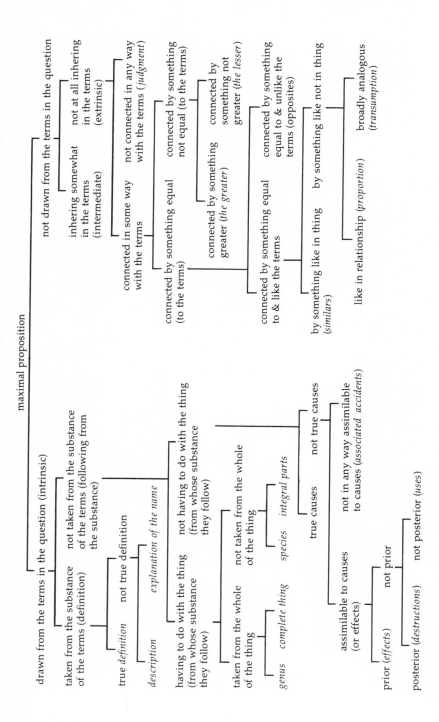

maximal proposition

not drawn from the terms in the question

- not at all inhering in the terms (extrinsic)
- inhering somewhat in the terms (intermediate)
  - not connected in any way with the terms (*judgment*)
  - connected in some way with the terms
    - connected by something not equal (to the terms)
      - connected by something not greater (*the lesser*)
      - connected by something greater (*the greater*)
    - connected by something equal (to the terms)
      - connected by something equal to & unlike the terms (opposites)
        - by something like not in thing
          - broadly analogous (*transumption*)
        - like in relationship (*proportion*)
      - connected by something equal to & like the terms
        - by something like in thing (*similars*)

drawn from the terms in the question (intrinsic)

- not taken from the substance of the terms (following from the substance)
  - not having to do with the thing (from whose substance they follow)
    - not true causes
      - not in any way assimilable to causes (*associated accidents*)
      - assimilable to causes (or effects)
        - not prior
          - not posterior (*uses*)
          - posterior (*destructions*)
        - prior (*effects*)
    - true causes
  - having to do with the thing (from whose substance they follow)
    - explanation of the name
    - not taken from the whole of the thing
      - integral parts
      - species
    - taken from the whole of the thing
      - complete thing
      - genus
- taken from the substance of the terms (definition)
  - not true definition
    - *description*
  - true *definition*

Differentia

The doctrine of the predicables is fundamental to Boethius's *De topicis differentiis*. Aristotle emphasizes four predicables: genus, definition, property, and accident;[1] Porphyry's *Isagoge* is devoted to five: genus, species, differentia, property, and accident.[2] There are, then, six predicables in all;[3] and though Boethius gives Aristotle's four as the predicables in *De top. diff.* (see 1177D10ff.), he often makes use of the other two as well in this treatise.[4]

Porphyry describes each of the predicables in a number of ways in an attempt to make clear what it is, but there are four sets of characteristics which I think basically distinguish the predicables among themselves. Boethius gives two of these when he is explaining the Aristotelian predicables (1177D12ff.). First, subjects have essences, and all predicates are either part of their subject's

1. See, for example, *Top.* 101b37ff.
2. Both men recognized the predicables they neglected.
3. For a discussion of these in detail, see "Differentia and the Porphyrian Tree" above.
4. Whether the predicables are linguistic entities was a moot point throughout the Middle Ages. In Boethius's work, although 'subject' and 'predicate' and words relating to the predicables are used ambiguously, generally they have to do not with linguistic entities but with the entities or characteristics signified by the expressions that constitute the grammatical subject or predicate of a sentence; and the same seems true for Porphyry's use of the words. For example, Boethius and Porphyry both say that if a differentia is destroyed or ceases to be, then its corresponding species is also destroyed, but not vice versa; if a species is destroyed, the corresponding differentia remains (Boethius, *In Isagogen*, ed. Samuel Brandt [Leipzig, 1906], pp. 328.21–329.3; *PL* 151B6–12; Porphyry, *Isagoge, Commentaria in Aristotelem Graeca* (*CAG*) IV, pt. i, p. 18.21–23). Just what Porphyry and Boethius think the ontological status of the predicables is, if they are not linguistic entities, is not clear. Porphyry says explicitly in the *Isagoge* that he means to avoid committing himself to one side or another on the question (*CAG*, pp. 1.8ff.). Boethius seems to take a conceptualist view of the predicables, intermediate between realism and nominalism (cf. *In Isag.*, ed. Brandt, p. 159.10ff.; *PL* 82B3ff.). In this discussion, I will follow Boethius's lead and use 'subject' and 'predicate' and words relating to the predicables ambiguously.

essence or not. Second, all predicates and so all predicables must be either greater than or equal to the subjects they are said of; no predicate is less than its subject.[5] A predicate is equal to its subject if it is predicated convertibly of the subject (see 1175C9ff.). For example, *risible* is a predicate equal to its subject *man* because it is predicated convertibly; man is risible, and, conversely, what is risible is man.[6] The point seems to be that an equal predicate is said of nothing other than the subject to which it is equal. A predicate that is greater than its subject, then, must be said of other things besides the subject in question; hence such a predicate is not predicated convertibly. A predicable, then, is either greater than or equal to its subject and either belongs or does not belong to its subject's essence.

Boethius uses these two sets of characteristics to distinguish and describe the four Aristotelian predicables. Genus is greater than its subject and is part of the subject's essence. Definition is equal to the subject and part of the subject's essence. Property is equal to the subject but not part of the subject's essence. And accident is greater than the subject and not part of the subject's essence.

Aristotelian predicables

Genus:	Greater	Part of essence
Definition:	Equal	Part of essence
Property:	Equal	Not part of essence
Accident:	Greater	Not part of essence

To distinguish the remaining two predicables, species and differentia, from the Aristotelian four, two more pairs of characteristics need to be added. First, a predicate can be predicated either of what is singular and individual or of what is common and general; that is, something can be said of Socrates, for example, or of the species *man*. According to Boethius, who is following Porphyry here, genus, differentia, property, and definition are said primarily of what is common and general and secondarily of what is individual. On this view, in a sentence such as 'Man is animal,'

5. Cf. 1175C14–D3 and my notes on the passage.
6. This particular touchstone for determining when a predicate is equal to its subject will not work when the subject is individual or singular. 'Socrates is running,' for example, does not convert. For an explanation of this difficulty, see below; the statements here involving predicables that are predicated convertibly should be taken as if the subject were not an individual but a species of individuals.

the predicate is being used in a way conceptually prior to its secondary, derived use in 'Socrates is animal'; that is, animal attaches to Socrates insofar as he is a man, but it attaches to man without any 'insofar as' rider. Species, on the other hand, is said only of individuals and not of what is common. Accidents fall into two groups; one resembles genus and the other resembles species in this respect. Accidents belong to their subjects either separably (that is, the subject may sometimes have the accident and sometimes not) or inseparably. Inseparable accidents are like genus: they belong primarily to what is common and only secondarily to individuals. Separable accidents, however, are said primarily of individuals and secondarily of what is common; being pale, for example, belongs first to Socrates and secondarily to the species *man*.[7]

One more pair of attributes is required to separate genus and differentia, which are so far the same, since both are greater than their subjects, part of the essence of their subjects, and said primarily of what is common.[8] To distinguish the two, a distinction needs to be made between predicating a thing in respect of what the subject is (*in eo quod quid est*) or in respect of what characteristics the subject has (*in eo quod quale est*). These two predications are often said to be answers to questions that might be expressed in colloquial English as 'What is it?' and 'What's it like?' If we ask what man is, the answer is animal; and if we ask what man is like, the answer is rational or two-legged or bilateral, and so on. This second answer, the response to the question 'What's it like?' can consist of characteristics that belong to the essence of the subject or of characteristics that are only accidental to the subject. Differentia is distinguished from genus because genus is predicated in respect of what its subject is and differentia is said in respect of the characteristics its subject has. Accident, too, is predicated *in eo quod quale est*; but, unlike differentia, it picks out characteristics that are not part of the subject's essence.

With this last pair of characteristics, we have enough to specify all the predicables and distinguish them from one another. The following table summarizes the results.

7. Porphyry, *CAG*, p. 13.10–21. Boethius, *In Isag.*, ed. Brandt, pp. 286–291 (*PL* 134C9–136C5).

8. Cf., for example, Porphyry, *CAG*, pp. 13.23 and 19.11–14, 9.7–16, and 13.10–14.12.

	in respect of what characteristic	in respect of what it is	of what is common	of what is individual	of the essence	not of the essence	greater than	equal to
Differentia	X		X		X		X	
Property	X		X			X		X
Accident	X		X*	X**		X	X	
Genus		X	X		X		X	
Species		X		X	X			X
Definition		X	X		X			X

*inseparable accident
**separable accident

With this foundation, I want to look at some problems that arise in connection with differentia and occasion confusion in *De top. diff.* The treatise is devoted to a discussion of differentiae, as the content and the title make plain, so that of all the predicables differentia has a special importance.

One of the most puzzling things in Book I of *De top. diff.* is a statement Boethius makes about differentia. In 1178B5ff. he argues that questions about differentia can be subsumed under questions about one of the four Aristotelian predicables. Differentia is either constitutive or divisive, he says. If it is constitutive, then it may be considered as the genus of the subject in question; if it is divisive, then it may be considered as the species of the subject. Hence, he says, differentia is used now in place of genus, now in place of species; and so all questions about differentia are equivalent to questions about genus.

More than one thing is puzzling or troublesome in this passage; to understand it, we need to have firmly in mind the nature of constitutive and divisive differentiae. A genus is divided into its species by divisive differentiae, and a species is constituted by its genus plus constitutive differentiae. Not every genus or species of a Porphyrian tree has both a constitutive and a divisive differentia, though. All subaltern genera or species have a constitutive as well as a divisive differentia, but the highest genus in a Porphyrian tree has no constitutive differentia, and the lowest species has no divisive differentia. Every differentia, however, is itself both constitutive and divisive; it constitutes a species of the genus it divides. The same differentia is constitutive of one species (which may be a subaltern genus) and divisive of some other genus (which may also be a subaltern species). So the constitutive differentiae of any given subaltern genus or species are distinct from its divisive differentiae. For a subaltern genus such as *animal*, the constitutive differentia is *sensitive* (that is, capable of perceiving), and the divisive differentiae are *rational* and *irrational* (that is, nonrational). Differentiae, furthermore, come in pairs, *rational* and *irrational*, for example; but as can be seen in the example of *animal* above, only one half of a pair is a constitutive differentia for any given genus or species, though the divisive differentiae are whole pairs.

So a constitutive differentia (considered as constitutive) attaches to species and a divisive differentia (considered as divisive) attaches to genera. Why, then, does Boethius say that a constitutive differentia is used in place of a genus and a divisive differentia in place of a species? In addition, since he takes the trouble to point out that the differentia is used now for the genus, now for the species, why does he conclude that all questions about differentia are equivalent to questions about genus? Some species are also genera, namely, subaltern genera; but lowest species are only species and not genera as well, and species and genus are very different, as Boethius explains in various places in his commentary on the *Isagoge*.

Porphyry's defining description of differentia, adopted by Boethius, is important for making sense out of this puzzle, I think. According to Porphyry, differentia is that which is predicated of more than one differing in species in respect of what characteristics each of them has.[9] Before we can use this description, we have to be sure what it means. Like many other statements about differentia, it seems susceptible of at least three interpretations, corresponding to three different senses of 'differentia' (labeled (1), (2), and (3) below).

It seems plausible that by 'differentia' Porphyry means either (1) a pair of characteristics, such as rational-irrational and mortal-immortal, or else simply (2) the affirmative characteristic of such a

---

9. "διαφορά ἔστι τὸ κατὰ πλειόνων καὶ διαφερόντων τῷ εἴδει ἐν τῷ ποῖόν τί ἐστι κατηγορούμενον." *CAG*, p. 11.7–8; see also Boethius, *In Isag.*, ed. Brandt, pp. 265–267 (PL 127A3–C6).

pair (rational, or mortal) which is predicated now affirmatively and now negatively of whatever is its subject. If the first, then, for every differentia there clearly must be at least two species since *one* differentia will be a *pair* of opposing characteristics, each of which is found in at least one species. If the second, then, since a genus will always be divided by one such differentia into two species, there will again be at least two species for each differentia. It is also possible, however, that Porphyry means each member of such a pair of characteristics to be a differentia in its own right; *rational*, for example, might be thought of as one differentia and *irrational* another. In this case, Porphyry's description of differentia says that any differentia is always predicated of more than one species, differentia here being (3) either the affirmative or the negative member of the appropriate pair of characteristics. Two things tell against this third interpretation of Porphyry's description. First, it is no longer so easy to see what in the nature of a differentia (understood in this third way) requires that it be predicated of more than one species. If this interpretation of Porphyry's description is correct, then it seems to be simply a matter of chance that the description is true; the world just happens to be such that characteristics such as *rational* or *mortal* are never found in only one species. Second, from what we know about the Porphyrian tree, it seems that some differentiae must be predicated of only one species; the differentia that constitutes a lowest species is apparently not a differentia for any other species. For all its difficulty, however, the third interpretation seems to be the one Porphyry and Boethius have in mind.

Many of the things Porphyry and Boethius say about differentia could support any of these three interpretations, but some of what they say definitely rules out the first, that a differentia is a pair such as *rational-irrational*. Porphyry, for example, says that a (divisive) differentia embraces or includes species, just as a genus does, but not as many as its corresponding genus (*CAG*, pp. 13.23–14.3). If the differentia were a pair such as *rational-irrational*, then any divisive differentia would include as many species as the corresponding genus; as many species are included under the heading *rational-irrational* as under the heading *animal*. Again, Boethius says that the same differentiae divide genera and constitute species.[10] But no species can be constituted by a pair of con-

10. *In Isag.*, ed. Brandt, pp. 259.1–260.5 (*PL* 124A7–C9).

traries. So a differentia cannot be a pair such as *rational-irrational* or *mortal-immortal*.

But neither can it be an affirmative property that is predicated affirmatively of some things and negatively of others. In some places Boethius talks of the affirmative and the corresponding negative property as two differentiae; for instance, in *In Isagogen,*[11] he speaks of *rational* and *irrational* as two differentiae. A little later,[12] he says that the genus *animal* is predicated of *horse* and *cow* as well as of *man* and *god* but that the differentia *rational* is predicated only of *man* and *god*. This latter passage indicates that some of the evidence in the preceding paragraph is of use here also. If a differentia were said affirmatively of some things and negatively of others, then a divisive differentia would not be said of fewer species than the corresponding genus is said of. If the differentia *rational* were predicated of some species affirmatively and of others—the irrational ones—negatively, then the differentia would embrace or include as many species as the genus *animal*. So the second interpretation of the description of differentia is not correct either; a differentia is not solely an affirmative characteristic that is said affirmatively or negatively.

What remains then, is the third interpretation. Each of the pair of contrary properties is a differentia; *mortal* is one differentia, and *immortal* is another. According to Porphyry's description, any differentia has to be predicated (affirmatively) of at least two species; *rational* and *irrational*, for example, must each be said of two or more species of things. So at least two different species have to manifest the characteristic of any differentia.

What about the difficulties attending this interpretation, which I mentioned earlier? First, does anything in the nature of differentia account for the fact that a characteristic such as *rational* is always predicated of more than one species? If we except for the moment the troublesome differentiae that constitute lowest species (and make another difficulty for this interpretation), then I think there is something in the nature of a differentia (and the Porphyrian tree) that does explain the fact that a differentia is always predicated of more than one species. All differentiae, except those we might call lowest differentiae, constitute subaltern genera. A differentia divides a genus and constitutes a species, but all the species constituted by differentiae, other than lowest species, are also

11. Ed. Brandt, p. 270.2–4 (*PL* 128C9-13).
12. Ed. Brandt, p. 293.13–15 (*PL* 137B6–9).

genera. Any genus has at least two species under it, and any species is constituted in part by its proximate genus. So since every differentia except a lowest differentia constitutes a subaltern genus, which in turn is part of what constitutes the species below it, every differentia constitutes at least two species. The genus *animal*, for example, has the constitutive differentia *sensitive* and is divided into the species *rational animal* and *irrational animal*. If we give the fully worked-out definitions for each of those two species, we will have *rational sensitive animate corporeal substance* and *irrational sensitive animate corporeal substance*. So the constitutive differentia (viz., *sensitive*) of the proximate genus (*animal*) is also constitutive of the two species under that genus. Hence, with the exception of lowest differentiae, all differentiae that constitute a species also constitute genera and in consequence are always said of more than one species. And so, still excepting lowest differentiae, the fact that Porphyry's description of differentia is correct is not an inexplicable matter of chance but rather a result of the structure of a Porphyrian tree and of the way in which a differentia functions.

The second difficulty for our interpretation of differentia picks up what the preceding explanation left unresolved. The difficulty arises because a differentia attaching to a lowest species appears to constitute that species and no other; as a result, these differentiae seem to be exceptions to the rule that all differentiae are said of more than one species. *Rational animal* for example, is the proximate genus for the lowest species *man*. *Rational animal* is divided by two lowest differentiae (*mortal* and *immortal*) into two species *mortal rational animal* (*man*) and *immortal rational animal* (*god*). Since these two species have no species under them, the lowest differentia of each of them seems predicated of only one species. At first glance, the description that says a differentia is always predicated of more than one species seems to be wrong. Several of the important medieval logicians who comment on this Porphyrian description ignore the problem;[13] Ockham says flatly that the description does not hold for lowest differentiae.[14] But the Boethian passages dealing with Porphyry's description do not

13. See, for example, William of Sherwood, *Introductiones Magistri Guilelmi de Shyreswode in logicam*, ed. Martin Grabmann, *Sitzungsberichte der bayerischen Akademie der Wissenschaften*, Heft 10 (Munich, 1937), pp. 47.22–48.12; and Peter of Spain, *Tractatus*, ed. L. M. de Rijk (Assen, 1972), pp. 20.35–21.14.

14. William Ockham, *Expositio in librum Porphyrii De praedicabilibus*, ed. Ernest A. Moody (St. Bonaventure, N.Y., 1965), p. 78.28–34.

admit of Ockham's qualification; Boethius says plainly in several places that a differentia is predicated of more than one species.[15] Aristotle and Porphyry, as well as Boethius, regularly describe differentia as greater than what it is predicated of.[16] But if differentia is a predicable that is greater than its subject, then any differentia must always be predicated of at least two species. If a particular differentia were predicated of only one species, then the propostion in which that differentia was predicated of its species would convert simply and the differentia would be a predicable equal to, not greater than, its subject.

It is important to notice, I think, that the two differentiae that are most frequently given as examples of lowest differentiae, namely, *mortal* and *immortal*, are in fact said of more than one species even though they are lowest differentiae. The lowest species *man*, in the genus *rational animal*, is constituted by the differentia *mortal;* but most if not all of the species in a different genus, namely, *irrational animal*, are also mortal. Someone might object that a characteristic such as *mortal* is a differentia when it is used to distinguish one species of rational animal from another but nothing more than an ordinary characteristic when it is used of irrational animals at a different level of the Porphyrian tree. But *mortal*, like any other differentia, is part of its subject's essence and answers the question 'What's it like?' rather than the question 'What is it?'; and these two things will be true of it whether it is said of rational or of irrational animals. Since these two characteristics are those generally used to specify differentia, it seems that a property that is a differentia at one level of the tree must also be a differentia of whatever else it is said of. Boethius, furthermore, explicitly discusses *mortal* as a differentia for the genus *irrational animal*.[17] The species *horse*, he says, as well as other species of irrational animals, is constituted by the differentiae *irrational* and *mortal*. And in another passage, when Boethius says that a differentia is never predicated of only one species, he cites as an example the differentia *mortal*.[18]

As for *immortal*, Boethius thinks that perhaps it is also a dif-

15. Cf. *In Isag.*, ed. Brandt, pp. 266.13–267.1 (*PL* 127B13–C5), 328.13–329.5 (*PL* 151A12–15), 331.18–332.6 (*PL* 152B11–C3), 335.1–336.2 (*PL* 153C3–154A3).
16. Cf. note 8 above and Aristotle's *Topics* 103b7–17, quoted in "Differentia and the Porphyrian Tree," above.
17. *In Isag.*, ed. Brandt, p. 256.10–12 (*PL* 123A8–10).
18. *In Isag.*, ed. Brandt, p. 266.13–15 (*PL* 127B13–14).

ferentia for the celestial bodies (he has already given it as a differentia for the species *god*) if, as some ancient views held, the celestial bodies are inanimate and hence irrational immortal bodies.[19] In this case, the differentia *immortal* is shared between species that differ not only in their proximate genus but also in all their genera up to the subaltern genus second from the top of the tree. All the differentiae constituting a subaltern genus are predicated of species that are hierarchically ordered under that subaltern genus. But for differentiae at the bottom of the Porphyrian tree, the species sharing a differentia seem not to be ordered one under another but rather to be scattered throughout different levels of the tree. As far as I know, neither in *Liber de divisione* nor in *In Isagogen*, the two Boethian works in which differentia is discussed at length, is any explicit explanation given for this wandering of lowest differentiae, that is, for the fact that the characteristics that are lowest differentiae also occur at other levels of the Porphyrian tree; and I do not see what such an explanation could amount to.

Boethius considers seriously the possibility that no irrational entities are immortal.[20] The only candidates are the celestial bodies, and Boethius does not altogether rule out the possibility that the celestial bodies are mortal (that is, perishable). The fact that he does not rule out the possibility is surprising, and his explanation is disconcerting. If celestial bodies are not immortal, then the differentia *immortal* is said of only one species, namely, *god*. In that case, Porphyry's description of differentia is false, and the classification of differentia as greater than its subject (which Aristotle, Porphyry, and Boethius all subscribe to) is incorrect. What Boethius says by way of explanation is this. It is possible that no irrational entities are immortal; and if so, then the differentiae *irrational* and *immortal* are not joined to produce any species. Nevertheless, *immortal* is by no means any the less a differentia, he says, because it *could* be coupled with *irrational* and then it *would* produce another species. It has the potentiality for forming another species when added to the genus *irrational animal* and therefore shows itself to be a differentia. What Boethius says here is disconcerting, of course, because it requires a very important revision in

19. *In Isag.*, ed. Brandt, p. 257.2–8 (*PL* 123B4–12). Boethius here seems, clearly, to be thinking of 'immortal' simply as equivalent to 'imperishable.'
20. *In Isag.*, ed. Brandt, p. 257.8ff. (*PL* 123B12ff.).

what has been said about differentia. If there is a differentia that is predicated actually of only one species, though it could be predicated of more than one, then differentia is not what is said of more than one differing in species, but rather what *could* be said of more than one differing in species. It is not what is greater than its subject, but what *could* be greater or what is *potentially* greater than its subject. Of course, in every case but that of certain lowest differentiae, the possibilities in question are actualized.

Boethius's discussion of the lowest differentia *immortal* is the only passage I know of in which what Boethius says clearly requires the Porphyrian description of differentia to be modified in the way I have just suggested. In many other passages on differentia, he speaks of differentia explicitly as that which *is* predicated of more than one differing in species.[21] It is unclear whether Boethius is being inconsistent in his views of differentia. If he is being inconsistent and means to hold the unmodified description of differentia, the problem of accounting for the fact that lowest differentiae are predicated of more than one species remains unsolved. If, on the other hand, he really means the description of differentia to be taken in its modified form because there are certain lowest differentiae that are in fact said of only one species, then the explanation I am about to give for one of the puzzles with which this chapter began will not work; and the problem of why a constitutive differentia always takes the place of a genus remains unsolved.

Whatever justification can be given for Porphyry's description of differentia, and whether or not Boethius means the description in its unmodified form, it should be clear now what the description amounts to. Armed with the description, then, let us return to the problematic passage in *De top. diff.*, where Boethius says that a constitutive differentia takes the place of a genus and that a divisive differentia takes the place of a species.

To begin with the constitutive differentia, we can see, using Porphyry's description of differentia, that though every single differentia must constitute a species, knowledge of one differentia alone is not enough to identify a species. Because every differentia is said of at least two species, we cannot pick out one particular species on the basis of a given differentia. Take, for example, the

21. Cf., for example, *In Isag.*, ed. Brandt, pp. 266.13–267.2 (*PL* 127B13–C5), 287.21–24 (*PL* 135A10–13), 328.18–20 (*PL* 151B2–5), 335.1–4 (*PL* 153C3–7).

constitutive differentia *animate,* which constitutes the species (subaltern genus) *animate corporeal substance.* Every species of a genus is constituted also by the constitutive differentiae of that genus.[22] So the constitutive differentia *animate* constitutes not only the species (subaltern genus) *animate corporeal substance* but also every species under that subaltern genus. *Man,* for example, is *mortal rational sensitive animate corporeal substance.* So, given only the differentia *animate,* we are not able to identify a particular species. We can pick out only the genus that comprises all the species sharing the differentia in question. And this will be the case even when the differentia at issue is a lowest differentia (if we take the Porphyrian description of differentia in its un-modified form) because every differentia is predicated of more than one species. So, given the Porphyrian description of differen-tia, Boethius seems right to say that a constitutive differentia takes the place of a genus.

What about the second part of Boethius's claim, namely, that a divisive differentia takes the place of a species? From what has been said about differentia, we can see that a differentia may con-stitute many species for every genus it divides. For example, al-though *animate* constitutes many species, it is a divisive differen-tia only when it comes into the Porphyrian tree to separate the genus *corporeal substance* into its species. *Corporeal substance* is divided into its two subaltern genera or species by two divisive differentiae, *animate* and *inanimate.* As a divisive differentia, then, *animate* picks out one of a pair of species into which the genus *cor-poreal substance* is divided, namely, *animate corporeal substance.* Here, too, Boethius seems right: a divisive differentia picks out or takes the place of a species.

What has just been said, though, is true only in case all the species that share a particular differentia fall under the genus

22. Both Porphyry and Boethius seem to use 'constitutive differentia' in a broad and a narrow sense, the former being much more common than the latter. In the broad sense, a constitutive differentia is any differentia that is part of the composi-tion of a species; in the narrow sense, it is that differentia which, when added to the proximate genus of a species, yields the definition of the species. These two senses are analogous to the two senses of 'genus,' the broader referring simply to any genus of a species and the narrower to the *proximate* genus of a species. I as-sume that Boethius has the broad sense of 'constitutive differentia' in mind when he says that a constitutive differentia takes the place of a genus, partly because I think the context suggests the broad sense and partly because the difficulties in the passage seem to be otherwise unresolvable.

which that differentia divides and the differentia is a divisive differentia for only one genus in the tree. Otherwise, if a differentia divides more than one genus in the tree, we will have the same problem we had with constitutive differentiae: given a particular divisive differentia, we will know that it picks out a species; but since it picks out more than one species, we will not be able to specify one individual species on the basis of a particular divisive differentia. And it seems clear that some differentiae divide more than one genus. The differentia *mortal*, for example, is a divisive differentia for the genus *rational animal*, but it also constitutes species falling under the genus *irrational animal* and so must be a divisive differentia for that genus as well.

In light of the preceding discussion, then, what Boethius says about constitutive differentiae taking the place of genera seems to make sense for all constitutive differentiae; but his view of divisive differentiae as taking the place of species seems to hold only for those differentiae that, unlike some lowest differentiae, do not divide more than one genus. It remains unclear how, if at all, differentiae that do divide more than one genus may be accommodated in Boethius's theory of differentia.

We are now in a position to deal with the last problem in this same passage in *De top. diff.* After Boethius's remarks about constitutive and divisive differentiae, he says that, though some differentiae take the place of the genus and some the place of the species, all questions in which the predicable is a differentia are equivalent to questions in which genus is predicated. We expect him to say that all questions about differentia are equivalent to questions about genus *or species.*

For Boethius, all constitutive differentiae are sufficient to specify only a genus and not also a species; so our concern that some questions about differentia reduce to questions about species rather than genus will concentrate only on divisive differentiae. Suppose we are considering the question whether a certain species is corporeal, where *corporeal* is thought of as a divisive differentia. Then this question might be thought of as equivalent to the question whether the species at issue falls under *corporeal substance.* But since *corporeal substance* is both a subaltern genus and a subaltern species, it seems correct to say that here, too, the question about differentia amounts to a question about genus. And such will be the case wherever the species picked out by the divisive differentia happens to be a subaltern genus. Since the species picked out by every divisive differentia except lowest divisive differentia is a subaltern genus, Boethius's claim that all questions about differentia are equivalent to questions about genus is vindicated, except for the differentiae that have consistently been the difficult cases, the lowest differentiae.

As for the lowest differentiae, if we assume that at least some lowest differentiae are predicated of only one species, as Boethius suggests *immortal* might be, then such a differentia (considered as divisive) is sufficient to identify one particular species, and a species that cannot in any way be thought of also as a genus. In this case, then, the lowest differentiae must, I think, be considered to be simply exceptions or counterexamples to Boethius's claim that questions about differentia are all equivalent to questions about genus. If, however, we take the Porphyrian description of differentia as applying to all differentiae, then even lowest differentiae make no trouble for Boethius's view. According to the Porphyrian description, even lowest differentiae are said of more than one species. In the case of a lowest differentia, at least one of the species of which the differentia is said is a lowest species; nonetheless, because the differentia is said of more than one species, the differentia alone is not sufficient to pick out a particular species. It can identify only the genus to which the various species it is said of belong. *Mortal*, for example, is a lowest differentia for the species *man* and also a differentia (whether lowest or not is unclear) for various species of irrational animals. So if we know of something only that it is mortal, we will not be in a position to identify any lowest species for it, that is, any species that is not also a genus; we will be able to give only the genus to which all the species of which *mortal* is said belong. In this case, then, Boethius's claim is justified: all questions about differentia are equivalent to questions about genus.

Bibliography

Primary Sources

Abelard. *Dialectica*. Ed. L. M. de Rijk. 2d ed. Assen: Van Gorcum, 1970.
—— *Scritti di Logica*. Ed. Mario dal Pra. 2d ed. Florence: La nuova Italia, 1969.
Adam of Balsham. *Adam Balsamiensis Parvipontanus: Ars disserendi. Dialectica Alexandri*. Ed. Lorenzo Minio-Paluello. (Twelfth Century Logic: Texts and Studies). Rome: Edizioni di Storia et letteratura, 1956.
Alexander of Aphrodisias. *In Analytica priora*. Ed. Maximilian Wallies. *CAG*, vol. II, pt. i. Berlin: G. Reimer, 1883.
—— *In Aristotelis Topicorum libros octo commentaria*. Ed. Maximilian Wallies. *CAG*, sup. vol. II, pt. ii. Berlin: G. Reimer, 1891.
Anonymous. *Rhetorica ad Herennium*. Tr. Harry Caplan. (Loeb Classical Library). Cambridge, Mass.: Harvard University Press, 1954.
Aristotle. *Topica et Sophistici elenchi*. Ed. W. D. Ross. Oxford: Clarendon Press, 1958.
—— *Topiques*. Books I–IV. Ed. and tr. Jacques Brunschwig. Paris: Les Belles lettres, 1967.
—— *Les Topiques*. Tr. Jules Tricot. Paris: J. Vrin, 1950.
Averroes. *Paraphrasis Topicorum*. In *Aristotelis omnia quae extant opera*. Venice, 1562. Vol. I, pt. iii. *Topicorum atque Elenchorum libri cum Averrois Cordubensis in eos media expositione Abramo de Balmes et Mantino interpretibus*. Reprint. Frankfurt am Main: Minerva, 1962.
Boethius. "A Critical Edition of Boethius' Commentary on Cicero's Topica Bk. I." Ed. A. Perdamo. Ph.D. dissertation, St. Louis University, 1963.
—— *In Perihermeneias*. Ed. Carolus Meiser. Leipzig: Teubner, 1880.
—— *Manlii Severini Boetii Opera omnia. Opera philosophica et Opera theologica*. Accurante J.-P. Migne. *Patrologiae latinae*. Vol. LXIV. Turnholt: Brepols, n.d.
—— *In Ciceronis Topica*. In *Ciceronis Opera*. Ed. J. C. Orelli and G. Baiterus. Zurich: Fuesslini, 1833. Vol. 5, pt. i.
—— *De hypotheticis syllogismis*. Ed. and tr. Luca Obertello. Brescia: Paideia, 1969.
—— *In Isagogen*. Ed. Samuel Brandt. (Corpus scriptorum ecclesiasticorum latinorum, 48). Leipzig: G. Freytag, 1906.
—— *Trattato sulla divisione*. Tr. Lorenzo Pozzi. Padua: Liviana, 1969.

Cassiodorus. *Institutiones.* Ed. R. A. B. Mynors. Oxford: Clarendon Press, 1937.

Cicero. *The Letters to His Friends.* Tr. W. G. Williams. (Loeb Classical Library). Vol. II. London: Heinemann, 1928.

—— *Topica.* Tr. H. M. Hubbell. (Loeb Classical Library). London: Heinemann, 1960.

Fortunatianus. "The Ars rhetorica of C. Chirius Fortunatianus." Ed. Mary Alene Brightbill. Ph.D. dissertation, Cornell University, 1930.

Galen. *Institutio logica.* Ed. C. Kalbfleisch. Leipzig: Teubner, 1896.

—— *Institutio logica.* Tr. J. S. Kieffer. Baltimore: Johns Hopkins University Press, 1964.

Garlandus Compotista. *Dialectica.* Ed. L. M. de Rijk. Assen: Van Gorcum, 1959.

Hugh of Saint Victor. "Le 'De grammatica' de Hugh de Saint-Victor." Ed. J. Leclercq. *Archives d'Histoire Doctrinale et Littéraire du Moyen-Age,* 14 (1943–1945), 263–322.

Isidore of Seville. *Isidori Hispalensis episcopi Etymologiarum sive Originum libri XX.* Ed. W. M. Lindsay. Oxford: Clarendon Press, 1911.

Lambert of Auxerre. *Logica.* Ed. Franco Alessio. Florence: La Nuova Italia Editrice, 1971.

Martin of Dacia. *Opera.* Ed. H. Roos. (Corpus philosophorum Danicorum medii aevi). Hauniae: G. E. C. Gad, 1961.

Peter of Spain. *Tractatus.* Ed. L. M. de Rijk. Assen: Van Gorcum, 1972.

Porphyry. *Isagoge.* Ed. Adolf Busse. *CAG,* Vol. IV, pt. i. Berlin: G. Reimer, 1887.

Quintilian. *Institutio oratoria.* Tr. H. E. Butler. (Loeb Classical Library). London: Heinemann, 1921.

Ralph Brito. "Quaestiones Radulphi Brithonis super libro Topicorum Boecij." MS. Brussels. Bibliothèque royale. Cod. 3540–47. Ff. 163v–195v.

Rhetores latini minores. Ed. Charles Halm. Leipzig: Teubner, 1863.

Tacitus. *Dialogus de oratoribus.* Ed. M. L. de Gubernatis. (Corpus scriptorum latinorum Paravianum). Turin: G. B. Paravia, 1949.

Theophrastus. *Opera quae supersunt omnia.* Ed. F. Wimmer. Leipzig: Teubner, 1854.

Thierry of Chartres. *Commentaries on Boethius by Thierry of Chartres and His School.* Ed. Nikolaus M. Häring. Toronto: Pontifical Institute of Mediaeval Studies, 1971.

—— *The Commentary of Thierry of Chartres on Cicero's De Inventione.* Ed. K. M. Fredborg. *Cahiers de l'Institut du Moyen-Age Grec et Latin* (University of Copenhagen), 7 (1971).

William of Ockham. *Expositionis in libros artis logicae prooemium et Expositio in librum Porphyrii de praedicabilibus.* Ed. Ernest A. Moody. St. Bonaventure, N.Y.: The Franciscan Institute, 1965.

William of Sherwood. *Introductiones Magistri Guilelmi de Shyreswode in logicam.* Ed. Martin Grabmann. *Sitzungsberichte der bayerischen Akademie der Wissenschaften.* Munich: 1937. Heft 10.

—— *Introduction to Logic.* Tr. Norman Kretzmann. Minneapolis: University of Minnesota Press, 1966.

Secondary Sources

Adamo, Luigi. "Boezio e Mario Vittorino traduttori e interpreti dell' 'Isagoge' di Porfirio." *Rivista critica di Storia della Filosofia,* 22 (1967), 141–164.

Alfonsi, Luigi. "Studi Boeziani." *Aevum,* 19 (1945), 142–157.

———. "Studi Boeziani (continua)." *Aevum,* 25 (1951), 132–146, 210–229.

Angelleli, Ignacio. "The Techniques of Disputation in the History of Logic." *Journal of Philosophy,* 67 (1970), 800–815.

Aubenque, Pierre. "La Dialectique chez Aristote." In *L'Attualità della problematica Aristotelica,* Atti del Conregno franco-italiano su Aristotele. Padua: Antenore, 1970. Pp. 9–31.

Barnes, Jonathan. "Property in Aristotle's Topics." *Archiv für Geschichte der Philosophie,* 52 (1970), 136–155.

Barrett, Helen Marjorie. *Boethius: Some Aspects of His Times and Work.* Cambridge: Cambridge University Press, 1940.

Berti, Enrico. "La Dialettica in Aristotele." In *L'Attualità della problematica Aristotelica,* Atti del Conregno franco-italiano su Aristotele. Padua: Antenore, 1970. Pp. 33–80.

Bidez, J. "Boèce et Porphyre." *Revue Belge de Philologie et d'Histoire,* 2 (1923), 189–201.

Biraghi, Luigi. *Boezio filosofo.* Milan: Boniardi-Pogliani de E. Besozzi, 1865.

Bird, Otto. "Dialectic in Philosophical Inquiry." *Proceedings of the American Catholic Philosophical Association,* 29 (1955), 234–246.

———. "The Formalizing of the Topics in Mediaeval Logic." *Notre Dame Journal of Formal Logic,* 1 (1960), 138–149.

———. "The Logical Interest of the Topics as Seen in Abelard." *Modern Schoolman,* 37 (1959), 53–57.

———. "The Re-discovery of the 'Topics': Prof. Toulmin's Inference-Warrants." *Proceedings of the American Catholic Philosophical Association,* 34 (1960), 200–205.

———. "Topic and Consequence in Ockham's Logic." *Notre Dame Journal of Formal Logic,* 2 (1961), 65–78.

———. "The Tradition of the Logical Topics: Aristotle to Ockham." *Journal of the History of Ideas,* 23 (1962), 307–323.

Bocheński, Innocentius M. *Ancient Formal Logic.* (Studies in Logic and the Foundations of Mathematics). Amsterdam: North-Holland, 1951.

———. *La Logique de Théophraste.* (Collectanea Friburgensia, vol. xxxii). Fribourg: Librairie de l'Université, 1947.

———. "Non-analytical Laws and Rules in Aristotle." *Methodos,* 3 (1951), 70–80.

Boh, Ivan. "Burleigh: On Conditional Hypothetical Propositions." *Franciscan Studies,* 23 (1963), 4–67.

———. "Paul of Pergula on Suppositions and Consequences." *Franciscan Studies,* 25 (1965), 30–89.

Bonnaud, R. "L'Education scientifique de Boèce." *Speculum,* 4 (1929), 198–206.

Brandt, Samuel. "Entstehungszeit und zeitliche Folge der Werke von Boethius." *Philologus,* 62 (1903), 141–154, 234–275.

Braswell, Bruce. "Godfrey of Fontaine's Abridgement of Boetius of Dacia's *Quaestiones supra librum Topicorum Aristotelis.*" *Mediaeval Studies,* 26 (1964), 302–314.

Braun, Edmund. *Zur Einheit der aristotelischen Topik.* Cologne: 1859.

Brennan, Rose E. "Dialectic in Philosophical Inquiry." *Proceedings of the American Catholic Philosophical Association,* 29 (1955), 246–258.

Brown, Sister Mary Anthony. "The Role of the Tractatus de obligationibus in Mediaeval Logic." *Franciscan Studies,* 26 (1966), 26–35.

Brunschwig, Jacques. "Dialectique et ontologie chez Aristote." *Revue Philosophique de la France et de l'Etranger,* 154 (1964), 179–200.

Cantin, Stanislas. "La Mémoire et la réminiscence d'après Aristote." *Laval Théologique et Philosophique,* 11 (1955), 81–99.

Cilento, V. *La Forma aristotelica in una "Quaestio" medievale.* (Filosofia e pedagogia, 36). Naples: Libreria scientifica editrice, 1961.

Collins, James. "Progress and Problems in the Reassessment of Boethius." *Modern Schoolman,* 23 (1945–1946), 1–23.

Courcelle, Pierre-Paul. "Boèce et l'école d'Alexandrie." *Mélanges d'Archeologie et d'Histoire,* 52 (1935), 185–223.

———. *La Consolation de philosophie dans la tradition littéraire, antécédents et postérité de Boèce.* Paris: Etudes augustiniennes, 1967.

———. "Etudes critiques sur les commentaires de la Consolation de Boèce (ixe–xve siècles)." *Archives d'Histoire Doctrinale et Littéraire du Moyen-Age,* 14 (1939), 5–140.

———. *Les Lettres grecques en occident de Macrobe à Cassiodore.* Paris: E. de Boccard, 1943. Tr. H. Wedeck as *Late Latin Writers and Their Greek Sources* (Cambridge, Mass.: Harvard University Press, 1969; 1st ed., 1948).

Crem, Theresa M. "The Definition of Rhetoric according to Aristotle." *Laval Théologique et Philosophique,* 12 (1956), 233–250.

Crifo, G. "L'*Argumentum ex contrario* in Cicerone e Boezio con particolare riferimento a Cicerone Top. 3.17." In *Hommages à Marcel Renard,* vol. I. Brussels: Latomus, 1969. Pp. 280–292.

Crocco, Antonio. *Introduzione a Boezio.* Naples: Empireo, 1970.

Dancy, Russell. *Sense and Contradiction: A Study in Aristotle.* Dordrecht and Boston: D. Reidel, 1975.

De Pater, Walter A. "La Fonction du lieu et de l'instrument dans les *Topiques.*" In *Aristotle on Dialectic. Proceedings of the Third Symposium Aristotelicum.* Ed. G. E. L. Owen. Oxford: Clarendon Press, 1968. Pp. 164–188.

———. *Les Topiques d'Aristote et la dialectique platonicienne: La Méthodologie de la définition.* (Etudes thomistiques, 10). Fribourg: Editions St. Paul, 1965.

De Rijk, L. M., ed., *Logica Modernorum,* vols. I and II. Assen: Van Gorcum, 1962 and 1967.

———. "A Note on Aganafat's *Thesaurus philosophorum* (?): An Unknown Arab Source of the Well-Known *Tractatus de modo opponendi et respondendi.*" *Vivarium,* 11 (1973), 105–107.

——. "On the Chronology of Boethius' Works on Logic." I and II. *Vivarium*, 2 (1964), 1–49, 125–162.

De Vogel, C. J. "Boethiana." I and II. *Vivarium*, 9 (1971), 49–66, and 10 (1972), 1–40.

——. "Boethius, der letzte der Römer." In *Aufstieg und Niedergang der römischen Welt*, sec. II, vol. III. Ed. Hildegard Temporini. Berlin and New York: De Gruyter, forthcoming.

Dickey, Mary. "Some Commentaries on the *De inventione* and *Ad Herennium* of the Eleventh and Early Twelfth Centuries." *Mediaeval and Renaissance Studies*, 6 (1968), 1–41.

Dietrich, Albert. "Die arabische Version einer unbekannten Schrift des Alexander von Aphrodisias über die Differentia specifica." *Nachrichten der Akademie der Wissenschaften in Göttingen*, I, Philosophisch-historische Klasse, 2 (1964), 85–148.

Douglas, A. E. The Aristotelian Συναγωγὴ τεχνῶν after Cicero, *Brutus* 46–48." *Latomus*, 14 (1955), 536–539.

——. "A Ciceronian Contribution to Rhetorical Theory." *Eranos*, 55 (1957), 18–26.

Duerlinger, James. "Συλλογισμός and συλλογίζεσθαι in Aristotle's *Organon*." *American Journal of Philology*, 90 (1969), 320–328.

Dürr, Karl. *The Propositional Logic of Boethius*. Tr. Norman Martin. (Studies in Logic and the Foundations of Mathematics). Amsterdam: North-Holland, 1951.

Ebbesen, Sten. "Manlius Boethius on Aristotle's Analytica Posteriora." *Cahiers de l'Institut du Moyen-Age Grec et Latin* (University of Copenhagen), 9 (1973), 68–73.

Eisenhut, Werner. *Einführung in die antike Rhetorik und ihre Geschichte*. Darmstadt: Wissenschaftliche Buchgesellschaft, 1974.

Ferrater Mora, José. "De Boecio a Alberto de Sajonia: Un fragmento de historia de la lógica." *Imago mundi* (Buenos Aires), 3 (1954), 3–22.

Foulquié, Paul. *La Dialectique*. Paris: Presses universitaires de France, 1949.

Fredborg, Karin Margareta. "The Commentary of Thierry of Chartres on Cicero's De Inventione." *Cahiers de l'Institut du Moyen-Age Grec et Latin* (University of Copenhagen), 7 (1971), 1–36.

Garin, E. "La Dialettica dal secolo xii al principio dell' Eta Moderna." In *Studi sulla dialettica*. Turin: Taylor, 1969. Pp. 112–137.

Gigon, Olof. "Cicero und Aristoteles." *Hermes*, 87 (1959), 143–162.

Gilby, Thomas. *Barbara Celarent: A Description of Scholastic Dialectic*. London: Longmans Green, 1949.

Giuliani, Alessandro. "The Aristotelian Theory of the Dialectical Definition." *Philosophy and Rhetoric*, 5 (1972), 129–142.

Goldschmidt, Victor. "Logique et rhétorique chez les Stoiciens." In *La Théorie de l'argumentation*. Louvain: Nauwelaerts, 1963. Pp. 450–456.

Grabmann, Martin. *Die Geschichte der scholastischen Methode*. Freiburg im Breisgau: Herder, 1909–1911.

——. "Kommentare zur aristotelischen Logik aus dem 12. und 13. Jahrhundert . . ." *Sitzungsberichte der preussischen Akademie der Wissenschaften*, Philosophisch-historische Klasse, 18 (1938).

Green-Pedersen, N. J. "William of Champeaux on Boethius's Topics according to Orleans Bibl. Mun. 266." *Cahiers de l'Institut du Moyen-Age Grec et Latin* (University of Copenhagen), 13 (1974), 13–30.

Grimaldi, William. "The Aristotelian Topics." *Traditio*, 14 (1958), 1–16.

———. "Aristotle *Rhetoric* 1391b29 and 1396b29." *Classical Philology*, 56 (1961), 38–43.

———. "The Enthymeme in Aristotle." Ph.D. dissertation, Princeton University, 1953.

———. "A Note on the πίστεις in Aristotle's *Rhetoric*, 1354–1356." *American Journal of Philology*, 78 (1957), 188–192.

———. "Rhetoric and the Philosophy of Aristotle." *Classical Journal*, 53 (1957–1958), 371–375.

———. *Studies in the Philosophy of Aristotle's Rhetoric.* (*Hermes:* Einzelschriften, 25). Wiesbaden: F. Steiner, 1972.

Guthrie, W. K. C. *A History of Greek Philosophy.* Vols. I–IV. Cambridge: Cambridge University Press, 1962–1969.

Hadot, Pierre. *Marius Victorinus.* Paris: Etudes augustiniennes, 1971.

———. "Marius Victorinus et Alcuin." *Archives d'Histoire Doctrinale et Littéraire du Moyen-Age*, 29 (1954), 5–19.

———. "Un Vocabulaire raisonné de Marius Victorinus Afer." *Studia Patristica*, I, 5th ser., 8 (1957), 194–208.

Hamesse, Jacqueline. *Auctoritates Aristotelis, Senecae, Boethii, Platonis, Apuleii, et quorundam aliorum.* I and II. Louvain: Publications du Cetedoc, 1972 and 1974.

Hamlyn, D. W. "Aristotle on Predication." *Phronesis*, 6 (1961), 110–126.

Hammer, Caspar. *Commentatio de Ciceronis Topicis.* Landavi: Formis Kaussleri, 1879.

Häring, Nikolaus. *Commentaries on Boethius by Thierry of Chartres and His School.* Toronto: Pontifical Institute of Mediaeval Studies, 1971.

Hayden, Dom Dunstan. "Notes on Aristotelian Dialectic in Theological Method." *Thomist*, 20 (1957), 383–418.

Hogan, James. "The Dialectic of Aristotle." *Philosophical Studies* (Maynooth), 5 (1955), 3–21.

Huby, Pamela M. "The Date of Aristotle's *Topics* and Its Treatment of the Theory of Ideas." *Classical Quarterly*, 56 (1962), 72–80.

Infante, D. A. "The Influence of a Topical System on the Discovery of Arguments." *Speech Monographs*, 38 (1971), 125–128.

Isnardi-Parente, M. "Per l'interpretazione di *Topici* VI 6, 145a19 sgg." *Rivista di Filologia e di Istruzione Classica*, 94 (1966), 149–161.

Janssens, Emile. "The Concept of Dialectic in the Ancient World." *Philosophy and Rhetoric*, 1 (1968), 174–181.

Jourdain, A. *Recherches critiques sur l'âge et l'origine des traductions latines d'Aristote.* Paris: Fantin, 1843.

Kapp, Ernst. *Greek Foundations of Traditional Logic.* New York: Columbia University Press, 1942.

Klein, Johann Joseph. *Dissertatio de fontibus Topicorum Ciceronis.* Bonn: C. et F. Kruegor, 1844.

Kneale, William, and Martha Kneale. *The Development of Logic.* Oxford: Clarendon Press, 1962.

Kretzmann, Norman. "History of Semantics." In *The Encyclopedia of Philosophy*. Ed. Paul Edwards. New York: Macmillan and Free Press, 1967. Vol. VII, pp. 358–406.

Leeman, A. D. *Orationis Ratio: The Stylistic Theories and Practices of the Roman Orators, Historians, and Philosophers*. Amsterdam: A. M. Hakkert, 1963.

Leff, Michael. "Boethius and the History of Medieval Rhetoric." *Central States Speech Journal*, 25 (1974), 135–141.

———. "Boethius's *De diff. top.*, Book IV." In *Medieval Eloquence. Studies in the Theory and Practice of Medieval Rhetoric*. Ed. James J. Murphy. Berkeley and Los Angeles: University of California Press, forthcoming.

Lloyd, A. C. "Genus, Species, and Ordered Series in Aristotle." *Phronesis*, 7 (1962), 67–90.

———. "Neoplatonic Logic and Aristotelian Logic." I and II. *Phronesis*, 1 (1955–1956), 58–72, 146–160.

Lohr, Charles. "Medieval Latin Aristotle Commentaries." *Traditio*, 23 (1967), 313–413; 24 (1968), 149–245; 26 (1970), 135–216; 27 (1971), 251–351; 28 (1972), 281–396; 29 (1973), 93–197; 30 (1974), 119–144.

Lugarini, Leo. "Dialettica e filosofia in Aristotele." *Pensiero*, 4 (1959), 48–69.

Madkour, I. *L'Organon d'Aristote dans le monde arabe*. Paris: J. Vrin, 1969.

Malcolm, John. "On Grabmann's Text of William of Sherwood." *Vivarium*, 9 (1971), 108–118.

Markowski, Mieczyslaw. "Les Questions de Jean Buridan sur les *Topiques* d'Aristote." *Mediaevalia Philosophica Polonorum*, 13 (1968), 3–7.

Mates, Benson. *Stoic Logic*. Berkeley: University of California Press, 1953.

McKeon, Richard. "The Methods of Rhetoric and Philosophy: Invention and Judgment." In *The Classical Tradition: Literary and Historical Studies in Honor of Harry Caplan*. Ed. Luitpold Wallach. Ithaca, N.Y.: Cornell University Press, 1966. Pp. 365–373.

McKinlay, Arthur Patch. "The 'De syllogismis categoricis' and 'Introductio ad syllogismos categoricos' of Boethius." In *Classical and Mediaeval Studies in Honor of E. K. Rand*. Ed. Leslie W. Jones. New York: Jones, 1938. Pp. 209–219.

———. "Stylistic Tests and the Chronology of the Works of Boethius." *Harvard Studies in Classical Philology*, 18 (1907), 123–156.

Merguet, H. *Lexikon zu den Schriften Ciceros*. Jena: G. Fischer, 1887–1894.

Merlan, Philip. "Ammonius Hermiae, Zacharias Scholasticus, and Boethius." *Greek, Roman, and Byzantine Studies*, 9 (1968), 193–203.

Michel, Alain. "Quelques aspects de la rhétorique chez Philon." In *Philon d'Alexandrie*. (Lyon 11–15 Septembre 1966. Actes publiés par R. Arnaldez, J. Pouilloux, C. Mondésert). Paris: Editions du Centre national de la recherche scientifique, 1967. Pp. 81–101.

———. *Les Rapports de la rhétorique et de la philosophie dans l'oeuvre de Cicéron*. Paris: Presses universitaires de France, 1960.

———. *Rhétorique et philosophie chez Cicéron: Essai sur les fondements philosophiques de l'art de persuader*. Paris: Presses universitaires de France, 1961.

Minio-Paluello, Lorenzo. "A Latin Commentary (?Translated by Boethius) on the *Prior Analytics* and Its Greek Sources." *Journal of Hellenic Studies,* 77 (1957), 93–102.

——. "The Methods of the Medieval Translators of Greek Philosophical Works into Latin." D. Phil. dissertation, Oxford University, 1949.

——. "Note sull' Aristotele latino medievale. X. I "Topici" nel X–XI secolo . . ." *Rivista di Filosofia Neo-scolastica,* 50 (1958), 97–116.

——. "Nuovi impulsi allo studio della logica: La seconda fase della riscoperta di Aristotele e di Boezio." In *La Scuola nell' occidente latino dell alto medioevo.* II (15–21 Aprile 1971. XIX. Settimane di studio del Centro italiano di studi sull' alto medioevo, Spoleto). Spoleto: Presso lasede del Centro, 1972. Pp. 743–766.

——. "The Text of Aristotle's *Topics* and *Elenchi:* The Latin Tradition." *Classical Quarterly,* 49 (1955), 108–118.

——. "Les traductions et les commentaires aristotéliciens de Boèce." *Studia Patristica* II, 5th ser. 9 (1957), 358–365.

Moody, Ernest A. *Truth and Consequence in Medieval Logic.* (Studies in Logic and the Foundations of Mathematics). New York and Amsterdam: North-Holland, 1953.

Moraux, Paul. "La Joute dialectique d'après le huitième livre des *Topiques.*" In *Aristotle on Dialectic. Proceedings of the Third Symposium Aristotelicum.* Ed. G. E. L. Owen. Oxford: Clarendon Press, 1968. Pp. 277–311.

Murphy, James Jerome, *Rhetoric in the Middle Ages.* Berkeley: University of California Press, 1974.

——, ed. *A Synoptic History of Classical Rhetoric.* New York: Random House, 1972.

Nacht-Eladi, S. "Aristotle's Doctrine of the differentia specifica and Maimon's Law of Determinability." In *Studies in Philosophy.* (Scripta Hierosolymitana, 6). Ed. S. H. Bergman. Jerusalem: Magnes Press, 1960.

Nitzsch, Friedrich. *Das System des Boethius.* Berlin: Wiegandt und Grieben, 1860.

Nuchelmans, Gabriel. *Theories of the Proposition.* Amsterdam: North-Holland, 1973.

Obertello, Luca. *Severino Boezio.* I and II. (Collana di monografie, 1). Genoa: Accademia ligure di scienze e lettere, 1974.

Ochs, D. J. "Aristotle's Concept of Formal Topics." *Speech Monographs,* 36 (1969), 419–425.

Oehler, Klaus. "Aristotle in Byzantium." *Greek, Roman, and Byzantine Studies,* 5 (1964), 133–146.

Orth, E. "De Ciceronis 'Topicis.' " *Helmantica,* 9 (1958), 393–413.

Ott, Ludwig. "Die Wissenschaftslehre im Topikkommentar des Adenulf von Anagni." In *Mélanges offerts à Etienne Gilson.* Toronto and Paris: Pontifical Institute of Mediaeval Studies, 1959. Pp. 465–490.

Owen, G. E. L., ed. *Aristotle on Dialectic. Proceedings of the Third Symposium Aristotelicum.* Oxford: Clarendon Press, 1968.

——. "Inherence." *Phronesis,* 10 (1965), 97–105.

Pagallo, G. "Per una edizione critica del ⟨⟨De hypotheticis syllogismis⟩⟩ di Boezio." *Italia Medievale e umanistica,* 1 (1958), 69–101.

Palmer, Georgiana Paine. *The τόποι of Aristotle's Rhetoric as Exemplified in the Orators.* (University of Chicago Dissertations, 158). Chicago, 1934.

Patch, Howard Rollin. *The Tradition of Boethius.* New York: Oxford University Press, 1935.

Perelman, Chaim. "La Méthode dialectique et le rôle de l'interlocuteur dans le dialogue." *Revue de Métaphysique et de Morale,* 60 (1955), 26–31.

Peters, F. E. *Aristoteles Arabus.* Leiden: E. J. Brill, 1968.

Pfligersdorffer, Georg. "Andronikos von Rhodos und die Postprädikamente bei Boethius." *Vigiliae Christianae,* 7 (1953), 98–115.

——. "Zu Boethius De Interpr. Ed. Sec. I, p. 4,4 sqq. Meiser nebst Beobachtungen zur Geschichte der Dialektik bei den Römern." *Wiener Studien,* 66 (1953), 131–154.

Pflug, Johannes. *De Aristotelis Topicorum libro quinto.* Leipzig, 1908.

Pinborg, Jan. *Logik und Semantik im Mittelalter.* Stuttgart-Bad Cannstatt: Frommann-Holzboog, 1972.

——. "Topik und Syllogistik im Mittelalter." In *Sapienter Ordinare: Festgabe für Erich Kleineidam.* (Erfurter Theologische Studien, 24). Ed. F. Hoffmann, L. Scheffczyk, and K. Feiereis. Leipzig: St.-Benno Verlag, 1969. Pp. 157–178.

Plebe, Armando. "La Retorica di Diogene di Babilonia." *Filosofia,* 11 (1960), 451–456.

——. "Retorica aristotelica e logica stoica." *Filosofia,* 10 (1959), 391–424.

——. "Retorica e semantica da Aristotele alla prima stoa." *Filosofia,* 11 (1960), 58–68.

Prantl, Carl. *Geschichte der Logik im Abendlande.* 4 vols. in 2 pts. Leipzig: S. Hirzel, 1855–1860.

Prior, Arthur Norman. "The Logic of Negative Terms in Boethius." *Franciscan Studies,* 13 (1953), 1–6.

Raphael, Sally. "Rhetoric, Dialectic and Syllogistic Argument: Aristotle's Position in 'Rhetoric' I–II." *Phronesis,* 19 (1974), 153–167.

Regis, L. M. *L'Opinion selon Aristote.* Paris: J. Vrin, 1935.

Reiley, Katherine Campbell. *Studies in the Philosophical Terminology of Lucretius and Cicero.* New York: Columbia University Press, 1949.

Rescher, Nicholas. "Al-Kindi's Sketch of Aristotle's Organon." *New Scholasticism,* 37 (1963), 44–58.

Riposati, B. "Quid Cicero de thesi et hypothesi in ⟨⟨Topicis⟩⟩ senserit." *Aevum,* 18 (1944), 61–71.

——. "Quo modo partitiones oratoriae cum topicis cohaereant." In *Atti I congr. stud. Cic.* Rome, 1961. Pp. 253–263.

——. *Studi sui 'Topica, di Cicerone.* Milan: Società Editrice "Vita e Pensiero," 1947.

Robert, Brother S. "Rhetoric and Dialectic according to the First Latin Commentary on the *Rhetoric* of Aristotle." *New Scholasticism,* 31 (1957), 484–498.

Roelants, H. "De methodologie van de Topika." *Tijdschrift voor Filosofie,* 28 (1966), 495–517.

Ross, W. D. "The Text of Aristotle's *Topics* and *Sophistici Elenchi.*" In *Mélanges de philosophie grecque offerts à Mgr. Diès.* Paris: J. Vrin, 1956.

Ryle, Gilbert. "Dialectic in the Academy." In *Aristotle on Dialectic, Proceedings of the Third Symposium Aristotelicum.* Ed. G. E. L. Owen. Oxford: Clarendon Press, 1968. Pp. 69–79.

——. *Plato's Progress.* Cambridge: Cambridge University Press, 1966.

Schneider, Bernd. *Die mittelalterlichen griechisch-lateinischen Übersetzungen der aristotelischen Rhetorik.* (Peripatoi, 2). Berlin and New York: De Gruyter, 1971.

Schrimpf, Gangolf. *Die Axiomenschrift des Boethius (De hebdomadibus) als philosophisches Lehrbuch des Mittelalters.* Leiden: E. J. Brill, 1966.

Shiel, James. "Boethius and Andronicus of Rhodes." *Vigiliae Christianae,* 11 (1957), 179–185.

——. "Boethius and Eudemus." *Vivarium,* 12 (1974), 14–17.

——. "Boethius' Commentaries on Aristotle." *Mediaeval and Renaissance Studies,* 4 (1958), 217–244.

Sichirollo, Livio. Διαλέγεσθαι—*Dialektik: Von Homer bis Aristoteles.* Hildesheim: G. Olms, 1966.

——. "Dialettica aristotelica e storia della dialettica." In *Festschrift H. J. Vleeschauwer.* Pretoria, 1960. Pp. 58–65.

——. *Storicità della dialettica antica.* Padua: Marsilio, 1965.

Slattery, Michael. "Genus and Difference." *Thomist,* 21 (1958), 343–364.

Smethurst, S. E. "Cicero's Rhetorical and Philosophical Works: A Bibliographical Survey." *Classical World,* 51 (1957–1958), 1–4, 24, 32–41.

Solmsen, Friedrich. "The Aristotelian Tradition in Ancient Rhetoric." In *Rhetorika.* Ed. Rudolf Stark. Hildesheim: G. Olms, 1968.

——. "Boethius and the History of the *Organon*." *American Journal of Philology,* 65 (1944), 69–74.

——. "Dialectic without the Forms." In *Aristotle on Dialectic, Proceedings of the Third Symposium Aristotelicum.* Ed. G. E. L. Owen. Oxford: Clarendon Press, 1968. Pp. 49–68.

——. *Die Entwicklung der aristotelischen Logik und Rhetorik.* (Neue philosophische Untersuchungen, 4). Berlin: Weidmann, 1929.

Sorabji, Richard. *Aristotle on Memory.* London: Duckworth, 1972.

Sprute, Jürgen. "Topos und Enthymem in der aristotelischen Rhetorik." *Hermes,* 103 (1975), 68–90.

Stangl, Thomas. *Boethiana vel Boethii commentariorum in Ciceronis Topica emendationes.* Gotha, 1882.

——. "Pseudoboethiana." *Jahrbücher für classische Philologie,* 29 (1883), 193–208, 285–301.

Stark, Rudolf, ed. *Rhetorika: Schriften zur aristotelischen und hellenistischen Rhetorik.* Hildesheim: G. Olms, 1968.

Stewart, Hugh Fraser. *Boethius.* London: W. Blackwood, 1891.

Stump, Eleonore. "Boethius's Works on the Topics." *Vivarium,* 12 (1974), 77–93.

Szabó, A. "Beiträge zur Geschichte der griechischen Dialektik." *Acta antiqua* (Budapest), 1 (1951–1952), 377–410.

Thielscher, P. "Ciceros Topik und Aristoteles." *Philologus,* 67 (1908), 52–67.

Thionville, Eugène. *De la Théorie des lieux communs dans les Topiques d'Aristote*. (Réimpression de l'édition 1855). Osnabrück: Zeller, 1965.

Thomas, Ivo. "Boethius' locus a repugnantibus." *Methodos*, 3 (1951), 303–307.

——. "Maxims in Kilwardby." *Dominican Studies*, 7 (1954), 129–146.

Thurot, Charles, *Etudes sur Aristote: La Dialectique et la rhétorique*. Paris: Durand, 1860.

Trevaskis, J. R. "Division and Its Relation to Dialectic and Ontology in Plato." *Phronesis*, 12 (1967), 118–129.

Van Aubel, Madeleine. "Accident, catégories et prédicables dans l'oeuvre d'Aristote." *Revue Philosophique de Louvain*, 61 (1963), 361–401.

Van den Driessche, R. "Sur le ⟨⟨De syllogismo hypothetico⟩⟩ de Boèce." *Methodos*, 1 (1949), 293–307.

Van der Weel, Richard L. "The *Posterior Analytics* and the *Topics*." *Laval Théologique et Philosophique*, 25 (1969), 130–141.

Van de Vyver, A. "Les Etapes du developpement philosophique du haut moyen-âge." *Revue Belge de Philologie et d'Histoire*, 8 (1929), 425–452.

Vennebusch, Joachim. "De venatione medii inter subiectum et praedicatum: Ein Abschnitt aus *De venatione substantiae, accidentis et compositi* des Raimundus Lullus." *Bulletin de Philosophie Médiévale* (Louvain), 14 (1972), 87–89.

Viano, Carlo Augusto. "La Dialettica in Aristotele"; "La Dialettica stoica." In *Studi sulla dialettica*. Turin: Taylor, 1969. Pp. 38–62, 63–111.

Viscardi, O. "Boezio e la trasmissione e conservazione della cultura greca in occidente." In *I Goti in occidente*. (Settimane di studio del centro italiano studi sull' alto medioevo). Spoleto, 1956. Pp. 232–243.

Wallies, Maximilian. *De fontibus Topicorum Ciceronis*. Berlin: A. Haack, 1878.

——. *Die griechischen Ausleger der aristotelischen Topik*. Berlin: A Haack, 1891.

Wilpert, Paul. "Aristoteles und die Dialektik." *Kant-Studien*, 48 (1956–1957), 247–257.

Wolfson, Harry Austryn. "The Problem of the Souls of the Spheres, from the Byzantine Commentaries on Aristotle through the Arabs and St. Thomas to Kepler." *Dumbarton Oaks Papers*, 16 (1962), 65–93.

Yates, Frances. *The Art of Memory*. London: Routledge and Kegan Paul, 1966.

——. "The Ciceronian Art of Memory." In *Medioevo e rinascimento* II. Florence: G. C. Sansoni, 1955. Pp. 871–903.

Index

C. General (exclusive of items listed in Index A or Index B)

Designed by R. E. Rosenbaum.
Composed by Vail-Ballou Press, Inc.,
in 10 point VIP Palatino, 2 points leaded,
with display lines in Palatino.
Printed offset by Vail-Ballou Press
Warren's Olde Style Wove, 60 pound basis.
Bound by Vail-Ballou Press
in Joanna book cloth
and stamped in All Purpose foil.

Library of Congress Cataloging in Publication Data
(For library cataloging purposes only)

Boethius, d. 524.
  Boethius's De topicis differentiis.

  Bibliography: p.
  Includes indexes.
  1. Dialectic. 2. Logic—Early   works   to   1800. 3. Aristoteles. Topica.
4. Joannes XXI, Pope, d. 1277. Summulae logicales. I. Stump, Eleonore, 1947–
II. Title. III. Title: De topicis differentiis.
B659.D582E5 1978   180   77-17275
ISBN 0-8014-1067-3

1499

67 — associated things not necessarily connected
68 — child. <u>40</u>

readily believable (probable)
    70
39   dy "probable"
46   dy "topic"

2009
181 facere fidem

CORNELL UNIVERSITY PRESS

Including COMSTOCK PUBLISHING ASSOCIATES

Dear Professor

Enclosed is a copy of the book you requested to examine in accordance with our
60-day approval plan.

If you decide to adopt the book for your
classes in a quantity of 10 or more copies,
just let us know and we will cancel your
invoice, inviting you to keep the book as
your desk copy. If not, you may purchase
the book for your personal use or simply
return it to us.

For your convenience, we are enclosing a
business reply envelope. Be sure to refer
to your invoice number in all future cor-
respondence.

Thank you for your interest in Cornell
University Press books.

Sincerely,

CORNELL UNIVERSITY PRESS

257-7000
124 ROBERTS PLACE, ITHACA, NEW YORK 14850 • *Phone* 607 273-5155 • *Cable* CORUPRES